PERFORMING POSTRACIAL

Reflections on Antiblackness, Nation, and Education through Contemporary Blackface in Canada

Blackface – instances in which non-Black persons temporarily darken their skin with make-up to impersonate Black people, usually for fun, and frequently in educational contexts – constitutes a postracialist pedagogy that propagates antiblack logics.

In *Performing Postracialism*, Philip S.S. Howard examines instances of contemporary blackface in Canada and argues that it is more than a simple matter of racial (mis)representation. The book looks at the ostensible humour and dominant conversations around blackface, arguing that they are manifestations of the particular formations of antiblackness in the Canadian nation state and its educational institutions. It posits that the occurrence of blackface in universities is not incidental, and outlines how educational institutions' responses to blackface in Canada rely upon a motivation to protect whiteness.

Performing Postracialism draws from focus groups and individual interviews conducted with university students, faculty, administrators, and Black student associations, along with online articles about blackface, to provide the basis for a nuanced examination of the ways that blackface is experienced by Black persons. The book investigates the work done by Black students, faculty, and staff at universities to challenge blackface and the broader campus climate of antiblackness that generates it.

PHILIP S.S. HOWARD is an associate professor in the Department of Integrated Studies in Education at McGill University.

Performing Postracialism

Reflections on Antiblackness, Nation, and Education through Contemporary Blackface in Canada

PHILIP S.S. HOWARD

UNIVERSITY OF TORONTO PRESS
Toronto Buffalo London

ISBN 978-1-4875-3672-5 (EPUB)

ISBN 978-1-4875-2529-3 (paper)   ISBN 978-1-4875-3671-8 (PDF)

Printed on acid-free, 100% post-consumer recycled paper with vegetable-based inks.

Library and Archives Canada Cataloguing in Publication

Title: Performing postracialism : reflections on antiblackness, nation, and
    education through contemporary blackface in Canada / Philip S.S. Howard.
Names: Howard, Philip S.S., 1964–, author.
Description: Includes bibliographical references and index.
Identifiers: Canadiana (print) 20220274339 | Canadiana (ebook)
    20220274436 | ISBN 9781487525293 (paper) | ISBN 9781487536725 (EPUB) |
    ISBN 9781487536718 (PDF)
Subjects: LCSH: Blackface – Canada. | LCSH: Racism against Black
    people – Canada. | LCSH: Racism in higher education. | LCSH: College
    students, Black – Canada. | LCSH: Canada – Race relations.
Classification: LCC FC106.B6 H69 2023 | DDC 305.896/071 – dc23

We wish to acknowledge the land on which the University of Toronto Press
operates. This land is the traditional territory of the Wendat, the Anishnaabeg,
the Haudenosaunee, the Métis, and the Mississaugas of the Credit First Nation.

This book has been published with the help of a grant from the Federation
for the Humanities and Social Sciences, through the Awards to Scholarly
Publications Program, using funds provided by the Social Sciences and
Humanities Research Council of Canada.

The book draws on research supported by the Social Sciences and Humanities
Research Council: SSHRC Insight Development Grant no. 430-2013-000432
and SSHRC Individual Connection Grant no. 611-2016-0429.

University of Toronto Press acknowledges the financial support of the
Government of Canada, the Canada Council for the Arts, and the Ontario Arts
Council, an agency of the Government of Ontario, for its publishing activities.

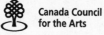

Canada Council
for the Arts

Conseil des Arts
du Canada

ONTARIO ARTS COUNCIL
CONSEIL DES ARTS DE L'ONTARIO
an Ontario government agency
un organisme du gouvernement de l'Ontario

Funded by the   Financé par le
Government   gouvernement
of Canada   du Canada

Canadä

MIX
Paper from
responsible sources
FSC® C016245

Contents

Acknowledgments

Authoring a book is a Herculean undertaking. While I take full responsibility for having authored this monograph, the designation "sole-authored" belies the multiple ways in which other persons make the book possible.

I would like to thank those who generously consented to participate in the studies that are the foundation upon which this book rests. It goes without saying, though I will not let it go without saying, that this book could not have existed without them. I particularly want to thank the students I interviewed, whose sharp insights and willingness to share so openly and engage so earnestly made this part of the research process most enjoyable as we built community for however limited a season.

I would also like to thank the several research assistants who supported me during this project with data collection, literature reviews, survey interpretation, transcription, and engaging in conversation about the study. These are: Aman Sium, Frédérique Bournot, Joel Reid, Judith Goodwin-Hall, Keisha Smith, Douglas Creighton, Marilyn Ize-Dukuze, Emily Yee Clare, and especially Desmond Miller, whose enthusiasm about this project was profoundly encouraging when the going was not necessarily smooth.

I am grateful to the following journals for permission to reproduce excerpts from the following previously published articles:

- Howard, P.S.S. (2018). A laugh for the national project: Contemporary Canadian blackface humour and its constitution through Canadian anti-blackness. *Ethnicities, 18*(6), 843–68.
- Howard, P.S.S. (2018). On the back of Blackness: Contemporary Canadian blackface and the consumptive production of post-racialist, white Canadian subjects. *Social Identities, 24*(1), 87–103.

Of course, I wish to thank my partner Haden, my son, my daughter, and my parents, who were deeply understanding and compassionate when this project called me away from time I ought to have been spending with them.

Last, but not least, I would like to thank the Lord Jesus, the source of my life and purpose, without whose inspiration and sustenance this project could never have been possible.

This book is dedicated to all the Black persons who make life, and do so richly, at the university and in Canada against all the odds.

PERFORMING POSTRACIALISM

Reflections on Antiblackness, Nation, and Education
through Contemporary Blackface in Canada

Introduction: Genesis and Intentions

Performing Postracialism is about blackface in Canada. It is equally about antiblackness, Canadian postracialism, and the Canadian university. Its point of departure is an examination of what I refer to as contemporary blackface in Canada – instances in which non-Black persons in the geopolitical space known to many as Canada today temporarily darken their skin with make-up to impersonate Black people – usually for fun, and frequently in educational contexts. *Performing Postracialism* employs these incidents as a lens through which to understand the broader institutional and national contexts in which they occur, in an analysis that prioritizes Black people's theorizing – both the quotidian forms that Black people use to understand our lives as we live them, and those more distilled forms of that theorizing produced by Black academics.

With regard to the specific practice of blackface, humour scholarship has examined how ambivalent racist jokes propagate racist rhetoric in contemporary times (Billig, 2001; Marwick & Lewis, 2017; Pérez, 2013, 2017; Weaver, 2011). There is also a well-developed literature analysing blackface minstrelsy of the nineteenth to mid-twentieth centuries in the United States (e.g., Cockrell, 1997; Hartman, 1997; Lhamon, 1998, 2003; Lott, 1993; Roediger, 1999) and, to a much lesser extent, in Canada (e.g., Best, 2008; Johnson, 2012, 2017; Nicks & Sloniowski, 2010), which addresses minstrelsy's relevance to white subject formation at a historical juncture most accept was overtly racist. However, little scholarship, and certainly no book-length project that I am aware of, has addressed how the embodied performance of blackface is constituted in the contemporary moment, and no scholarship looks at this phenomenon in contemporary Canada. This gap in the literature mirrors the tendency in scholarly and popular circles to consider contemporary blackface solely as it relates to historical minstrelsy in the United States. Black communities' concerns about contemporary blackface are therefore largely dismissed as belonging properly to another time and place, and contemporary blackface in Canada is recast as harmless fun. Indeed, the existing literature does not address the persistent allure and ostensible humour of blackface in the present, how this might make sense in a national context that declares itself multicultural and egalitarian, or why it is so popular in educational settings. This book endeavours, in part, to answer these questions by exploring how contemporary blackface in Canada is produced by *current* racialized relations *in Canada*. Guided by the data upon which it is based, the book works within a discursive framework that understands antiblackness as rooted in relations of slavery, and as casting Blackness[1] continually as the antithesis of Western conceptions of the Human[2] (see, e.g., Sexton, 2016; Walcott, 2014c; Wilderson, 2003; Wynter, 1994b, 2003) to be discussed further in Chapter 1. The outcome of two Social Sciences and Humanities Research Council of Canada (SSHRC)–funded research projects[3] investigating blackface incidents in the last fifteen to twenty years in Canada, this book's central premise is that contemporary blackface is more than a simple matter of racist (mis)representation. Rather, contemporary blackface, its ostensible humour, and the conversations around it instantiate extant formations of antiblackness in the nation state and in educational settings. Further, contemporary blackface functions as a postracialist pedagogy, propagating and normalizing antiblack logics through the very claim to have overcome them. *Performing Postracialism* particularly attends to educational contexts as sites where blackface frequently occurs, to examine their institutional complicities in broader relations of Canadian antiblackness. The book ends with a meditation on the fugitive learning that Black members of university communities

---

1 I define "Blackness" as the state of being Black in the world. This is, of course, not a biological or genetic definition. Rather, it is related to how people of African descent are positioned in the contemporary post-Columbus world. It is also a non-monolithic political identification that informs the various ways in which Black people make/ live Black life in this historical moment.

2 Throughout this book, I capitalize the word "Human" when I intend to refer to the West's (but increasingly global) socially constructed understanding of humanity. This is what Sylvia Wynter (2003) refers to as "our present ethnoclass (i.e., Western bourgeois) conception of the human, Man" (p. 260) that is defined against whatever it might mean to be Black (p. 44).

3 SSHRC Insight Development Grant no. 430-2013-000432: Racial Humour in the Post-racial: A Critical Race Africology of Canadian Blackface Incidents, and SSHRC Individual Connection Grant no. 611-2016-0429: The Arts Against Postracialism: Strengthening Resistance Against Contemporary Canadian Blackface.

engage in that allows and fosters Black life amid the climate of campus blackface and other forms of antiblackness there.

Postracialist Blackface

Books such as this one are always the result of many incremental moments that initiate questions and analysis. It is therefore almost impossible to pinpoint exactly when a book project begins. If pressed to identify such a moment, I might say that I first started thinking carefully about contemporary blackface in the heady early days of the Barack Obama presidency in the United States. We already knew about the constraints of the presidency for Obama (see Howard, 2010), and the near impossibility that it could meaningfully address the unique oppressive conditions that Black people face. Regrettably, we had already seen Obama position himself in postracial terms – particularly through his 18 March 2008, "A More Perfect Union" speech during his bid for the US Democratic Party nomination. Many of us held lurking fears about how he might be bound to further, rather than challenge, the American colonial project. Nevertheless I was, like many others were, still basking in what it meant, at least symbolically, that it had become possible for a Black man to be president of the United States.

We were not far into the Obama presidency before racist resentment erupted forcefully – both specifically against the person of Obama in representational (Howard, 2014a) and more substantive terms, and against Black people and Black life in general. I became particularly interested in the ways that this racist backlash frequently expressed itself through ostensible humour. Every so often we would see yet another internet meme, party incident, cartoon, or editorial – allegedly all in good fun – that drew on the most racist of tropes.

Blackface featured frequently at this time as part of the unfolding backlash against Blackness. This practice has a long history in the tradition of blackface minstrel shows, which emerged in the United States of the early nineteenth century as a wildly popular form of entertainment. Unbeknownst to many, minstrelsy was also widely practised and enjoyed beyond the United States, and specifically in Canada (Best, 2008; Johnson, 2017; Le Camp, 2005; Nicks & Sloniowski, 2010).

Of course, antiblack humour has never not been a thing since the days of slavery, and I am under no illusion that there had ever been any let-up in the structural antiblackness that undergirds the capitalist, colonial world order. Blackface as one vehicle for caricaturing Black people also never fell completely out of vogue. While minstrel shows occurred much less frequently after the Civil Rights movements of the 1960s – though they did not altogether disappear (Le Camp, 2005; Pérez, 2016) – the practice of "blacking up" outside the context of minstrel shows has endured. As Johnson (2012, p. 14) writes, blackface "is not a 'figure' that disappeared and then reemerged; it has always been present and accounted for, but only recently widely disseminated through YouTube ... Facebook," and other forms of social/electronic media. Nevertheless, in the moment just after Obama's election, I had the impression that I was seeing a sharper, more overt edge to this humour and the incidents of blackface than had been typical during, say, the decade before, and it appeared that we were seeing them more frequently. For some reason, blackface seemed to be a medium of choice in the Obama moment to provoke, to flout norms of acceptable public expression, and to register political and racial resentment. Thus, at the very moment that the United States was claiming to have become postracial, racist expression was proliferating, as though the lid that had repressed unapologetic public expression of an abiding antiblackness had been blown off. It occurred to me that this was not coincidental.

As someone living in Canada, which perpetually positions itself as more racially progressive than the United States, and where the idea of having transcended racism has long held sway in the national mythology, I was further struck by the ways I was hearing Canadians position themselves in this moment. The mood seemed to me to be "Congratulations, America, on finally catching up to our progressive standards!" – even as it would not be until 3 October 2020 (more than a decade later) that Canada could say that it had a Black leader of any federal political party, and even though Canadian prime minister Justin Trudeau after his 2015 election declared his to be the most diverse federal cabinet ever while it did not have a single Black member (Foster, 2015; Walcott, 2019). Even more interesting was the way that blackface incidents were gaining popularity here in tandem with what was happening in the United States. I took note of the ways that post-racial claims and racist humour were coinciding here as there.

There were two Canadian blackface incidents that particularly caught media attention at that time. The first was during Halloween 2009, when four white students at the University of Toronto appeared in dark makeup, one wearing a "dreadlock" wig, to portray the Jamaican bobsled team as depicted in the Disney movie *Cool Runnings*. They were accompanied by a racialized student who had painted his face chalk white to represent the team's coach (Mahoney, 2009). The second, essentially depicting a lynching, occurred in October 2010 at the Royal Canadian Legion in Campbellford, Ontario (CTV News, 2010). In both cases the blackface wearers were awarded prizes by their peers.

As importantly, in both cases the perpetrators denied that what they did was racist.

These are, however, not the only incidents of blackface to take place in the recent past in Canada. Among other incidents reported in the media are those in Winnipeg nightclubs (Benedictson, 2013; CBC News, 2014c); one by a Toronto drag queen (Prestwich, 2013); those involving public officials and politicians of all stripes who wore blackface prior to being in office (e.g., Bowe, 2019; CBC News, 2018; Kelland, 2017; Shah, 2019), not the least significant of which were three occasions that came to light in late 2019 in which Prime Minister Justin Trudeau had earlier worn blackface (CBC News, 2019); multiple portrayals of Canadian hockey-player P.K. Subban (e.g., CBC News, 2015; Petchesky, 2010); those by Dutch heritage communities in several provinces that persist in portraying the blackface character Zwarte Piet (e.g., CBC News, 2016b; Crawford, 2017; Huffington Post Canada, 2013; Larsen, 2019; Prestwich, 2016); and numerous performances by Quebec comedians (e.g., Béland, 2012; Dunlevy, 2016; Ravary, 2013).

As a scholar in the field of education, I was intrigued that, in addition to the above, so many of the Canadian blackface incidents occurred in association with educational institutions – that is, at schools and universities. In addition to the University of Toronto incident mentioned above, there were incidents at Queen's University (MacMillan, 2005); Wilfrid Laurier University (HueyFreeman222, 2007); HEC Montréal, the business school of the Université de Montréal (Montpetit, 2011); the 2012 Montreal student protests (Morgan, 2012); Mayfield Secondary School in Caledon, ON (Karstens-Smith & Rushowy, 2013); Brock University (CBC News, 2014b); Collège de Montréal in Montreal (TVA Nouvelles, 2017); Citadel High School in Halifax (CTV Atlantic, 2019); John Rennie High School in Pointe Claire, QC (CBC News, 2020); and it is worth noting that all of Justin Trudeau's blackface incidents occurred in education contexts. The above are by no means exhaustive lists, for once we began interviews for this project, we heard of numerous other campus blackface incidents that participants had witnessed but that had not garnered media attention.

The discussions that followed these incidents, both online in comments under media articles and in person, frequently justified blackface in post-racial terms as harmless and non-racist, sometimes with reference to the "progress" marked by Obama's presidency, and certainly with reference to Canada's reputation for being the friendly, non-racist North. Taking all these realities together, then, some of the objectives that motivated my research into contemporary blackface in Canada were to understand the mechanisms that repeatedly return people to blackface performance, the discursive context(s) within which these contemporary blackface incidents in Canada are performed, articulated, justified, and apologized for in a postracialist climate; and why educational contexts in Canada seem to foster the performance of blackface.

Meanwhile, Black People's Voices

However, my concern with blackface perhaps goes back further to a graduate class on race and racism I took almost a decade earlier in which I was introduced to Eric Lott's (1993) *Love and Theft*. Lott argued that the extreme popularity of blackface minstrelsy in the nineteenth-century United States was informed by white people's (particularly white working-class people's) ambivalent relationships to Blackness – involving both desire and aversion. As cogent as the analysis was, I remember experiencing a deep unease with it that I struggled to articulate.

The dissatisfaction I felt then would arise again as I later reviewed other minstrelsy literature, which includes Cockrell's (1997) *Demons of Disorder* and Lhamon's *Raising Cain* (1998) and *Jump Jim Crow* (2003). I realized that collectively this work, predominantly authored by white scholars in music, theatre, and performance genres, seemed puzzlingly preoccupied with complicating minstrelsy. It appeared motivated by a peculiar need to make minstrelsy something other than "just racist," positing it instead as a confluence of more fundamental nationalist, class, ethnic, and gender relations, and as resistance to white elite culture in the formation of new white identities. Like Lott (1993, p. 15), most of these authors felt that a "we" of the contemporary moment were blinded by our contemporary views on race and that "we," in a form of presentism, were therefore wont to impose a monolithic view of blackface minstrelsy that was not true to how white people who earlier performed and enjoyed minstrelsy would have felt. However, this approach requires one to overlook, where it does not expressly contradict, the views of the *Black* thinkers who wrote during minstrelsy's heyday. Indeed, the first chapter of Lott's (1993) book opens with Frederick Douglass's unequivocal 1848 condemnation of minstrelsy, which Lott then anachronistically uses to characterize "our" view at the time of his writing (p. 15). Lott proceeds to challenge Douglass's position, later misreading Du Bois's and James Weldon Johnson's correct identification of minstrelsy as, in part, an appropriation of Black culture as though they amounted to endorsements of the practice (p. 16).

The tenor of this work goes further to what are, in my assessment, rather dangerous ends. For example, in a 2012 chapter, Lhamon makes specific connections between blackface and the election of Barack Obama, much as I have above, but with a peculiar twist that aligns with the dominant narrative of the scholarship on minstrelsy that I have been describing. Lhamon applies his analysis of minstrelsy to the entirety of social arrangements of the Jim Crow era in the United States. In a genealogy of the term and concept, Lhamon (2012) argues that "Jim Crow" originally had an integrationist meaning, rather than the segregationist meaning that is now almost exclusively and indisputably understood when the term is used. Lhamon proposes that blackface minstrelsy and (his version of) Jim Crow – indelibly intertwined through T. D. Rice's minstrel anthem *Jump Jim Crow* – were the vehicles through which an interracial desire was forged, eventually leading to the country's de jure rejection of segregation, and ultimately to the possibility of the Obama moment. For Lhamon:

> Jim Crow is the fetish figure that tangles these American oppositions, demanding that we untie them. To learn that knot is to understand the contrarieties in American life – *something beyond the disgust and shame and horror at the cruel facts*. It is to acknowledge the intense waves of emotional release, manifested in tears, that coursed through the country on election day, November 4, 2008, and again on inauguration day, January 20, 2009. Down the tracks of those tears, Americans were releasing pent-up shame and longing tamped tight for centuries. Those tracks reenact and retell a story running from Jim Crow through Barack Obama. (p. 24, emphasis added)

While my fascination in the Obama moment was with the revival of blackface, where blackface appeared to serve seamlessly as an apt vehicle for expressing indignation at the Obama presidency, Lhamon read the same moment as an opportunity to redeem not only minstrelsy and blackface, but also Jim Crow.

Similarly, C.M. Cole (2012) in the chapter "American Ghetto Parties and Ghanaian Concert Parties" in the same collection, wonders whether blackface ghetto parties, popular on US university campuses, are

> a performance of disavowal – a disidentification with places, identities, and lived realities to which the upwardly mobile college student does *not* aspire. Or ... a performance of identification, a grasping for authenticity in a media-saturated world, and a sign that even the most elite college students see that a neoliberalized future has now put them in the "ghetto" too. (p. 249, emphasis in original)

For me, whether it is Cole's ability to wonder about the most white-supremacist of parties and imagine a level racial playing field within neoliberal, racial capitalism or Lhamon's ability to imagine an unproblematic (if complex) desire for Blackness driving an ostensible agenda of racial harmony through as currently uncontroversially racist a project as Jim Crow, these are examples of the kind of argument that is incessantly made about blackface and minstrelsy in mainstream minstrelsy scholarship. These readings require us to look "beyond ... the cruel facts" (Lhamon, 2012, p. 24). But we cannot all equally afford, nor do we all equally desire, to do so. This tendency in the literature is, for me, part of a broader, dangerous leaning towards giving the benefit of the doubt to white supremacy while dismissing Black people's analyses, and towards disregarding antiblackness's violent and deadly effects on us. I wonder whether it is generally clearer now in 2021, as I write, that blackface expression has not led to harmony; that it was indignant backlash rather than repentant desire for racial unity that found such impunitive expression through blackface during the Obama years and beyond, and that eventually brought America to the Trump presidency and a call to "make America great (that is, white) again"?

However, while mainstream minstrelsy scholarship is dominated by these perplexing voices, there have always been Black voices. There were those who spoke out in no uncertain terms against blackface at the height of its popularity – such as Douglass, who referred to white minstrels as "the filthy scum of white society, who have stolen from us the complexion denied to them by nature" (cited in Lott, 1993, p. 15), and Ellison (1958) in *Change the Joke, Slip the Yoke*, who noted that the "white man's relish is apt to be the black man's gall" (p. 104). Then there have been later analyses, particularly the chapter "Innocent Amusements: The Stage of Sufferance" in Saidiyah Hartman's (1997) *Scenes of Subjection*, that have focused less on whiteness than on the foundational antiblackness of blackface and its impact on Black people. As Hartman writes:

> Overwhelmingly the donning of the blackface mask reiterated racial subjection, however much this subjection might provide a liberatory vehicle for white working-class consciousness or a sense of white integrity and wholeness effected by the policing of racial boundaries. In blackface, as elsewhere in antebellum society, the fashioning of whiteness in large measure occurred by way of the subjugation of blacks. The illusory integrity of whiteness facilitated by attraction and/or antipathy to blackness was ultimately predicated upon the indiscriminate use and possession of the black body. (p. 32)

I have been deeply impacted by these analyses.[4] Rejecting a dubious academic impartiality, I wish in this book to speak in concert with the voices of those whose bodies position us as the primary targets of blackface humour, and who refuse to allow assertions of complexity to speak louder than our own embodied readings of the phenomenon.

Blackface Incidents as Lens to Examine Canadian Education

In addition to contributing to the blackface literature, this book contributes to the scholarship examining the intersections of Blackness, schooling, and academia in Canada. Book-length projects in this regard include Dei's (1996) *Anti-racism Education*, Dei, Mazzuca, McIsaac, and Zine's (1997) *Reconstructing Dropout*, and James's (2005) *Race in Play* and (2012) *Life at the Intersection*. These, focused primarily on Ontario, accompany a host of other books, articles, and reports concerning other provinces (e.g., Black Learners Advisory Committee [BLAC], 1994; H.M. Codjoe, 2001; McAndrew et al, 2006), examining Black teachers' experiences and pedagogies both historically and in the contemporary moment (e.g., Aladejebi, 2012, 2015b; Cooper, 2002; A. Henry, 1992; Howard, 2014b; Howard & James, 2019), Black students' experiences (e.g., H.M. Codjoe, 2001; Lafortune & Balde, 2012; McPherson, 2020; Solomon & Palmer, 2004), pedagogies with/for/by Black students (e.g., H. Codjoe, 2006; Mogadime, 2000), and community-led initiatives intended to address the failings of state schooling in meeting the needs of Black students – specifically African-centred schooling (e.g., Dei, 1995; Dei & Kempf, 2013; hampton, 2010; A. Henry, 1993; Howard, 2013, 2014b). Some of this work takes up the dynamics of diaspora, migration, and being/becoming Black in the context of schooling (e.g., Ibrahim, 2014, 2019). However, most of this work focuses primarily on schooling at the K–12 levels in Canada.

There is a much less extensive literature that addresses the university context. Bannerji, Carty, Dehli, Heald, and McKenna's (1991) *Unsettling Relations* and Henry and Tator's (2009) edited volume *Racism and the Canadian University* include various anti-racist and feminist (which are not, of course, mutually exclusive) meditations on the academy. With the exception of Carty's (1991) Black Marxist feminist analysis, which remains highly instructive today thirty years after its first publication, these volumes largely do not specify Black experience,

---

4 Non-Black scholar David Roediger writes another impactful analysis in this vein in the chapter "White Skins, Black Masks" in his book *The Wages of Whiteness* (1999).

or more accurately do not name Black experience even when this is what is under consideration. There are, of course, a diversity of racially informed experiences of the university, all deserving of scholarly attention. However, it is important that Blackness and Black experience do not become invisible under larger catch-all terms such as "race," and it is important to avoid a "people-of-colour blindness" whereby Black people's experiences are used to make the case for change (as they are in Henry and Tator's introduction) but where that specificity is lost when solutions are considered (Dumas, 2018; Sexton, 2010; Vargas, 2018). In *Racism in the Canadian University*, Hernandez-Ramdwar (2009) rightly indicts the ways in which racial distinctions are employed by the state to uphold white supremacy in ways that particularly affect students from the Caribbean, but does not sufficiently problematize the ways in which the failure to consider the distinct workings of different processes of racialization also maintains the status quo and promotes antiblackness.

Several studies do specifically examine Black people's experience in the Canadian university, addressing, for example, students' experiences of navigating the university (e.g., Bullen, 2007; Mogadime, 2002; Wane, 2009), including how Black women faculty contribute to caring for Black students (Bernard et al., 2000). Some of this work, particularly more recent work in the Quebec context (e.g., Agbaire, 2019; Magnan et al., 2021), study the experiences of Black people at the university within the theoretical framework of microaggressions – a conceptualization that, in my view, fails to capture the endemic nature of antiblackness (though even this intervention is welcome in the Quebec provincial context where the government halts even at admitting the existence of systemic racism [CBC News, 2017; Shingler, 2018; Williams, 2020]). These more liberal analyses are complemented by historical analyses that focus on the fraught relationships between Canadian universities and Black people, such that the university is constituted by these relationships (e.g., Austin, 2013; Cooper et al., 2019; hampton, 2020). An important strand of scholarship at the intersection of Blackness and the university is that which takes up Black Studies and its defining, yet defiant, relationships with the Canadian university, Canadian Studies, and the nation state (e.g., Austin, 2007, 2013; hampton, 2020; Hudson & Kamugisha, 2014; Walcott, 2000, 2003b, 2014a; Walcott & Abdillahi, 2019).

Two recent books are of particular note in relation to *Performing Postracialism*. The first of these is Eternity Martis's (2020) *They Said This Would Be Fun*. This layered autobiography of Martis's experiences as a Black woman undergraduate student at Western University is the only account of its type of which I am aware. It specifies gendered antiblackness, and gives the reader an intimate picture of how these relations overdetermine Black students' experiences at Canadian universities, forestalling any hope they might hold of having the enjoyable, away-from-home, rite-of-passage experience that attending university is made out to be. Of particular note in relation to this book is how white students use blackface, among many other techniques, to produce Black unbelonging. Also important are Martis's accounts of surviving this hostile climate through forming community with other Black people at the university.

The second recent book is rosalind hampton's (2020) study of McGill University, *Black Racialization and Resistance at an Elite University*, which hampton refers to as an institutional/political activist ethnography. Its importance is in the way that it traces, largely by way of interviews with Black people and an examination of McGill artefacts, how "Canadian settler nationalisms" (p. 104) play out at the university in relation to Black people, and how Black people have resisted within/out and against these formations.

Performing Postracialism makes a contribution to this educational literature, and speaks alongside these recent books. It attends to the long postracialist moment in Canada, as I signal above. Blackface serves as a vehicle through which to examine the postracialist national consciousness, and how its discourses coalesce around this highly contested phenomenon. Through blackface and its discourses we gain access to the ways in which antiblackness is instantiated in the settler-colonial nation state and its institutions, what it might mean to navigate this contradictory postracialist climate as a Black person, and especially how Black people struggle against, occasionally fall for, and/or make life in spite of its seductions. In this vein, *Performing Postracialism*'s exploration of blackface incidents and the discourses around them simultaneously examines the dynamics of antiblackness as it plays out in Canadian university and other education institutions.

Methodology

Participants and Data

The first study upon which this book is based is a three-year study of blackface in relation to incidents taking place since roughly 2005 on university campuses and beyond in Canada. I conducted interviews and focus groups at seven universities. Student participants were recruited through cooperating university courses and student unions as well as by word-of mouth, directing them to a link to a voluntary online survey that asked their views about blackface at university, its impacts, and whether/how it should be addressed by administration. From among the students indicating interest in participating further, the research team invited focus group participants representing a broad range of locations (e.g., self-identified race, gender, age, year in studies, discipline) and the range of responses to the survey. The students selected were encouraged to invite friends. Across the seven campuses, the research team conducted ten focus groups open to all students (comprising a total of fifty-six students).

I crucially wanted to prioritize Black people's knowledge in trying to understand the meaning of the blackface phenomenon and how it is experienced within the context of mainstream post-race discourses. Therefore, we also reached out to campus Black student organizations (BSOs) where they existed, and were able to arrange focus groups on three campuses for executive members of these organizations and members they wished to invite. These sessions involved a total of thirteen students—eight identified as women and five as men. We conducted three individual interviews with Black students (all identifying as men) who were unable to make any of the focus groups, and two individual interviews with Black students in focus groups who requested follow-up interviews to share further information. We therefore spoke to a total of thirty Black students who either participated in the general focus groups, the BSO focus groups, or the interviews. Thirteen identified as women and seventeen as men. Of the forty-two students who were not Black, thirty identified as women and twelve as men.

We conducted individual interviews with thirteen administrators and staff (three identified as men and ten as women) whose roles included a social justice mandate and/or who were tasked with responding to blackface incidents that had occurred. We also interviewed seven faculty members (one man and six women, including two Black women) involved in responding to campus blackface incidents.

In addition to the data from interviews and focus groups, the study examined online media articles about blackface incidents in Canada. We gathered as many articles about each incident as were generated by search engines and that we could find in print media such as university and community newspapers until the data on each incident seemed to saturate. Since blackface incidents continued to occur after the project began, articles were collected on an ongoing basis. We collected and analysed a total of 104 articles covering some twenty incidents reported in the media over the last seventeen years. Photographs of the blackface incidents as well as reader comments on the media articles were included as data.

A smaller second study was conducted in relation to arts-based events I held across four university campuses intended to mobilize knowledge from the first study above. Details about these events are described more fully in Chapter 9, which is the only chapter in which these data are used (alongside data from the first study). Here we conducted a focus group with the five Black artists who participated in this project, with Black students from the Black student organizations on each campus who assisted with the planning and execution of the events, and gathered written feedback through online and paper surveys from attendees at the events and art installations.

Epistemological Foundations and Data Analysis

As a result of travel constraints and funding limitations, the seven universities included in this study are all in Ontario and Quebec, two among the Canadian provinces with the highest proportions of Black persons. Each of the universities at which we conducted interviews was associated with a contemporary blackface incident that we learned of through the media or by word of mouth. These campuses were not selected supposing that they were exceptional because of their association with blackface incidents, but so that participants might have a common reference point. My conviction is that antiblackness is embedded within overarching social, institutional, and discursive structures; therefore, while not representative of all Canadian universities in a statistical sense, the data collected on these seven campuses together offer insight into larger university and societal structures, and the broader societal discourses around blackface to which individuals have access. Throughout these pages, I discuss where there are specificities to these discourses that might be related to the province in which they occur.

As noted above, this study insists on the salience of the experiences of Black people with regard to issues that affect them. In the introduction to *Dusk of Dawn*, one of his many treatises on Black life and antiblackness, W.E.B. Du Bois (1940) wrote:

> The problem of the future world is the charting, by means of intelligent reason, of a path not simply through the resistances of physical force, but through the vaster and far more intricate jungle of ideas conditioned on unconscious and subconscious reflexes of living things; on blind unreason and often irresistible urges of sensitive matter; of which the concept of race is today one of the most unyielding and threatening. I seem to see a way of elucidating the inner meaning and significance of that race problem by explaining it in terms of the one human life that I know best. (p. 5)

In so saying, Du Bois highlighted the salience of the testimonies of Black people in articulating the conditions of our lives. Years later, Patricia Hill Collins (2000) would insist upon "lived experience as a criterion of meaning" in Black women's lives (p. 275), identifying Black experience not only as data for analysis, but as the site from which to undertake analysis. Another way of saying this is that Black experience is generative of the necessary theory that makes Black life possible, and that it challenges paradigms that always already disregard Black life, never mind the possibility of Black thought. As bell hooks (1994) notes:

> When our lived experience of theorizing is fundamentally linked to processes of self-recovery, of collective liberation, no gap exists between theory and practice. Indeed, what such experience makes more evident is the bond between the two – that ultimately reciprocal process wherein one enables the other. (p. 26)

More than a standpoint epistemology, this is a methodology taking up Black thought/experience/theory in a way that calls not for its insertion into existing dominant forms of thought, but rather lays bare the anti-blackness that militates against Black being, indicts the fantasy of the possibility of inclusion, and sketches out Black life beyond that which is predicated on its negation without making Black life and thought analogous to white positionality (Hartman & Wilderson, 2003, p. 187; Moten, 2013).

One reviewer of this book in manuscript suggested that the perspectives shared by participants in the study represent only a narrow subset of Black perspectives on the matter – that of "university students belonging to or with pathway towards the middle class." The reviewer suggested the students' articulation of their experiences might in fact be atypical, and not representative of a majority of Black persons' understandings of blackface. Since the respondents were all university students at the time of the interviews, there could be some truth to this suggestion, which would be substantiated by studies of Black students in Canada that suggest, unsurprisingly, that Black students gain access to a kind of critical analysis that they often do not have before entering university (Bullen, 2007, p. 156; Hernandez-Ramdwar, 2009, pp. 108–9). It is important to also say that such a relationship should not be presumed without caution. Other work suggests that gaining a university education may in fact militate against critical Black perspectives in favour of ones more aligned with white middle-class perspectives (see e.g., Gosine, 2002, 2008; Rollock et al., 2012). Further, the reviewer's suggestion aligns with a view that critical Black perspectives are developed in the university and flow outward, rather than with the more accurate view that radical Black thought is created in struggle, forged through the experiences of Black people, thereafter flowing into the university, not without risk to the integrity of that thought (Kelley, 2016b). In any case, as will become clear in the chapters that follow, while the participants do narrate their experience of blackface in similar terms, these are not analyses that they speak of as having learned in classes. Indeed, many struggled to articulate what to them was a visceral or embodied reaction to blackface, and worked it into words as they spoke to us. Their perspectives also held resonance with the widely held perspectives of Black persons outside of the university context (whose relationships to the university I admittedly cannot speak to) who write media articles, comment on media articles, and otherwise express objection to blackface.

With respect to dominant discourses, the study used critical discourse and critical visual analysis (e.g., Aiello, 2006; van Dijk, 1991, 1993, 2000; Wetherell & Potter, 1988), to understand the discursive contexts within which blackface is produced and challenged. Media reports are always artefacts of the social contexts in which they are produced and largely represent elite perspectives (van Dijk, 2000), though given the opportunity for readers to comment electronically, sometimes quite unguardedly, on media articles published online, we can gain access to a greater range of perspectives – including more unapologetic forms of dominant discourse than the "polite," postracialist, racist discourse often characterizing Canadian media, as well as oppositional discourses. Articles in Black community newspapers and some comments from Black people responding on mainstream media articles gave access to other sources of Black opinion.

Images of incidents of contemporary blackface in Canada were also analysed. These were usually amateur photographs posted on social media and/or reproduced in online media articles. Analysis did not focus on the composition of the photographs, but rather on the blackface costuming within them and what they might say about how Blackness is conceived of. I have deliberately not included any photographs of blackface incidents in this book, understanding fully the antiblack violence that these images reinflict at each fresh viewing. I have preferred to, where necessary, describe the incidents such that the descriptions always appear alongside my critique and exposure of their antiblack, white-supremacist character.

All data were subjected to an inductive analysis to identify themes within and across the different categories of data. It goes without saying that my theoretical orientations and embodied experience guided me in the identification of themes, and before this in the construction of the study. Nevertheless, the themes I began to identify also directed me, in turn, to further relevant theoretical literature of which I had not been aware. I engaged this literature for its explanatory power in relation to the study data. It was placed in conversation with, rather than imposed upon, the data – a process that is reflected in the structure of the chapters that follow. I resist both orthodoxy – an approach that squeezes life into theory rather than engaging theory as it makes it possible to understand the terms of our living; and the demand for orthodoxy, often imposed from without. Thus, for example, while I cite some Afropessimist scholarship, I do not, and likely never will, embrace the Afropessimist reading of social death to describe Black life in all its richness – even as it is beleaguered by antiblackness. To say that Black people are evicted from dominant notions of the Human, barred from political community, and subject to premature death is not, for me, tantamount to a lack of life, but rather to the promise of life lived on different terms. Similarly, I do not embrace a reading of racism and antiblackness that makes them mutually exclusive, even while I acknowledge that they are not the same. I am fully of the opinion that antiblackness needs to be thought on different terms than racial domination of non-Black people of colour as an antagonism that is "ontological and gratuitous as opposed to merely ideological and contingent" (Wilderson, 2003, p. 229). However, this is not the same as saying that antiblackness is not related to skin colour and embodied characteristics, and therefore that it is not in broad terms a kind of racialization. Neither I nor Afro-pessimists claim that race is inapplicable to Black people

This way of working might, to some, appear to violate a purist approach to theoretical literature and perhaps even disquiet some of the scholars I engage. I have become comfortable in inhabiting this location of uncertainty (the exact coordinates of which are likely to shift for me in the future as I continue to do this work) to the extent that my engagement allows me to read the data and the experience of participants with integrity rather than manipulate them to suit a predetermined set of theoretical claims.

My Learning

I have learned immensely through writing this book and through the research projects associated with it. I am grateful for the many friends and colleagues who have encouraged me along the way, doggedly expressing confidence in my gut motivations. Yet this project has given me no end of trouble in terms of trying to justify its worthiness.

I was asked why I was interested in the actions of a few ignorant white folk, and why this was worth examination. Some well-meaning white colleagues even attempted to school me about why working on the issue of blackface was misguided. "The goal of anti-racist, anti-colonial work," one white colleague felt he need to remind me, "is not to make more apologetic or careful white supremacists, but to take down white supremacy." There is an inherent assumption here, he may not have noticed, that my main audience would be white. But then, some Black colleagues also were apprehensive that I might be hoping to offer an easy liberal fix for universities dealing with blackface, or were worried about the value of my research when there are so many more violent things happening to Black people in the contemporary moment that are worthy of attention. Disheartening as these challenges were, they forced me to identify why this project was important to me, and the value I hoped it would have. More importantly, in working through these critiques I have learned to listen, and my political and theoretical commitments have been sharpened. I have come to be able to articulate more clearly my reasons for this project.

I situate this project in a desire to listen – really listen – to Black people. Blackface is a phenomenon that has existed for at least two hundred years, and several generations. Black people have, since the beginning, been deeply disturbed and outraged by these acts in ways that defy the superficial reading of blackface as *just* the work of foolish white people. These feelings were an indication to me of the deep psychic offence of blackface. Paying attention to the reactions of Black people suggests doing the close analytical work to discover how and why this is of such deep concern, rather than coming to some simple conclusion that Black people have better things they ought to think about and put their energies into. Many of my participants confessed a difficulty articulating exactly the reason for their offence at blackface, and that this was exacerbated by incessant Canadian claims to the diminishing significance of race. My hope is that this work will share the words and concepts – grounded in interviews with Black people, and drawn through the lens of Black scholarship – that will help us to articulate and own our indignation. In this way, this is a project for us and by us.

Second, I take up Saidiya Hartman's challenge (1997, p. 4) to look not only to spectacular instances of antiblack violence, but to trace antiblackness in the everyday and in that which escapes recognition because it is considered pleasurable. In this way we expose the "terror of the mundane" (Hartman, 1997, p. 4), the everyday ways that we are violated but are expected to overlook.

Third, and related to the second, through my research I have now learned that blackface is really not so easily separated from physically violent antiblackness, as I argue throughout this work. Mustaffa (2017, p. 723) identifies blackface specifically as a form of violence connected to the very same logics against which movements for Black life of our day are organizing. This relationship becomes starkly evident in the Canadian context if we consider what it might mean that members of law enforcement, an institution deeply implicated in the enclosure, control, incarceration, and premature deaths of Black people in Canada, are also significantly represented among Canadian perpetrators of blackface not associated with universities (CTV News, 2010; Eggerston, 1995; Kelland, 2017; Le Camp, 2005). We might also think about why an individual somehow saw fit to show up in blackface, asserting his right to do so, during protests in Toronto in the wake of the deaths in police custody of George Floyd and Regis Korchinski-Paquet (D'Sa, 2020). In the end, it is clear to me that blackface and antiblack humour bridge the psychic, the interpersonal, and the structural, tapping into the deep motivations, desires, and libidinal currents that are the very source of the egregious acts of hatred, abuse, and murder of Black people. My hope is that this book makes the multiple relationships between antiblack violence and death and the antiblackness of blackface and its ostensible humour evident and comprehensible.

Summary of Chapters

Performing Postracialism is divided into two parts and nine chapters. Part 1, consisting of Chapters 1–4, examines the broad implications and meanings of blackface and its production through the antiblack structures of the broader Canadian postracialist, settler-colonial project. My intention here is to make a comprehensive statement about blackface from a Black Studies perspective. I engage existing Black Studies scholarship and other critical race literature, placing it in conversation with empirical work to understand Black people's deep objections to blackface and the gap between this objection and the ways that non-Black, often white, publics take up blackface.

Chapter 1, "Contemporary Blackface in Canada as Performance of Antiblackness," analyses the reactions of Black study participants to blackface, drawing attention to their frequent references to slavery and other systems of historical racial violence, thus demonstrating that they experience blackface on these terms. Drawing on Saidiya Hartman's 2007 concept of the "afterlife of slavery" and her 1997 analysis of blackface minstrelsy in the United States, the chapter argues that blackface appropriates the Black body and Black identities, thereby re-inscribing the relations of slavery, which depend on the exchange value of the Black body. These factors announce the inherent antiblackness of contemporary blackface, and its animation by the antiblack pillars of the Canadian settler-colonial project.

Chapter 2, "What's the Joke? The Black Body as White Pleasure in Canadian Blackface," examines both Black and non-Black participants' understandings of the ostensible humour of contemporary blackface. Employing Weaver's (2011) concept of embodied racism, it argues that the humour of contemporary blackface depends upon an antiblack libidinal economy (Wilderson, 2010, p. 7), and a socially embedded, psychic association of the Black body and its commodification with white pleasure (Hartman, 1997) founded, again, in the relations of slavery and its afterlife. The chapter further argues that this humour is intensified in/through the Canadian postracialist national discourse of multiculturalism that makes Blackness perpetually foreign and out of place in Canada.

Chapter 3, "Defending Blackface: Performing the 'Progressive,' Postracialist Canadian," analyses public online debates about blackface as represented in reader comments on electronic media articles about blackface. Drawing on this data in relation to Goldberg's analyses of racial neoliberalism (2009), postracialism (2012), and the concept of racial dis-appearance (2012), I argue that discourses around contemporary blackface in Canada are postracialist in their tendency to juxtapose racist expression with claims to racial transcendence, and that this discourse helps to shore up ostensibly progressive, (usually white) Canadian subjectivities. The chapter positions this identity-making dynamic within a broader Canadian practice of constructing its national mythologies partially through revisionist understandings of the nation state's relationship to Blackness.

Chapter 4, "Pornotroping Performances: Overt Violence, Un/Gendering, and Sex in Contemporary Blackface," wraps up Part 1. It is an exploration of incidents of contemporary blackface in Canada that portray overt antiblack violence, and simultaneously an examination of the place of gender in Canadian blackface. The chapter grew organically from my observation that gender seemed to be made relatively insignificant in the visual presentation of blackface in Canada. As is my general approach throughout this book, I work up from the data to incorporate theoretical literature that might prove explanatory. Working with Spillers's (1987) formulation of the pornotrope, the chapter traces the ways that ungendering and violence as well as the scopic/spectacular are inseparably intertwined in contemporary blackface. The chapter argues that in the postracialist context of Canada, antiblack violence is always haunting even the most seemingly innocuous blackface incident. Consequently, the *performance* of antiblackness and enfleshment is *performative*, instantiating, in the performance, the very relations it portrays.

Part 2 of the book focuses in on how the relations and structures discussed in Part 1 play out in the specific context of Canadian universities and schools, sites where blackface frequently occurs in Canada. It contributes to the scholarship on higher education in Canada by using blackface and the circumstances that surround it as a site from which to understand the antiblackness that characterizes Canadian education. Chapter 5, "Blackface at University: The Antiblack Logics of Canadian Academia," juxtaposes interviews with Black participants, who invariably connect their experiences with blackface to a wider climate of antiblackness throughout their schooling, with interviews with university administrators. I draw on McKittrick's (2006) meditation on Blackness as surprise in Canada and Wynter's (1979) discussion of the Sambo figure to explain the constitutive antiblackness of the current Canadian university, and what we might call the predictable unpredictability of blackface there. The chapter argues that the tropes of blackface and the antiblackness of discourses of intelligence and rationality are compatible, thus accounting for the ritual recurrence of blackface at Canadian educational sites. I assert that the stubbornly postracialist claims of the university to be a site of progressive rationality continually reproduce the motivations for blackface in all its antiblack meanings, as well as why it must always be considered surprising.

Chapter 6, "'Making Them Better Leaders': The Pedagogical Imperative, Institutional Priorities, and the Attenuation of Black Anger," further analyses interviews with university administrators where they speak about how they have dealt with blackface incidents on their campuses. The chapter argues that despite the universities' institutional claims to equity, the pedagogical imperative in their procedures and eventual responses to blackface instantiate the universities' deeper commitment to serving the interests of whiteness, and to producing ostensibly progressive, postracialist white citizens out of blackface perpetrators. These priorities necessarily involve constructing Black reactions to blackface as outrageous, attenuating Black indignation, and ultimately disregarding the interests of Black members of the university community. The chapter ends by imagining what institutional responses might resemble if conceived through a commitment to eradicate Black suffering.

Chapter 7, "Learning to Get Along at School, or Antiblack Postracialism through Multicultural Education," considers the narratives of Black students we interviewed who reflected on their pre-university education. It lays bare the ways in which pre-university schooling, structured by the broader structures and discourses of Canadian multiculturalism, seduces students into a post-racism view of Canada. This priming works seamlessly with the discourses of the university to inform relationships among students at university. Black students are pressured to negate their embodied, familial, and community knowledges in order to get along with their non-Black peers, and non-Black students are set up to resent and reject their Black peers who are unwilling to sugarcoat the way they experience the world. The chapter concludes with a reiteration of the importance of the kinds of education that take place in Black families and communities to pre-empt and counter schooling's postracialist seductions.

Chapter 8, "The Costs of Belonging for International Students," examines the perspectives of the two Black students who said they were not offended by blackface and/or who participated in blackface performances with their white peers. They both happened to be international students, though they did not represent the views of other Black international students we interviewed. These two students both connected their lack of objection to blackface to what they feel is a Black essentialism imposed on them by other Black students. The chapter complicates their claims, focusing on the seduction to commit to post-racism that international students may already face, parallel to what Canadian students experience pre-university.

Chapter 9, "Fugitive Learning: Countering Postracialism and Making Black Life at University," is interested in fugitive learning, or learning as marronage (Patel, 2016; N. Roberts, 2015) as a form of Black life-making and a jurisgenerative practice of freedom (Harney & Moten, 2015, p. 85) that takes place at the university. It attends to the initiatives that students participate in related to challenging blackface and the broader postracialist iterations of educational violence. It highlights the ways in which fugitive Black learning is constituted of much more than whatever information might be gathered in these moments, but rather is constituted by ways of being in these spaces. Concluding the book, it highlights the ways in which, at university as beyond, Black freedom must be taken, and is taken in each moment we make Black life, by living in flagrant refusal of the constraints of an antiblack world.

This book goes to press at a time when many universities, in the wake of the assassination of George Floyd and the subsequent uprisings against antiblackness across the globe, are making statements concerning, and in some cases endeavouring to address, antiblackness in their institutions. This book and the study on which it is based have not been framed as interventions towards such a reforming of the university, convinced as I am about the inherent inability of the university as currently conceived to actually follow through (Kelley, 2016b). Nevertheless, the study and this book do offer critical insights into the ways in which the Canadian nation state, its universities, and its schools are implicated in antiblackness. Its contribution is towards understanding further how the problem of blackface and the antiblackness of schools and universities in Canada is conceived. As such, my aspiration is that it will inform the ways in which Black people can continue to engage in struggle and take up space as free at the university and beyond. I also hope that it will contribute obliquely towards the long goal of reimagining and recreating the university on terms that do not always already mean Black subjugation. That there is crucial work of this sort that already takes place within and against the university makes such a vision not totally unimaginable, however long it may take, for those not already hopelessly given to the status quo. This kind of radical futurist imagination is what has always kept the work of Black freedom alive.

PART ONE

Blackface in the Context of the Canadian Settler-Colonial Nation State

1 Contemporary Blackface in Canada as Performance of Antiblackness

This chapter introduces us to the findings of the study, by introducing us to the Black participants' reactions to blackface. It argues that they experience blackface as taking from them – specifically, as stealing their bodies and identities – and highlights their frequent references to slavery and other systems of historical racial violence to describe what they feel blackface does. Drawing on Saidiya Hartman's (2007) concept of the "afterlife of slavery," and building from her analysis of blackface minstrelsy in the United States, the chapter shifts the analysis of blackface from the limited terms of minstrelsy, representation, and stereotype within which it is usually discussed in the public sphere to one that offers a more precise framework for articulating its offence.

The Offence of Blackface

As discussed in the introduction, this book has its beginnings in Black outrage at blackface, and my interest in the disturbing ways that it shows up in the context of postracialism. Of course, I am by no means the only Black person who is profoundly disturbed by contemporary blackface, and the Black participants in this study also speak of being disturbed by it. Most Black participants[1] I interviewed have an initial automatic negative reaction when they encounter blackface. This reaction varies in intensity. Some participants, like Gary at University 5, have a very strong negative reaction: "Like, you feel it almost spiritually, viscerally,

---

1 There were thirty-five Black participants in this study, only three of whose responses do not fit the pattern I am describing here. The exceptional cases will be discussed in Chapter 9.

that this is a problem, but we can't find the words" (U5S1).[2] For participants like Gary, blackface is profoundly disturbing in a way that they feel in their bodies, in the depths of their being. Patrick at University 7 reported feeling nauseous, "physically sick" from his encounter with blackface and its aftermath.

Other Black people I spoke to have a more indeterminate reaction that we could call "off visceral." Using terminology like "not visceral, but ...," they describe their reaction to blackface by positioning it in proximity to, but not quite as, an embodied response. For them it is also a profound reaction, but perhaps one that they feel less intensely, and therefore not in a physical way. Still other Black people have a reaction that is milder: "What the hell?" or "That sucks!" or "It pissed me off!" As with the others, their reaction is clearly negative – here experienced as intense irritation.

This range of reactions is not surprising and might, at first, seem to indicate a range of levels of offence to blackface. However, as we explored the topic further in our conversations, it was clear that these Black participants all found blackface deeply offensive, and the ways in which they described the source of the offence was far more consistent than the range of their initial reactions might suggest. They almost uniformly understand blackface as "taking" parts of themselves, and experience this as a violation, a personal affront, regardless of whether they had experienced blackface in person, confronted it visually via some form of media, or heard about it.

This sense of being stolen or stolen from was complex, and like their reactions to blackface, coalesced along a spectrum of references from the overtly physical to the less so. Quite notably, several participants experienced blackface as an appropriation of their own bodies. For example, in a student focus group at University 2, Valerie shares:

> Well, it kind of sucks because they painted their face black and, like, I am Black. ... You know – like how do I explain this? I feel like they're taking a part of me and making it into a costume. (U2BSOFGP2)

Valerie experienced blackface as though her very skin was being snatched for the perpetrators to wear. Much like Gary's above, Valerie's

---

2 Identifiers such as "U5S1" indicate the interview or focus group from which a quote has been taken. It first indicates the university, then the type of conversation and the participant in that conversation. Thus, "U2BSOFGP2" indicates University 2, Black Student Organization focus group, participant no. 2; "U3FGP3" indicates University 3 Focus Group, participant no. 3; and "U5S1" indicates University 5, solo interview no. 1.

struggle to find language to adequately articulate what an encounter with blackface is like suggests the way in which, for them, the encounter lacks a parallel. Therefore, available language offers few metaphors that capture how they experience blackface.

In a focus group at another university, Ginika expresses a similar feeling that blackface snatches parts of the Black body:

> But what I find *really* offensive is the Afro. I don't know if they're trying to be Black or something, but they have this Afro hair, that is basically a black person's hair, and they come out with that look for Halloween. And to me it's quite offensive! (U1BSOFGP3)

"Afro wigs" and other accoutrements mimicking Back people's hair or Black people's hairstyles are often, though not always, a part of contemporary blackface portrayals, and Ginika experiences these instances as another form of appropriation of the Black body. That is, in the context of blackface – the mimicking of Black skin – Ginika's sense of offence is intensified by this seizure of Black hair that, she emphasizes, once belonged (whether actually or symbolically) to a Black person.

For other Black participants, blackface steals a part of them that is less clearly physical, yet in a transaction that they find just as disturbing. For example, Vera, also at University 1, says:

> I found it offensive because it takes my identity as a Black person into something that's comedy or fun or something they can just put on or put off whenever they want as opposed to the fact that my identity as a Black person is not something I can change or put off or, you know, turn it into something that's fun. (U1BSOFGP5)

Vera indicates here that she experiences blackface as a seizing of her identity as Black in a process that, in the same moment, effaces her personhood.

The dynamic of seizure that the participants express is, of course, connected in a particular way to notions of consent. Notably, the participants do not speak of blackface as borrowing or sharing, but as "taking." The metaphor is one of theft. Fundamentally, that which is stolen is taken against the will of the owner, and may then be used in ways that the owner does not, and would not, authorize.

This theme of the theft of identity recurs where Black respondents discuss blackface incidents that mimic Jamaicanness, which are quite popular in the Canadian context. The appropriation of Jamaican identity in blackface clearly involves the seizure of skin as discussed above, and most often includes the seizing of hair, as perpetrators wear wigs of various types to mimic the ways in which Rastafarians wear their hair. Black participants – particularly those with Jamaican heritage – feel that blackface that references Jamaicanness also seizes their identities as Black Jamaicans. Ava, the only Black participant in a focus group at University 3, states:

> To be completely honest just leave Black people alone! And like specifically – this is just from my own personal experience because I am Jamaican – leave Jamaicans alone! I can never understand how people feel so entitled to my culture and entitled to do these things when they don't know anything about anything. (U3FGP3)

In these instances, Black people express the ways in which blackface simultaneously appropriates their identities and at the same time exhibits a disconnect from whatever it might really mean to be, in this case, a Black Jamaican. Lance, at University 2, feels similarly about blackface that references Jamaicanness:

> I guess I don't like people in general taking Jamaican culture and making it such a trivial thing. … They are just taking it as if it's, uh, whatever, and they can wear stuff that's a part of me and they can just take it and make it a joke almost. (U2BSOFGP1)

Lance's statement here aptly expresses the ways that Black participants throughout this study feel about the entire dynamic of theft they see in all instances of blackface. What is particularly salient here is that whether it is a Black identity or a part of the Black body that is appropriated, the Black people who participated in this study are repeatedly and almost uniformly concerned that blackface constitutes a theft of (parts of) themselves, and as such, a violation of their being. While participants occasionally indict the paraphernalia that often accompanies blackface portrayals – such things as novelty marijuana joints, Kentucky Fried Chicken buckets, monkeys, and bizarre clothing, all racist tropes used in blackface costumes that serve to intensify the ridicule almost invariably inherent in contemporary blackface in Canada – it is not those aspects that participants experience as the fundamental offence. This is a crucial point, as quite often non-Black people who attempt to justify blackface identify these stereotypical markers, which are over and above the alteration of skin colour, as constituting the line between, to them, "harmless, ignorant" blackface and "harmful, racist" blackface. What Black people in this study tell us challenges this reasoning, instead placing the primary focus on non-Black people's efforts to take on Blackness through an easy appropriation of cherry-picked parts of Black bodies or Black identities that they consider to be representative of the whole. Black people's indignation, then, is principally directed at the presumption that Black identities and Black bodies are, in part or in whole, available for the taking and the wearing. For them, the other aspects of blackface costuming that draw on stereotypes are important, racist, and offensive but largely secondary to the more fundamental seizure of Blackness.

Transience, Disregard, and Entitlement

In our conversations with Black people, they spoke of additional layers to the ways that they experience blackface. Above, Vera mentions that those who wear blackface consider her identity as "something they can just put on or put off whenever they want as opposed to the fact that my identity as a Black person is not something I can change or put off." Like Vera, other Black people in this study mention this dynamic of putting on and putting off. Njeri at University 1 raises this as well:

> It's the first time I've heard of [blackface], but my first year during Halloween I saw posters of – I think it was a Zulu person in Zulu attire – and it was like cautioning every other person not to dress like them, saying, "We are not a costume. Please don't do this." And I was shocked! I was like, "People actually do that?" It's like people just come in and out of it! and I'm like, "Black people are not a costume. [Blackness] is not something you can actually wear for your Halloween and then walk out and show it off, and then tomorrow you're white again!" (U1BSOFGP4)

Both Vera and Njeri point to an inherent transience of the blackface act that reduces Blackness to a wearable commodity one can frivolously put on as an accoutrement and just as easily discard at whim in an easy return to whiteness. For them, this transience compounds the dehumanizing effects of the blackface act. Ava also speaks about blackface's temporary forays across racial lines, and the return to being white, saying:

> It is offensive because they think it's something that they get to put on and take off afterwards. Because at the end of the day you still end up white. The only person that it hurts in the room is the people who are still being stigmatized and stereotyped on these very narrow-minded assumptions of what blackness is. (U3FGP3)

The nuance Ava adds here is that the carefree, temporary engagement with Blackness through blackface for a moment of fun not only fails to constitute any meaningful engagement with what it means to be Black, but also leaves negative consequences in its wake for Black people for whom Blackness is not an external accoutrement they decide to wear or not wear. The derisive ways that the Black body is represented through these acts, then, not only flow from but also help to reinforce the racist contempt Black people face daily.

Throughout, we see this contrast between the transience of blackface and the ways in which embodiment as Black fixes Black people for particular kinds of treatment in a white-supremacist world. What the Black participants object to, then, is the kind of tourism (a metaphor they use in several instances) through their bodies and identities that does not, and cannot, take seriously the realities that attend Black life (whether Black suffering or Black joy). Vera says: "There's so much racial discrimination, racial oppression and inequality that when somebody does something like this it's as though they're making fun of the whole situation that Black people as a whole are going through." Vera's comment captures a shared sense among Black participants that the engagement with Blackness attempted by those who wear blackface really goes no further than a fetishistic, passing relationship with a conjured-up understanding of Blackness, and takes no interest in actual Black people.

This non-engagement with Black communities is the almost exclusive pattern of blackface incidents. For example, in 2014 at Wilfrid Laurier University a fraternity party advertised as a "Jamaican Me Crazy" event was cancelled by the dean of students in response to pressure from Black people and their allies, who felt it was likely that blackface and other disparaging representations of Jamaicans would be featured. The executive director of the students' Public Interest Research Group highlighted the non-engagement with Black communities, saying: "The way they described Jamaica, the fact that they were advocating for costume-use, the way the event was described. *And they had no partnership with actual Caribbean groups and there are multiple on campus.* Those were all warning signs to me" (Severin, 2014, emphasis added, erroneously attributed to A. Denuzzo online). Further, even after blackface incidents, blackface perpetrators rarely seek out relationships with Black people or take their objections seriously. Again, the 2014[3] Laurier

---

3 Exceptionally, in a 2007 blackface incident at Wilfrid Laurier University, there appears to have been some genuine effort on the part of the perpetrators to understand and change (see comments on HueyFreeman222, 2007). Though sparked and sustained by the efforts of Black people and their allies, at least in this instance there appears to have been some remorse.

incident is an example. Brie Berry, a student at Laurier at the time, wrote in the campus newspaper:

> And what reparations has Pi Kappa Alpha taken [since the cancellation]? Have they worked with the Diversity and Equity Office? Have they gone in to speak with the Association of Black Students? … No, instead a patronizing article is written, which at its core is not about fighting intolerance or promoting equality. It's about misplaced entitlement to a culture that they felt could be used for profit. (Berry, 2014, erroneously attributed to D. Saad online)

This lack of interest in meaningful engagement with Blackness is demonstrated not only by blackface perpetrators but also by the much wider group of those who defend blackface in disregard of Black objection. The transience of blackface, along with these kinds of responses, announce a categorical dismissal of Black people and their concerns, only reinforcing the climate of disregard that constitutes the background for participants' feelings of being stolen from. The casting off of the blackface costume, the inevitable concluding moment of the transient blackface act, aptly represents the disregard of Black people

Dissection, Reduction, and Metonym

In this section, I discuss the matters of reduction/dissection and metonym inherent in blackface acts, and the ways in which they compound the offence that they cause to Black people. Typically, those who wear blackface expend very little effort to convincingly portray Black people. Few other elements that might arguably constitute a good impersonation are employed, and even the imitation of Black hair and complexions are most often grotesque and far from lifelike. This lack of effort is particularly evident where the blackface performance intends to portray a specific Black personality. Here there is normally little effort towards either impersonating aspects of their character or credibly imitating their physical characteristics. For example, a photograph provided by one Black participant of a blackface incident in which the perpetrator ostensibly intended to pay tribute to singer-songwriter Barry White showed the perpetrator had unrealistically darkened his skin to a macabre, pallid grey, stuffed his suit jacket to suggest White's body type, then inexplicably donned a wig of mid-back-length dreadlocks draped over his shoulders. Of course, anyone with a genuine interest in Barry White would know that he most often wore his hair in a shoulder-length Jheri curl when not in the cropped straight perm he

had at the height of his popularity. Nevertheless, somehow this perpetrator presumed dreadlocks would adequately serve the purposes of
his impersonation.

Instances in which blackface has been used in Canadian theatrical
productions, such as in 2014 at the Théâtre du Rideau Vert, display a
similar lack of effort to create convincing portrayals. This is, of course,
immediately apparent in the rejection of the obvious path of hiring Black
actors to play these parts in the first place. This is then compounded by
the fact the portrayals are seldom any more convincing than amateur
blackface.

Make no mistake: on the whole, Black participants in this study consider all blackface offensive. I am therefore not suggesting that a blackface portrayal is redeemed by the extent to which it might be considered
"accurate." What I am drawing attention to is the way in which blackface uses unpersuasive caricatures of black skin and hair to, *on their
own*, do the work of representing Black people in a kind of visual short-
hand that lays bare the glib way in which these "pieces" are ultimately
intended to stand in for the whole Black person. If blackface performs
the "taking" of discrete "parts" of Black identities and Black bodies in
a transaction that Black people do not authorize (and who could authorize this kind of stealing of the self?), we should be careful not to miss
the violent dynamic of dissection and dismemberment therefore also
inherent in blackface.

There are two integrally related aspects to this violence. First, blackface constitutes the violation of the integrity of the Black body, rendering it a buffet from which one can select and consume fragments of
Black physicality to wear for a fleeting moment of pleasure. More than
symbolic or epistemic violence, this negates the idea of an inviolable,
whole Black body. Rather, it violently undoes the Black body, reducing
it to pieces, and rendering those pieces available for consumption. In
the process, the Black body is displaced from the notion of personhood.

Second, considering the dissection of Black bodies alongside the lack
of effort to create a "realistic" portrayal and alongside blackface's inherent transience, we might also notice the ways in which blackface entails
a series of metonymic substitutions. For example, black skin and dreadlocks = Rastafarian = Jamaican, or more precisely, Jamaican is *only* Rastafarian, which is nothing more than black skin and dreadlocks. Analo-
gously, Blackness is no more than a Black body is no more than skin and
hair. Indeed, the logic undergirding these blackface portrayals is that
a Black person is easily signalled by, and reduced to, these elements –
primarily skin and hair. The blackface perpetrator operates under the
presumption that these fragments *are* what constitute being Black. This

practice is, then, a visual representation of colour-blind logic whereby Blackness is equal to the superficial visible differences represented by Black skin and hair. Its logic erases the historicity of Blackness, and the racist desires and structures that frame conditions of life for Black people. Again it represents a refusal of engagement with Black people. Black life/humanity/experience is deconstructed, and reconstructed from digestible fragments intended to represent the whole, in ways that cast aside the uncomfortable injustices that (Canadian) whiteness would rather not consider.

As we discussed this in a focus group at University 2, Sonji expressed frustration at the kind of dismissal that blackface represents, and identified it as participating in a broader climate that engages with Black culture but dismisses Black people. She spoke at length in the group about how she has experienced this dismissal from people who, like blackface perpetrators, engage with Blackness – in this case, through Black popular culture such as hip-hop. Sonji relates an experience of being at a campus party where a Kendrick Lamar track was playing, and noting her non-Black colleagues' obliviousness to the liberatory intent of the track while they sang along exuberantly. She recalls how these same colleagues later disengage when she attempts to talk about Black life:

> I'm just like, "You guys don't even understand this is a song for Black people to rise!" And I'm kind of like, "You guys don't understand this; you guys don't care!" And I get that vibe even in my studies. No one cares about your Black issues! ... If you speak on Black issues ... it's like somehow you are racist, or somehow you are too focused on Black people. It's kind of like, "Okay you are too focused on this! You are making a big deal out of nothing!" It's like your experiences aren't even valid; you get that kind of feeling. (U2BSOFGP3)

This is an experience that Sonji has on campus both within and outside of her courses. In later chapters I will explore further the antiblackness of university contexts. For the moment, the point is that Black participants experience blackface as an overt performance of a broader social and institutional (pseudo)engagement with Blackness that trivializes, reduces, violates, and disregards it.

Entitlement and Disregard

Another matter arising in conversations with Black participants is that of white entitlement. For these participants, the seizure of the Black body and Black identities that constitutes blackface is based in a sense of non-Black, especially white, entitlement to Blackness. Across all sources of data for this research – whether interviews and focus groups, or published statements by Black communities and groups, or media responses to blackface articles online – Black people object to this sense of entitlement that blackface represents for them. Black people feel that non-Black people largely dismiss their concerns about blackface in favour of asserting this ostensible right to wear blackface as long as *they* don't think it's a problem. For example, in one instance where a secondary school vice-principal wore blackface for Halloween, a Black parent shared with me:

> To add fuel to the fire, my son attends that school, and he is among the very few Black students there. A friend of his [also Black] went directly to the VP on that day and told him that his costume offended him. The VP responded, "Oh well," and walked away. (SGFG1)

We see this dynamic reproduced on a broad scale way beyond such individual interactions given that every contemporary instance of blackface is vociferously condemned by Black communities while large numbers of non-Black people expend a lot of energy to justify blackface, and their right to continue using it, despite Black objection. For instance, when Radio-Canada, the station that carries the Quebec comedic year-end review *Bye-Bye*, required *Bye-Bye* producer Louis Morissette to use a Black actor instead of a white actor in blackface, Morissette responded with deep entitlement. He found this requirement an imposition on his artistic freedom, and wrote an op-ed piece to this effect that referred to those who object to blackface as annoying mosquitos (Dunlevy, 2016). Ultimately, Morissette hired a Black person, but still put him in blackface to play the role (Durocher, 2016).

The sense of entitlement defies any critical perspectives about blackface that may be shared with those who possess that sense of entitlement. Efforts to educate them about the fraught history of blackface and the impacts it has on Black people in the present are generally to no avail. As Sharon, a Black staff member at University 1, says:

> It's about privilege, right? So, "my privilege to do whatever I want. I was tickled by this and I don't want to be critical about it, and if you force me to be critical about it then I have to give something up and I don't want to give that thing up." (U1A3)

Zawadi, a student at University 2, is much more forthright: "I think there's that sense of entitlement that people think that they can! Feeling

like 'Well I can do that!' They can because they are! It's white supremacy!" (U2FG2P4).

Contemporary Blackface as Instantiation of the Afterlife of Slavery

Considering these themes – the seizure and dissection of Black bodies and identities, the non-Black sense of entitlement to do so, and the
disregard of Blackness that makes light of the realities of Black life –
it is not surprising that for several participants, blackface conjures up
notions of slavery and other historical structures of violence against
Black people such as Jim Crow in the United States and European colonialism more generally.

In one interview, a white participant, Sarah, describes a discussion
that took place among herself, her Black colleague, June, and the principal of the school their children attended. After an event where another
parent had worn blackface to a school event, Sarah and June, both parents of Black children, had come to meet with the principal to discuss
why they found the incident problematic, and to demand that an apology be made to the community and that informational and educational
activities be implemented to explain the problem with blackface. Sarah
relates:

> So [the principal] agreed at the end of the meeting that she would issue an
> apology. "But just explain to me" – she looked at both of us – "somebody
> putting paint on their face to make their skin darker, what does that mean
> to you?" And June looked her in the eye and said, "It reminds me of the
> history of the enslavement of my people," just like that! (U5F1)

What is immediately noticeable about June's response as reported by
Sarah is her direct association of contemporary blackface with slavery. Interestingly, June does not mention minstrelsy, or the many other
forms of racial ridicule that Black people have experienced historically
to which contemporary blackface could be compared. Rather, for June
blackface is offensive because of the way it is haunted by slavery.

Several other Black participants also make this kind of direct connection
between blackface and slavery. For example, Tim at University 2 says:

> You need that historical reference there so they would know what's wrong
> with it. … you need to have that understanding. You can't just say, "Forget
> the past and let's just move forward," because there's so many – slavery,
> all those kinds of things, have their roots in society today so it's just impos-
> sible to negate it and just move forward. (U2FG1P3)

This response is particularly salient coming from Tim, who also expresses the opinion that perhaps it is best to not "dwell on the past," but rather to just focus on relating to each other well in the present. Yet he, too, makes this direct connection between blackface and slavery without mentioning minstrelsy. He warns that we cannot forget the history of slavery and "those kinds of things." For him, it is impossible to properly understand the present within a framework that erases the history of slavery.

Other participants say blackface specifically reminds them of lynching. With regard to an encounter he had on campus with a fellow student in blackface, Kevin at University 2 reflects:

> What comes to my mind when I think about blackface? I think violence! I think lynching! I think Jim Crow, or whatever! So him doing that thinking it's Lil Wayne, you know [*voice changes as though to speak to the person in blackface*], "I don't blame you. I don't think you're the worst person in the world. But this is what it means to me. This is what it means to millions of other people regardless of your intent. This is not OK!" (U2FG2P2)

Similarly, Zawadi says:

> The way I respond to blackface, it's never okay! … It's violent. It's very violent … Those images of people being lynched, all the violence – the lynchings, all of the historic ugliness that came with the [US] South, and North America – all of these things come into play when someone puts on blackface. It triggers all those pictures; it evokes all those memories in people.

In all these instances, the participants indicate that, for them, these violent conditions are not somehow over, but rather cast a shadow over their lives in the present. This sense of enduring circumstances stemming from the violent conditions of slavery is summed up in Reva's response to blackface:

> It makes me think like they see us as less of a person. Even though we have been out of slavery, and these things are like transforming, and things are supposedly supposed to be better, it's like, "Is it really getting better?" Maybe we are free, but we're not free mentally because these things are still happening." (U1BSOFGP2)

Reva poses a poignant challenge to the ways in which dominant contemporary ways of relating to Black people pose as "better" or as entirely new and different when, for her, they feel embedded in the same will to dehumanize Black people. While acknowledging that conditions of life for Black people today are clearly not identical to those during the days in which enslavement of Black persons was legal, Reva broaches the notion of "better" circumstances with a double conditional, sharing that she feels she lives in an in-between place of unfreedom, or not-quite-freedom.

I am interested in the ease with which these participants make direct connections between contemporary blackface, on one hand, and slavery and related antiblack structures with their attendant violence. In contrast to some participants (such as Gary and Lance, mentioned at the beginning of this chapter) who struggle to find language to adequately express how they experience blackface, these participants find a way to articulate their experience with blackface by making reference to slavery.

I find scholar Saidiya Hartman's (2007) notion of the afterlife of slavery helpful for thinking this through. Hartman has famously written:

> If slavery persists as an issue in the political life of black America, it is not because of an antiquarian obsession with bygone days or the burden of a too-long memory, but because black lives are still imperiled and devalued by a racial calculus and a political arithmetic that were entrenched centuries ago. This is the afterlife of slavery. (p. 6)

Black participants such as June, Kim, Kevin, Zawadi, and Reva appear to experience blackface as part of this persistence of the relations of slavery – what Black scholars also refer to as antiblackness. Further, it seems clear that though Hartman specifically cites the US context, for these participants the notion of the "afterlife of slavery" describes conditions for Black people in Canada as well. The participants' responses not only defy the erasure of the fact of Canadian slavery in the past, but emphasize that this history is still salient today. They also reassert these historical and ongoing relations as an important framework for understanding the contemporary experiences of Black people in Canada, and specifically, in this instance, blackface.

I am interested, then, in what it is about contemporary blackface in Canada that might conjure up notions of slavery for some participants, and the ways in which such a framework might be compatible with the other responses of the larger group of Black people in this study who are offended by blackface. For this, we must first clarify what the logics are that constitute the afterlife of slavery.

Antiblackness: Slavery's Afterlife and Its Logics

Black Studies scholars have long investigated the processes and logics of the transatlantic slave trade and the enslavement of Africans in
the modern world. These scholars insist that it is erroneous to regard
slavery simply as an exploitation of workers for free labour, for to do
so is to miss the deliberate techniques of dehumanization that made it
possible to repeatedly kidnap, buy, sell, torture, rape, maim, mutilate,
murder ... (the list, however long, can never adequately communicate
the fullness of the evil) other human beings with impunity for centuries.
As Hortense Spillers (1987) has noted:

> That order, with its human sequence written in blood, represents for its
> African and indigenous peoples a scene of actual mutilation, dismember-
> ment, and exile. ... their [the enslaved's] New-World, diasporic plight
> marked a theft of the body – a willful and violent (and unimaginable from
> this distance) severing of the captive body from its motive will, its active
> desire. Under these conditions, ... the captive body reduces to a thing,
> becoming being for the captor; ... I would make a distinction in this case
> between "body" and "flesh" ... before the "body" there is the "flesh,"
> that zero degree of social conceptualization ... Even though the European
> hegemonies stole bodies ... we regard this human and social irreparability
> as high crimes against the flesh ... If we think of the "flesh" as a primary
> narrative, then we mean its seared, divided, ripped-apartness, riveted to
> the ship's hole, fallen, or "escaped" overboard. (p. 67)

Spillers here describes the foundational abominations of New World
enslavement. In a first moment, slavery and its agents sought to reduce
Black humans to property – that is, people to "bodies," and bodies to
(mere) indeterminate "flesh" through mechanisms of violence, terror,
and death. More than a process that marked the boundaries between
bondage and freedom, in this first moment the slaveholder's objective is the obliteration of Black subjectivity. As Sexton (2016) contends,
"slavery is not a loss that the self experiences – of language, lineage,
land, or labor – but rather the loss of any self that could experience
such loss" (p. 591). As such, slavery renders Black people not primarily
as exploited workers, though, of course, the enslaved did work, but as
flesh – a particular kind of property (Wilderson, 2003). Enslavement
thus constituted a fundamental assault against the humanity of Black
people.

In an intertwined second moment, the techniques of slavery relegate
the Black body, ontologically, to the status of "being for the captor"

(Spillers, 1987, p. 67). Having been made flesh by the alchemy of wanton violence, this "being for the captor" is not a person with sovereignty over her own body, but property whose purpose is whatever its owner decides it shall be. African people, having now become (Black) flesh, are understood as subservient to the will and whim of the white slaveholder – not as a human struggling under coercive and oppressive human relations, but as flesh that has no say in the terms of its use, and further, no voice that the relations of slavery could recognize in the first place (Wilderson, 2003). The Black body is reduced to the state of "fungible" commodity (Hartman, 1997, p. 21) – that which can be accumulated and exchanged.

These processes make Blackness the foil against which white people came to know themselves within the Atlantic world not simply as free, as Toni Morrison (1992) has long argued, but as Human (e.g., Hartman, 1997; Walcott, 2014c; Wilderson, 2003; Wynter, 1994b, 2003). As the scholars cited here explain, definitions of liberty, freedom, and human rights – that which defined the Enlightenment Human – emerged in the "Western" world at the very time during which the enslavement of Black people was a normalized global reality. Thus, as these Enlightenment values developed, an equally well-developed antiblack logic was also elaborated that allowed these realities to exist together, ultimately making these "universal" Human values inapplicable to Black people. In other words, Blackness is established firmly outside the limits of the Enlightenment discourses of the Human, placing the concept of Blackness and this construct of the Human into irreconcilable antagonism. These Enlightenment discourses of the Human persist today, as the means through which people might claim subjectivities as Human. As such, Hartman and other Black scholars argue that the logics and desires undergirding the economy of slavery persist into the present – even after various legal declarations of emancipation and the end of slavery – to make these exclusive constructed Human subjectivities possible. It is these logics, from the slave trade into the present, that we call antiblackness. Antiblack epistemological and libidinal economies are continually, repeatedly, habitually, incessantly, and compulsively mobilized to that end.

The persistence of antiblackness exposes the supposed sea changes from slavery to freedom to be non-events, that is, non-performative failures to constitute the kind of total transformation that is typically imagined, such that we live enduringly in slavery's "afterlife" (Hartman, 1997, p. 116, 2007, p. 6). A stark instance of the non-performativity of this kind of non-event (Hartman, 1997, p. 116) is revealed in the relationship between slavery and lynching in the United States. Lynching exploded as a practice after the American Civil War and the Emancipation Act, which made it illegal (de jure at least) to own slaves. But the violence of lynching was nothing but a continuation of the deadly violence of slavery, and was a way to shore up the dehumanization and subordination of Black people who were now, by law, ostensibly free. The new nomenclature for this antiblack terror was only made necessary because, on the books, such violence was disallowed, though law enforcers often participated in lynchings – sometimes openly, sometimes clandestinely – where they did not orchestrate them. As such, the distinctions between the violence of slavery and the violence of lynching are only technical. For Black people in the United States during these times, then, emancipation was experienced, for all intents and purposes, as a non-event.

Antiblackness is therefore far more than racism against Black people, a narrower concept that might be reserved for instances of bigotry, whether individual or systemic, directed against Black people (Sexton, 2008). Antiblackness is the condition upon which Humanity is contingent in modern/post-Columbus society (Wynter, 1994b, 2003).

Connecting Contemporary Blackface in Canada to the Afterlife of Slavery

With this understanding of the afterlife of slavery – the way that it structures the contemporary – we can return to our consideration of Black responses to contemporary blackface. How compatible might this lens/framework that some participants advance be with the broader set of themes that are the subject of this chapter? Alternatively, we could ask, how might these themes return us to this matter of slavery and its afterlife? Indeed, what might such a framing offer us?

We can start by asking whether the references to slavery, lynching, and Jim Crow function differently in the participants' narratives to signal separate epochs. A look back at the participants' words suggests little if any distinction. For example, Tim mentions "so many – slavery, all those kinds of things"; Kevin says, "I think violence! I think lynching! I think Jim Crow, or whatever"; Reva cites "slavery, and these things"; and Zawadi speaks of "the lynchings, all of the historic ugliness." The participants use these terms in close proximity to each other, and speak of them as constituting a larger whole: "all the historic ugliness," "or whatever," "all those kinds of things." The meanings of the various terms in their responses are qualitatively indistinguishable. We therefore cannot conclude that they intend to signal different phenomena, or different degrees of violence, violation, subordination, or unfreedom.

I suggest that this is not careless referencing or a lack of specificity on their part. Instead, this slippage among terms highlights the "non-eventness" of the ostensible breaks between the violent eras they cite. The participants use these terms interchangeably to speak to the seamless continuity of antiblackness in all these periods.

We also note the reference to lynching and Jim Crow in the United States on the same terms as slavery, which participants know happened in Canada. This connection to slavery is made by Black people in Canada from several backgrounds: Reva and June were born in the Caribbean, Zawadi on the African continent, and Kevin and Tim in Canada. This indicates to us that the sensibilities they have developed based on their experiences in Canada are independent of these diverse origins, but signal a global phenomenon identifiable in their specific local experiences in Canada. They all, despite their diverse backgrounds, experience this antiblackness, and discern it in blackface. The participants who make the comparisons to slavery view this seamless antiblackness as the primary conceptual framework for understanding blackface. They select it over a dislocated reference to minstrelsy, as though minstrelsy were an isolated practice, historically sealed off from its past and future.

Applying this insight to the broader themes identified above, we have seen that Black participants experience blackface as a taking of (parts of) their bodies and of their identities. Hartman (1997) has long written about post-bellum minstrelsy in the United States that "the donning of blackface restaged the seizure and possession of the black body for the other's use and enjoyment ... [and] cannot be extricated from the relations of chattel slavery" (p. 31). It is therefore not difficult to see how contemporary blackface might also be considered to metaphorically seize upon and steal the Black body, and in this way resonate with the dynamics of enslavement. However, the links between the logic of slavery and the dynamics that Hartman identifies go far beyond metaphor. The climate of disregard for Black people within which contemporary blackface occurs – one that easily dismisses Black people's vociferous opposition to blackface – underscores the logics and desires of slavery. Contemporary blackface's dynamic of stealing is woven of the way it takes the Black body without any regard for what Black people might think about it, or for the concerns and conditions of actual Black life. This is, of course, perfectly congruent with the logics undergirding the capture and coercion of black bodies under slavery, and starkly announces the antiblackness of contemporary blackface.

The notion that Blackness can be appropriated with no respect for Black sentience is at the heart of participants' identification of blackface with the desires of slavery's afterlife. Antiblackness concludes that whiteness has access to Blackness, and particularly the Black body, at will and with impunity. Reduced to "being for the captor" (Spillers, 1987, p. 67), our humanity is negated, and thus our consent is neither sought nor considered relevant.

Further, if blackface cannot be separated from the seizure of the Black body in slavery, then the dynamic of dismemberment inherent in contemporary blackface cannot be separated from the transmutation of the Black body to flesh inherent to the relations of slavery. Blackface's dismemberment of the Black body, and the disarticulation of these parts from real Black bodies, from Black personhood, and therefore from Black volition, repeat the negation of Black subjectivity that Hartman, Spillers, and Sexton identify as central to the relations of slavery. In speaking of blackface as taking parts of themselves, then, Black participants are identifying and resisting the antiblack relations that negate their humanity and reduce the Black body to fungible flesh.

That Black people dare to have an opinion about blackface is always already considered excess, and this is evident in the sense of white entitlement that the participants perceive. Where white people speak of the *freedom* to participate in blackface, and speak of admonitions not to participate in blackface as encroachments on their *freedom* (whether understood as freedom of expression, as artistic license, or as some other imagined Human right), this cannot be disentangled from the antiblack processes by which whites know themselves as free, indeed as Human, by knowing themselves as *not* Black. The claiming of freedom and rights in this manner is necessarily at odds with Black people's prerogative to assert *our* freedom and full humanity.

Of course, the claim that contemporary blackface performs the relations of slavery and its afterlife is bound to raise the spectre of blackface perpetrators' intentions. It is now a rather elementary anti-racist claim that it is not so much intentions as impact that counts in racist circumstances. Yet this maxim requires further development with regard to antiblackness and its specificities, and therefore in the context of blackface. Thinking again about the ways in which the participants focus primarily on the appropriation of the body rather than on the racist stereotypes often added to a blackface portrayal, we see that the issue is not what one does once one has appropriated the Black body – whether one intends homage or ridicule, or is even unaware of one's motives. Rather, the issue is the presumption of access to the Black body in the first place – that "*you* can choose to do what *you* wish with the black body" (Hartman & Wilderson, 2003, p. 188, emphasis added). Under these conditions, asking whether one has racist intentions is beside the point, and misses how blackface invokes the entitlement that makes the Black body ontologically available for the taking.

In sum, Black participants' responses in this study make it clear that the participants in this study – both those who articulate it as such and those who do not – experience contemporary blackface in Canada as a performative instantiation of the afterlife of slavery.

Beyond Cultural Appropriation: The Problem of Analogy

Thinking contemporary blackface in Canada through the framework of slavery's afterlife, which understands the uniqueness of antiblackness, provides a clearer framework for articulating its offence. We have already seen how it identifies the offence as antiblackness – much more than racist representation. Understanding blackface as antiblackness therefore also helps us avoid the conceptual problems that arise by way of analogy, or what Sexton (2010) calls "people-of-color-blindness" – that is, regarding antiblackness as simply one of many types of racism or, even more problematically, as just one form of a generic oppression that humans inflict on other humans (Sexton, 2010; see also Howard, 2020).

As I mentioned early in the chapter, some participants struggle to find a suitable way of describing their experiences with blackface, for example where Gary says:

> A lot of us don't have the language, a lot of us have difficulty articulating what's the problem. Like you feel it almost spiritually, viscerally, that this is a problem, but we can't find the words because our conversation is underdeveloped on race, on representation. (U5I1)

The antiblackness framework urges us to go further than Gary to say that, in fact, public discourse is underdeveloped *precisely because* it thinks blackface within the narrow parameters of race and representation. In the case of blackface, the pitfalls of analogy present themselves in the tendency to identify blackface as one example of a phenomenon of cultural appropriation.

Cultural appropriation has been broadly defined as "the use of a culture's symbols, artifacts, genres, rituals, or technologies by members of another culture" (Rogers, 2006, p. 474). This broad definition is used by some who justify blackface on the basis that "borrowing" between cultures is normal human activity and the substance of innovation. It is not difficult to see how blackface might come to be erroneously understood as cultural appropriation by those who imagine contemporary blackface to be the same as blackface minstrelsy (which did involve varying degrees of appropriation and bastardization of Black cultural forms), and who imagine this as minstrelsy's only offence. Yet this hasty comparison misses the significance of the act of "blacking up" in minstrelsy as an act of appropriation of the body, as well as the secondary significance of cultural mimicry, if it appears at all, in contemporary blackface in Canada.

It is not only those who would defend blackface who refer to it as cultural appropriation; some who object to it also do so. Most of these would consider power imbalance to be central to their conception of cultural appropriation, thus capturing a more specific idea that some have labelled "cultural *exploitation*: the appropriation of elements of a subordinated culture by a dominant culture without substantive reciprocity, permission, and/or compensation" (Rogers, 2006, p. 477, emphasis added). This version of cultural appropriation may well be applied accurately to instances in which people with no connection to a particular way of life wear its cultural or ceremonial attire out of context – especially in the carnivalesque context of costuming. For example, we saw this at Queen's University in 2016 where large numbers of white students costumed themselves as Buddhist monks, Mexicans wearing prison jumpsuits, Saudi men wearing the keffiyeh, and Viet Cong soldiers wearing the douli traditionally worn by Chinese labourers in East and Southeast Asia (CBC News, 2016a). This kind of costuming, with stereotypical and one-dimensional cultural representations, is clearly racializing, serving to mark these groups as quaint and inferior within problematic discourses of civilization, development, progress, and respectability. Yet as disturbing as these instances are, they are not the same as blackface, where what is seized and worn is Black skin and hair meant to stand in for the bodies of Black people. To make this distinction is not to mark one practice as more egregious than the other, but rather to highlight a crucial qualitative difference.

As our Black respondents have taught us, and as a Black Studies analysis of antiblackness insists, what is fundamentally at issue in blackface is the access to Black *bodies*. In some rare instances, body appropriation shows up in the mimicry of non-Black racialized people. A white comedian playing the part of a Quebec lawyer born in Cambodia squinted to represent the latter's eyes (Dunlevy, 2016), and there are costumes available on eBay that mimic the tattooed skin of a Samoan character from a Disney movie. These too need to be thought about in terms of dismemberment, and I find them as reprehensible as blackface. Importantly, these exceptions prove the rule that body appropriation occurs more readily to portray Black people because of the structures of slavery's afterlife, which position the Black *body* ontologically as available for appropriation. The offence of blackface is not so much that it marks Blackness as inferior (which is the case with all racist mockery) as that it rehearses the expulsion of the Black from the realms of humanity altogether, making the Black body into a fungible commodity. Any inferiorization resulting from the blackface act is gratuitous – a foregone consequence of the reduction of the Black body to flesh.

Understanding that blackface cannot properly be considered to be cultural appropriation also helps us to rethink the value of "My Culture Is Not a Costume" campaigns for discouraging blackface. The "My Culture Is Not a Costume" posters attempt to prevent offensive Halloween costuming on university campuses, and often present instances of blackface under this rubric. But to make blackface fit within this campaign, these posters generally add appropriative dress such as stereotypical representations of hip-hop culture or African traditional dress (such as the Zulu attire in the poster mentioned by Njeri earlier) and divert attention from the appropriation of the body. As such, "My Culture Is Not a Costume" campaigns fail by missing, at the very least, the uniqueness of the appropriation of the body. They might even inadvertently authorize blackface that does not involve the appropriation of attire. More importantly, these campaigns fail in that they commit the same error as blackface by making the Black body equivalent to clothing, and thus in regarding the Black body as wearable commodity. "My Culture Is Not a Costume" therefore does not address the antiblackness of blackface.

Conclusion

This chapter has discussed the reactions of Black participants in the study to blackface. The vast majority of Black participants in this study (thirty-two out of thirty-five) experience blackface as an appropriation of their bodies and identities in a way that, for them, reinflicts the violence of the terms of slavery. This violence is exacerbated by both the dissection of the body inherent in such acts and the sense of entitlement with which both perpetrators and defenders of blackface approach the phenomenon. As such, I have argued that contemporary blackface in Canada cannot properly be considered cultural appropriation or simply a matter of racist representation. Rather, by its nature, it appropriates the Black body and Black identities, thereby reinscribing the relations of slavery, which depend on the exchange value of the Black body.

The exchange involved here is not usually monetary, though to the extent that contemporary blackface is performed professionally, or that amateur blackface performers receive cash prizes of appreciation from their peers, the monetary cannot be dismissed. More significant are the returns in terms of white pleasure and humour as well as a particular egalitarian Canadian identity, both animated by the antiblack pillars of the Canadian settler-colonial project. These returns are the subject of the next two chapters.

2 What's the Joke? The Black Body as White Pleasure in Canadian Blackface

Down at the deep dark bottom of the melting pot, where the private is public and the public private, where black is white and white black, where the immoral becomes moral and the moral is anything that makes one feel good (or that one has the power to sustain), the white man's relish is apt to be the black men's gall. (Ellison, 1958, p. 104)

If Black people experience blackface as antiblackness, indeed if the violence of the relations of slavery are deeply woven into blackface logics, it is just as clear that many white and non-Black persons experience blackface as pleasurable. Contemporary blackface in Canada is performed almost exclusively in contexts of ostensible humour, fun, and entertainment. That this is the context in which blackface occurs is easily confirmed by a scan of media accounts of blackface incidents in Canada, which demonstrates that contemporary blackface in Canada occurs primarily during Halloween parties, campus carnivals, frosh events, sporting events, comedy fests, theatre performances, and comedy revues (e.g., CTV News, 2010; Dunlevy, 2016; HueyFreeman222, 2007; Montpetit, 2011; QMI Agency, 2014; Ravary, 2013). Importantly, blackface performers are not the only ones who find blackface fun. In fact, those who wear blackface have frequently been rewarded with approval by their audiences. Indeed, in 2009 at the University of Toronto and in 2014 at Brock University, students wearing blackface to portray the *Cool Runnings* film version of the Jamaican bobsled team received

An earlier version of this chapter appears in Howard, P.S.S. (2018). A laugh for the national project: Contemporary Canadian blackface humour and its constitution through Canadian anti-blackness. *Ethnicities*, *18*(6), 843–68. https://doi.org/10.1177/1468796818785936.

cash awards from, respectively, an elected U of T student representative and the Brock student union (CBC News, 2014b; Mahoney, 2009). And, appallingly, in 2010 two white men – one in blackface led by a noose by the other, who wore a US confederate flag and a costume mimicking Ku Klux Klan robes – won the prize for most original costume at a party in Campbellford, Ontario (Dempsey & Allen, 2010). The air of amusement, along with these monetary recognitions, indicate the consensus in these arenas that blackface is something that those who perform it, and those who consume the performances, consider pleasureable.

It is worth a brief detour here to clarify that which is *not* the argument of this chapter. There are many who take the humour context of blackface as evidence that contemporary blackface cannot be racist[1]. According to this reasoning, humour and racism are incompatible: that which is done for "good fun" cannot at the same time cause harm. This is a rather superficial claim that ignores the role of humour in disparagement, to which anyone who has encountered the playground bully can attest. In any case, humour theorists have long challenged the notion that humour and racism are incompatible. They have advanced three theories of humour that are useful in analysing racist humour: superiority theory, relief theory, and incongruity theory.

Superiority theory holds that humour is constituted through the inferiorisation of an out-group (Billig, 2001; Morreal, 2005; see Plato and Aristotle in Weaver, 2011). Thus, in the case of antiblack jokes, non-Black people take pleasure in ridiculing Black people in order to establish their own ostensible superiority.

Relief theory posits that humour is a response to imposed social constraints, to which we may usually acquiesce for an ostensible common good, but that limit our freedom to do what we might sometimes prefer to do. Humour, according to this theory, is associated with temporary, carnivalesque respite from these social constraints that operate in more normative social settings (Bakhtin, 1984; Freud, 1960; Morreal, 2005, p. 68; Mueller et al., 2007). Those who understand racist humour through relief theory suggest that the pleasure of racist humour is derived from the temporary opportunity to express racist sentiments that would otherwise be deemed unacceptable – whether one actually holds them or not. However, there are limits to understanding racist humour as carnivalesque, since carnivals normally allow the socially less powerful to make fun of the socially more powerful (Mueller et al., 2007). Therefore, in racist humour where less-powerful groups are the butt of the joke,

---

1 We will see examples of this claim in Chapter 4.

relief and superiority objectives become indistinguishable, and prompt us to ask who it is that might be seeking relief from norms against racist expression and why.

Incongruity theory posits that humour results from experiencing the unexpected juxtaposition of concepts that are normally unrelated, thereby creating unexpected relationships among them. Double entendre is a central feature of this kind of humour, and humour researchers have analysed these incongruities in overtly racist humour (Billig, 2001; Weaver, 2010a, 2011). Others have further argued that incongruity is a central feature of the racist humour we encounter in contemporary postracialist times (Goldberg, 2012; Howard, 2014a; Pérez, 2013; Weaver, 2010b). Humour arising from incongruity finds particularly rich ground in postracialist societies that claim to be racially egalitarian but in which racism remains a key feature of how they are structured. Racist humour in this context navigates a tenuous line between overt racism and what might pass as harmless racial jesting. It depends on the ambiguity created around the joker's intentions in performing racist material in a society in which "serious" racism ostensibly no longer exists (Pérez, 2013, p. 483). The humour context therefore becomes a preferred means of engaging in racist rhetoric (thereby advancing racist ideas) while denying racism (Pérez, 2013; Weaver, 2011).

Overall, then, these theories debunk the claim that humour cannot be racist, and this chapter will not further focus on that argument. Indeed, the question about *whether* contemporary blackface is harmless humour circumvents more fundamental questions about *why* it is considered humourous and *how* blackface humour might be constituted through antiblackness. It is to this project that I now turn. How can we understand the intertwining of antiblackness and non-Black/white pleasure in blackface? How is it historically constituted? What circumstances make recourse to the Black body alluring when humour is the objective? And given that this book is concerned with blackface that occurs in the geopolitical space known as Canada, what are the peculiarities of Canadian antiblackness, and how might they constitute the "humour" of Canadian blackface? What are the conditions – historical, contemporary, and local – within which contemporary blackface "humour" in Canada becomes legible as such?

In this chapter, I argue that the conditions of possibility for contemporary blackface in Canadian humour are an antiblack libidinal economy dependent upon the tropes of biological racism, and a socially embedded, psychic association of the Black body with pleasure that was entrenched through slavery's relations of domination. I further argue that contemporary blackface humour in Canada is constituted

and intensified by the specific modalities of antiblackness and postracialist social relations in Canada – matters that, in part, characterize the
contemporary Canadian colonial project.

Blackness and Blackface as Unexamined Humour

To begin, I draw attention to the reflex manner in which many non-Black,
usually white, people find Black people inherently humorous, and the
way that, from the perspective of Black people, this humour seems to be
embedded in what they are willing to believe about Black people.

In a focus group conversation at University 5, Black people discussed
what they found to be an uncanny and disturbing degree of pleasure
that white people seem to take in instances where Black people are
being parodied. It is not that Black people cannot sometimes enjoy
humour where they are the butt of the joke. Yet they feel uncomfortable
with the degree of pleasure that white people – often their friends and
acquaintances – take from these situations, which to them seems exces-
sive. They are perturbed that white people find these instances so very
hilarious. In this conversation, Norman at University 5 refers to Key
and Peele's "Pegasus" skit[2] (which did not include blackface) to explain
his discomfort with blackface humour:

> I find a lot of Key and Peele skits very, very funny. This one I didn't find
> that funny. But what I found noticeably striking was that I was watching
> it with Caucasian friends, incidentally, and they found this skit, out of all
> of them, to be the most hilarious skit of all. And for me, I sort of had an
> unease with that because I thought to myself, "What is it that they find that
> funny about it?" ... So it got me thinking. ... I was wondering if part of the
> reason why the friends around me were laughing so hard is maybe some
> part of unconscious racial bias in the sense that they actually believe that
> people who live within ghettos or those communities could believe [that] ...
> I found myself in this sort of uneasy position, because I found the skit funny,
> but not laugh-out-loud funny, not rolling-on-the-floor funny. (U5BSOFGP1)

---

2 What is perhaps particularly interesting about this skit is that it is apparently based
 on a real news story about a 2006 "leprechaun sighting" in the Chrichton area of
 Mobile, Alabama (NBC 15, n.d.; https://www.youtube.com/watch?v=K1ljOcl39PQ).
 One of the key players in Chrichton, Demarco Morissette, and another Chrichton
 resident later claimed to be responsible for the hoax (Wavywebsurf, 2018). What truly
 happened may remain a mystery, but the larger phenomenon is that the joke is largely
 one played by a Black community on reporters, to which reporters are susceptible
 because of what they are willing to believe and report about Black people.

In the same conversation, Kim recounts a similar experience she had – this time with blackface – as the only Black person in her otherwise white high school class:

> I was about sixteen, and we were watching a movie, *Of Mice and Men*. … There was like blackfaced actors in it and I strongly recall the members of my class just found it hilarious. They were really laughing, because the actors that were impersonating Black people were kind of caricatural. It was very over the top and very dramatized. So they found it very funny … they just thought it was just really funny. I remember feeling a sense of unease seeing that people could think that Black people could actually act that way in a way that's so unlike the way we normally act. (U5BSOFGP6)

These participants struggle to understand how and why their white colleagues find these incidents that parody Black people so outrageously funny, and feel it has to do with embedded racist beliefs about Black people. In other words, for them, the roots of this humour are racist.

Kevin at University 2 independently refers to the same dynamic:

> Just in the same way that the Chappelle show, Chappelle had to stop – Some of his sketches were so on point and so powerful, but maybe the majority of the people watching them didn't understand what was going on and were just laughing at it in the same way that people laughed at minstrel shows a hundred years ago or less. So that's what makes it so tricky for me. (U2FG2P2)

Indeed, it is not clear whether Kevin was aware, but in an appearance on the Oprah Winfrey show Dave Chappelle explains his sudden departure from his wildly popular show and from a fifty-million-dollar contract. He recounts that his epiphany occurred in relation to a skit into which he had written a character in blackface – an image he admits is "difficult" but that he had chosen as the "visual personification of the n-word" to make a point about racial motivations hiding within people. He says:

> So then when I'm on the set and we're finally taping the sketch, somebody on the set that was white laughed in such a way – I know the difference between people laughing with me and people laughing at me. And it was the first time I'd ever gotten a laugh that I was uncomfortable with. Not just uncomfortable, but like, "Should I fire this person?" (Oprah Winfrey Network, 2019 at 7:52)

Chappelle, like the participants above, suspects that the degree of pleasure that white audiences get from humour with Black people as the subject is founded in racist beliefs about and attitudes towards Black people, and constitutes a racist offence. In Chappelle's case, it was worth giving up a fortune to uphold Black dignity and not abet this dehumanizing racist humour.

As we see above, this association of humour with Blackness is exacerbated when blackface is involved. Indeed, blackface perpetrators often announce the humour as though it were self-evident, clearly associating the humour directly with the representation of the Black body. For example, an online commentator makes this unexamined connection:

> It's funny ... I remember when I was a kid I dressed up like Cito Gaston – painted face and all ... All in good fun. (User *Pete Kic*, Comment on Toronto Mike, 2010)

Similarly, a drag queen fired from a Pride event in Toronto in 2013 objected: "The people I asked at Crews & Tangos [club] thought it was hilarious that I was dressed as a big, fat, black woman" (Prestwich, 2013) in what comes across as an ostensibly unchallengeable justification of his actions. Thus, blackface wearers and their audiences appear to be neither self-reflexive nor critical about the reasons they and others might take such pleasure in blackface, or about how the Black body comes to be regarded as humorous in these circumstances. They are able to claim innocence of racist mockery, even as they admit to the pleasure of blackface. The commonsensical nature of these associations of the Black body with humour suggest deep foundations powerful enough to motivate their behaviour, while remaining beyond conscious critique.

Embodied Racism: The Black Body and/as White Pleasure

In order to understand this unexamined relationship between blackface and humour, I turn to a discussion of the unique historical relationships among Black embodiment, antiblackness, pleasure, and humour.

In antiblack humour, there is an intense focus on corporeality to an extent that appears to exceed that in racist humour targeting people who are not Black (Howard, 2014b; Pérez, 2016, p. 45; Weaver, 2010a, 2011, Modood as cited in Weaver 2013, p. 126). To describe it, Weaver (2011) has proposed the concept of *embodied racism*, which he defines as

> a racism that focuses on parts of the body, on phenotype or on corporeality. It is a racism with an order-building and hierarchical propensity, and is

an invention of modernity alongside the development of race and biological racism. Embodied racism contains many of the themes and stereotypes of biological racism but lacks the systemic totality that biological racism exhibited in earlier periods of modernity. It appears as a contemporary racism that does not display the dominance of early biological racism. (p. 414)

While I agree with the overall concept, I disagree with Weaver's claim that embodied racism is a less dominant or attenuated form of biological racism. I argue, instead, that it persists today as a specific form of biological racism, which when applied to Black people is grounded in an antiblack libidinal economy. While embodied racism adapts to its temporal and spatial locations, it is continuous with earlier forms, and is as systemic and totalizing as ever – even if most people embroiled in it do not openly declare, or even consciously recognize, their commitment to it.[3] Nevertheless, I find the concept of embodied racism particularly useful for understanding contemporary blackface humour.

To further theoretically frame the ways in which, historically, the corporeal has occupied a privileged place in antiblackness, and the ways in which the domination of Black people has historically produced white pleasure and shaped antiblack humour, I also identify the historical relationships between white pleasure and the Black body entrenched during slavery. Saidiya Hartman, in *Scenes of Subjection* (1997), examines slavery's antiblack violence in its more dissembling forms, looking particularly at instances of apparent lightheartedness. For example, she examines instances in which the enslaved sang en route to slave auctions, or for slave-owners' entertainment during plantation celebrations. Hartman's analysis disrupts the dominant reading of these scenes as instances of uncomplicated *Black* enjoyment to contend instead that they constituted *white* pleasure produced by white domination *of* Black people resulting from the presumption of Black insentience. What Hartman lays bare here is the antiblack "libidinal economy" – which Frank Wilderson (2010) describes as the "distribution and arrangement, of desire and identification … anxieties, pleasures, appetites, revulsions, and phobias" (p. 7) – that organized plantation relations. Within it, two conflations occurred.

First, white pleasure and the domination of Black people became largely indistinguishable, and "enjoyment defined the relation of the

---

3 I make this argument more thoroughly in Howard (2018), which is an earlier version of this chapter.

dominant race to the enslaved" (Hartman, 1997, p. 23). Slave-owners assigned themselves the prerogative to coerce the enslaved, under threat of physical violence, to perform merriness and thereby to participate in obscuring their dehumanization. This was an important performance of white power and identity – from both of which slave-owners could reap a sordid pleasure of superiority, even as consuming the coerced performances augmented that pleasure (Hartman, 1997, pp. 7–8). Thus, the pleasure of being racialized as white, a pleasure experienced in the body (Farley, 1997, p. 484), was produced through the relations of slavery and the domination of Black people.

Second, the Black body *became* pleasure for the white subject. Resorting repeatedly to the body of the slave for "white enjoyment, in all of its sundry and unspeakable expressions" (Hartman, 1997, p. 23) afforded forms of racialized and sexualized pleasure that were simply impossible without access to the Black body. Scenes of subjection compounded self-serving white fantasies of Black insentience – that Black people were jovial and did not experience violence, pain, and indignity in the ways that white people did. This fantasy produced Blackness as the epitome of devil-may-care abandon; as the ability to transmute adversity into ecstasy (p. 22), while multiplying the violence inflicted upon Black people – a tendency that persists today (see, e.g., Howard, 2020). Thus, the violence of slavery central to the production of Black people as flesh is synonymous with pleasure's unruly and indomitable excess, paving the way for white pleasure to be appropriated through (proximity to) Black bodies.

Slavery's Canadian Themes

While slavery in Canada operated on a much smaller scale than in the United States, and was not associated with plantations, Canada has its own 206-year history of slavery. However, Canadian nation-building narratives actively erase Canada's history of slavery and/or re-present it as fundamentally "kinder" than slavery in the United States. These denials and sugar-coatings make detailed treatises like Hartman's more difficult to produce in Canada given a scarcity of material with which to work, and make it necessary to outline how Hartman's analysis applies to Canadian slavery. Hartman sets out to re-read slavery's scenes of subjection. In Canada, scenes of subjection can only be re-read once one has unearthed what we might refer to as slavery's subjected scenes – the general occlusion of the historical fact of slavery in the territories now referred to as Canada. Yet the existing evidence does allow some inductive conclusions.

The small population of enslaved Africans in British North America (now Canada), dating back to the early 1600s, dramatically increased with the arrival of white, slave-owning British Empire Loyalists circa the 1760s (Winks, 1997, p. 28).[4] White loyalists were attracted to, and appeased by, the passage of laws that upheld their slave-holding rights here (Cooper, 2006, p. 91). In this way, American and British North American attitudes and practices towards enslaved Black people informed each other, and were more similar than they were different.

We also know that the enslaved changed hands frequently during this time, and that some of these sales happened in public markets (Cooper, 2006, p. 89; Winks, 1997, p. 27). The small communities in which these took place made it likely that potential buyers would know something of both the character of the slaves they might purchase and their efforts to resist enslavement (Nelson, 2017; Winks, 1997, p. 50). To facilitate these transactions, Canadian slave-owners therefore had as much incentive as their American counterparts to coerce the enslaved into feigning contentment and merriment.

Finally, since generally only the elite could afford to own slaves, slave-owning became a mark of affluence, social standing, and respectable Humanity in British North America. Being seen with one's slave(s) visually marked this status (McKittrick, 2006, p. 113). Therefore, it is quite probable that enslaved Black people would have become accoutrements that whites could parade around to flaunt this status. Doing so would generate the same embodied pleasure of whiteness of which Hartman speaks.

Overall, then, the differences between slavery in the United States and Canada do not undermine the applicability of Hartman's analysis in Canada. Rather, Canadian slavery replicated (where it did not aggravate) the conflations of the Black body, white domination, and white pleasure.

From Slavery to the Present

The powerful relationships among Black embodiment, humour, and white pleasure did not end with slavery; they have continued in several forms since. Nineteenth-century blackface minstrelsy, in both Canada and the United States and indeed throughout the "Western" world, is

---

4 I draw reservedly and reluctantly on Winks at appropriate points in this book, for whereas Winks does record information about Black people in Canada, the book itself is, at best, condescending where not itself antiblack in its tone.

a most relevant example in the context of this book's central concern, and indeed Hartman applies her arguments directly to minstrelsy. The extensive literature on minstrel shows (e.g., Johnson, 2012, 2017; Lhamon, 1998; Lott, 1993; Roediger, 1999) outlines their complexity, describing the ways in which, by caricaturing Black bodies and appropriating Black culture, white men constructed representations of Blackness against which they could know themselves as superior. Minstrelsy was simultaneously a carnivalesque form of humour allowing white working-class men to poke fun at white elites, challenge class relations, and establish their own gendered national identities (Lott, 1993; Nicks & Sloniowski, 2010, p. 286; Pérez, 2016; Robinson, 2012; Roediger, 1999, p. 123). However, it is crucial not to read the complexity of the intertwined race, class, gender, and nationalist relations that produced this entertainment as mitigating the antiblackness at the core of blackface and its ostensible humour (Hartman, 1997, p. 29; Pérez, 2016, p. 930; Roediger, 1999, pp. 123–4). Rather, antiblackness was both the material from which minstrelsy's class politics was woven and the shared grammar upon which the broad appeal of minstrelsy was built.

In the early twentieth century, as minstrel shows lost popularity, they were largely replaced by, or continued by way of, animated films (Kenrick, 2010; Robinson, 2012; Sammond, 2015), which continued to draw upon embodied racism, where not specifically on blackface iconography, to produce humour and entertainment. As a YouTube search for the term "racist animated film" will quickly confirm for the reader, embodied racism was evident even in children's films, where the bodies of characters such as Buckwheat in *The Little Rascals*, Sunflower in Disney's *Fantasia*, and Mammy Two Shoes in *Tom & Jerry* (to name just a few examples) were the fulcrum around which racist humour and pleasure turned. Indeed, scholars have argued persuasively that Mickey Mouse is a minstrel (Sammond, 2015, pp. 3–5; Willis, 1991, p. 107). If this is true, since Mickey Mouse is synonymous with the Disney franchise which is, in turn, synonymous with ostensible wholesome mainstream family fun, then here again the Black body continues to be made into white pleasure.

Sean Mills, in a chapter entitled "Sex, Race, and Sovereign Dreams" in his *A Place in the Sun* (2016), speaks particularly poignantly to the relationships between conceptions of Black sexuality, the Black body, and the settler-colonial context in Canada within the broader context of colonial racist logic, but looking particularly at how this played out in Quebec in the complex, deeply gendered relationships of desire and revulsion between white francophone Quebeckers and Haitians (largely Haitian men). This discussion speaks to the libidinal economy attached to the Black body, operating in Quebec and Canada as much as elsewhere, and from which we cannot separate the practice of black-face. The particular context of Quebec, and its ambivalent historical relationships with Blackness founded in Quebec nationalism and the appropriation of Blackness on the one hand, while maintaining a racial hierarchy between white Quebecers and Black people (particularly Hai-tians) on the other (Mills, 2016), is perhaps not unrelated to the fact that Quebec is the only province in the last twenty years[5] in which blackface has continued to occur openly in theatres and on televised programs.

Overall, then, contemporary embodied humour (Weaver, 2011) such as blackface, preoccupied as it is with Black corporeality, cannot be pre-sumed innocent, and warrants analysis.

Peeling Back Blackface: Layers of Embodied Racist Pleasure

It is not surprising, then, that within the performance of contemporary blackface, which Black people easily identify as antiblackness, we might see this embedded libidinal current that associates the Black body with pleasure. This shows up in the data from this study where, for example, a non-Black focus-group participant at University 5, and one of the few participants who openly supported blackface, recounts her experience:

> PARTICIPANT: Last Halloween my sister dressed up as Bob Marley ... I mean my sister happens to be the whitest person in my family [*chuckle*] and to us that was funny ...
>
> INTERVIEWER: So she actually used dark makeup?
>
> PARTICIPANT: Dark makeup, a wig, and a big, big joint [*chuckle*] ... Honestly it was hilarious because of my sister's physical appearance, naturally speaking. It was really such a contrast, it was funny ... It's like a metamorphosis visually ... I don't know if I were to do it, if it was going to be as funny.
>
> INTERVIEWER: Because you think she's a lot lighter than you, complexion-wise?
>
> PARTICIPANT: Oh, my sister is definitely a lot lighter than me! (U5FG1P5)

Evidently, for this participant, the humour of her sister's blackface is drawn directly from skin-colour contrasts. Consistent with what

---

5 In 1998 and again in 1999, the musical *Jolson* was performed at the Royal Alexandria Theatre in Toronto, during which at least four characters appeared in blackface (Le Camp, 2005, p. 28).

incongruity theory might suggest, this participant finds the humour of this incident to be generated by juxtaposed incongruous elements – in this case her sister's white skin vs. Marley's darker skin. As such, the performance becomes less funny the less visually white the black-face wearer is. Yet significantly, the participant does not mention, say, nationality, height, musical talent, gender, or any of the many other possible factors that might differentiate the blackface wearer from Bob Marley. Indeed, while on all of these other factors, the respondent is likely as different from Marley as her sister, she suspects that, if she were to attempt the same portrayal, it would not be as humorous. In other words, these factors do not invoke humorous incongruities. Not even the wig and joint would have recuperated the coveted humour response. In her estimation, this is entirely because she is not as white-complexioned as her sister.

According to this participant, then, the humour is specifically and solely located in incongruities associated with the presentation of Black-ness. We see the same investment in racial difference and its contribu-tion to humour in several other instances, as in this online comment about a blackface incident: "What made the whole thing more humour-ous was the only Black guy played the only white guy as well. But it was all for fun!" (User *Rob*, Comment on Urback, 2009).

That these respondents identify skin-colour difference as the source of blackface humour suggests that they perceive an incongruity – much more than difference – between white and Black skin. There is little that is inherently funny or incongruous about colour differences. Dressing up as a blue apple for Halloween, for example, is not likely to produce any appreciable humour though we do not expect apples to be blue. Rather, it is the hierarchical significance that an antiblack society places upon the visual and embodied presentation of Black-ness, rooted in embodied racism, that informs the incongruity, and therefore the humour. In a society primed with embodied racism, the Black body signifies by its visibility. Embodied racism makes it such that Black bodies have not signified, and do not signify, what white bodies do since Blackness is deemed the foil against which not only whiteness but Western Humanity itself can be known – that is, an ostensible absence of subjectivity (Spillers, 1987; Walcott, 2014c; Weheliye, 2014b; Wilderson, 2003; Wynter, 2003). Herein lies the real source of incongruity. The pleasure that blackface wearers and their audiences experience is produced by the presentation of the Black body – particularly where one expects a white one. It is about a failure of signification undergirded by the ways that a racial logic conjures up ideas of an incommensurability between Blackness and white/Human subjectivity made visible through embodiment. This is why although stereotypical accoutrements are often present in blackface portrayals (such as the wig and joint in the Marley example), they are only secondary in generating the humour of contemporary blackface in Canada. The presentation of Blackness through darkening white skin, on its own, serves to conjure up the apparent pleasurable sensations of white/Human subjectivity in a racial hierarchy.

There is another dimension to the embodied humour in contemporary blackface. Weaver applies the term "embodied racism" to contemporary antiblack jokes on the internet – the humour of which, he suggests, is dependent upon verbal references to Black embodiment (Weaver, 2011). Contemporary blackface takes this embodied racist humour a step further, by embodying the referent. Here, non-Black people do not simply tell jokes *about* the Black body, but rather *become* the joke by wearing the Black body. Blackface is a performance – that is, it is embodied by definition. Blackface therefore becomes a quintessential expression of embodied racism's humour. If, as we have seen, the Black body is overdetermined as white pleasure, then what better way to experience that pleasure than by temporarily becoming the Black body? This opportunity to embody the tropes of embodied racism produces the intense pleasure blackface wearers apparently experience.

Of Metamorphosis: Fear and Humour in Contemporary Blackface

There are yet further layers to the constitution of blackface humour in the account of the Marley impersonation, where the respondent speaks about metamorphosis. Blackface seems to afford a moment of Black becoming – a transmutation into something one would otherwise never be. A white focus-group participant surmises about this in a general application to racial difference:

> You have this desire to participate in, like, temporary – maybe it's like exotic or different … you kinda want to know what it's like. Like, I'm not saying that's how I feel, but I can see why someone would have the desire *to be* someone who comes from a different experience than yourself. (U1FG2P3, emphasis added)

A similar sense of metamorphosis achieved through blackface (though to different effect) can be found in John Howard Griffin's account of his own blackface-esque escapade in the 1960s, which he hoped would afford him an "authentic" experience of Blackness. Looking at himself in the mirror for the first time after darkening his skin, Griffin writes:

> The transformation was total and shocking. I had expected to see myself disguised, but this was something else. … I knew now there was no such thing as a disguised white man, *when the Black won't rub off*. … I became two men, the observing one and the one who panicked, who felt Negroid even to the depth of his entrails. … For a few weeks I must be this aging, bald Negro; I must walk through a land hostile to my color, hostile to my skin. (Griffin, 1961, pp. 11–12, emphasis added)

Griffin's effort, however fraught, was to genuinely pass for an extended time as Black in the segregated southern United States. The fear he expresses results from the sense that he had lost the security of identity – the protection from antiblack violence – that the bodily presentation of whiteness normally afforded him. The fear also results from the way he imagines he had become Black inwardly as well as outwardly – a disordering of his very being. It is as Ralph Ellison (1958) had earlier surmised with respect to minstrelsy:

> When the white man steps behind the mask of the trickster his freedom is circumscribed by the fear that he is not simply miming a personification of his disorder and chaos, but that he will become in fact that which he intends only to symbolize; that he will be trapped." (p. 218)

In contemporary blackface, however, where the effort to pass as Black is much less earnest than Griffin's, where the Blackness *will* rub off, making the return to white personhood imminently accessible and assured, security of racial place is not threatened. Instead, under these conditions, white subjectivity felt as pleasure is secured. A comment from a non-Black participant in a focus group at University 2 gives further insight into this relationship between security of identity and the fleeting experience of contemporary blackface:

> I think even more common than blackface costumes is going as the opposite gender, and I've done it … In a way it almost makes you feel more feminine when you dress up like a boy; it's like, "Ha ha, I'm still a girl." And I think maybe sometimes white people are, like, subconsciously just wanting to exploit that difference of like, "Oh, I look like I'm Black but, tee hee, I'm still white underneath." (U2FG1P6)

This participant suggests that playing at Blackness through contemporary blackface is about the pleasure of confirming one's whiteness, and that this contributes to the humour and laughter (thus "tee hee"). As in slavery's scenes of subjection, white people experience pleasure from the security of their racial positionality, which in this case is facilitated by wearing blackface. In contemporary blackface, then, pleasure and fun are accumulated by crossing racial boundaries and pretending to risk this positionality, knowing all the while that a safe return to whiteness is guaranteed.

While it is usually, but not always, white people who perform blackface, for others the logic outlined above still applies, particularly since it is not only whiteness but a sense of Humanity and respectability that blackface secures. For non-white, racialized people who participate in blackface, the performance secures them a toehold on this Humanity and respectability (Fellows & Razack, 1997) however mitigated it might be by, and perhaps especially because of, their non-whiteness. The pleasure of blackface, then, whether performed by white or other non-Black people, draws upon, and teaches, the power and violence of antiblack social relations in a postracialist pedagogy.

Antiblackness in Contemporary Canada

To say that embodied racism is a long-standing, totalizing biological racism that exists across the "Western" world is not to suggest that it is not shaped by the temporal and spatial locations in which it exists. What, then, are the features of antiblack racial formation in contemporary Canada, and how does it inform contemporary blackface in Canada?

It is always important to declare that the geopolitical space we now know as Canada is the subject of a long-standing settler-colonial project that is sustained by ongoing colonial relations. These relations differently racialize and affect various social groups. Primarily, in order for the Canadian state to continue to pretend to legitimate access to the land upon which it exists, Indigenous peoples must be made to disappear along with their originary claims as guardians of the land (Nichols, 2014; Wolfe, 2006). This is effected through several policy frameworks – among them the Indian Act and the Official Languages Act – which appropriate territory, give the state control over definitions of Indigenousness, and install Europeans of French and English heritage as the founders of the nation whose fabricated founder status is used to claim entitlement to the fullest benefits of citizenship (Cannon,

2007; Haque, 2012). Simultaneously, Canada's immigration policies, and the combined political and discursive expressions of its Multiculturalism Act, frame Black and other racialized people solely as recent immigrants who live here as "supplicants" because of the benevolence of white Canadians rather than as contributors to life and society here (Thobani, 2007, p. 252; Walcott, 2014b). These ideas are underscored through multiculturalist discourse that refers especially to racialized Canadians by hyphenated references to countries of "origin" outside of Canada, regardless of individuals' actual place of birth[6] (Jackson, 2004; Walcott, 2001, p. 127, 2014b, p. 129). Overall, racialized groups are positioned as having tenuous claims to citizenship, and certainly as having no legitimacy to make anti-racist claims against the state or Canadian civil society. This helps to produce the myth of a Canada where race ostensibly is not, and has never been, an issue.

For Black people specifically, evidence of our long presence here since the 1600s is actively erased both materially and symbolically (see, e.g., McKittrick, 2002; Walcott, 2003a), and the afterlife of Canadian slavery persists through the multiple mechanisms by which Black labour is appropriated to build the nation state while Black people simultaneously experience barriers to citizenship through Canadian labour and immigration law (see, e.g., Bashi, 2004; Calliste, 1994; Lawson, 2013), being perpetually regarded as out-of-place and a poor fit for the Canadian body politic (e.g., Walcott, 2014c).

Ironically, however, Canada constructs itself as progressive and racially egalitarian (explored further in Chapter 3), and Canada's relationship to Blackness has been integral to constructing Canada as beyond racism (Cooper, 2006). This has been enacted first through silencing and distorting the history of Canadian slavery and Canada's integral involvement in the Atlantic economies that both upheld and were upheld by the relations of slavery (Cooper, 2006; Poole, 2012; Walcott & Abdillahi, 2019). This has been accompanied by selective historical accounts of the Underground Railroad to Canada. This hegemonic narration of Canada's role as safe destination on the Underground Railroad focuses on a short time period, especially between the 1851 Fugitive Slave Act and the 1865 Thirteenth Amendment in the United States, during which time Canadian territory provided greater security than the northern United States for those fleeing slavery in the South (Bakan, 2008; Winks, 1997, p. 142).

---

6 Though hyphenated labels are sometimes used by/for white Canadians, they are usually reserved for recent immigrants, and do not racialize whites – or rather, help to racialize them as white.

These trends, then, make Canada ideologically postracialist – that is, it functions through racist social relations while denying and claiming to have overcome them (Goldberg, 2009, 2012, 2015). Thus, while racist, colonial, social relations continue to structure the state and civil society, Canada officially, like a majority of Canadians, claims to have transcended racism, antiblackness, and colonialism, if it admits to a racist, colonial history at all. These historical and extant antiblack formations in Canada organize contemporary blackface in Canada, and inform its humour.

Working the Edge: Humour's Zenith

In this section, I argue that the deniability that characterizes the postracialist climate adds to the pleasure and humour of contemporary blackface in Canada.

As discussed above, the superiority theory of humour suggests that racial humour is derived from the sense of ascendency gained by inferiorizing racial "Others." This dynamic operates in contemporary blackface in Canada. For example, Jules, a Black student in a focus group at University 4, suggested an explanation for the racist stereotypes accompanying two specific blackface incidents that took place at Canadian universities. In one at Hautes Études Commerciales (HEC) Montréal, the perpetrators carried monkeys and make-believe bags of marijuana, and in the other perpetrators simulated smoking three-foot novelty marijuana joints and wore dreadlock wigs with Kentucky Fried Chicken buckets as hats. Jules hypothesizes:

> In these kinds of competitions … people try to push things to the extreme. To win, to get points, you have to exaggerate. You have to go very, very far. So, for me, that somewhat explains everything. It explains the enormous joints, the weed in a bag, the KFC. It explains all the stereotypes that they could find, and they piled them up – one on top of the other. So you get points the more elaborate your costume is. (U4FG1P8)

This excerpt speaks to the ways in which humour is harvested as one journeys deeper into the realm of racist expression and ridicule ("going very far"). Blackface wearers secure positive attention from their peers (represented here by "points") by accumulating antiblack signifiers. Thus, racist discourse, and the libidinal economy that conflates antiblackness and pleasure, organize the humour. A non-Black, Latinx student, Antonio at University 2, develops this idea further, indicating the ways that the desire for notoriety through humour informs the excesses of racist expression in contemporary blackface:

> To go back to the point of humor and like getting close to the edge … you're only gonna be remembered if you go to that boundary and draw some looks and stuff. Like no one would remember if you just dressed up as Superman or something like that. So shock value in our culture is a really big part of getting attention. (U2FG1P7)

Evidently, those who perform blackface make deliberate calculations to go far enough to "draw looks" and to incite "shock." The degree of humour and notoriety to be had is related to the degree of antiblackness performed, suggesting a deliberate effort to enter the territory of offence.

However, this participant also introduces the notion of a "boundary" or "edge," to which several participants across three focus groups refer. In postracialist climates, racial expression must be carefully coded and managed, placing limits on the extent to which one can admit deriving humour from racist ridicule (see Pérez, 2013, 2016). The metaphorical "edge" appears related to this postracialism and what might be deemed "acceptable" racial expression. Referring to the edge, a white student at University 2 says:

> And by going to the edge, the edge of acceptability, they might think that it's more likely that they'll win the contest. I think they anticipate that, definitely anticipate that debate. (U1FG1P4)

Two things stand out here. First, blackface wearers apparently anticipate *both* approval (to win contests) *and* debate, suggesting either that controversy is considered a reasonable price to pay for approval or, more insidiously, that controversy is an important component of the humour. Second, as in the excerpt before it, here humour is found *at* "the edge." It might be tempting to understand this "edge" humour through the lens of relief theory as the result of a carnivalesque flouting of norms of racial decorum imposed by a society that claims racial egalitarianism. However, to flout normative boundaries is to rupture, transgress, and exceed them. In these excerpts, however, humour is found by "getting close" to and flirting with "the boundary." Humour is found *at* "the edge" rather than beyond it, an assertion with which all the narratives of the participants who discuss "the edge" agree.

Zawadi at University 2 addresses the relationships among the deniability and humour that are possible at "the edge":

I think for the most part people who do these kinds of things are trying to agitate, to get a reaction, to channel their racism ... and say, "Oh, it's Halloween!" ... otherwise why else of all the things you could do, and of all the things you can be and dress-up in, why the colour of a people? Why be that particular thing – especially when you know there are these tensions? And it happens in universities! These are not stupid people! They know they are not in spaces where there are no racial tensions.

Zawadi's assessment dovetails with the assertion above that blackface wearers anticipate debate and controversy at the "edge of acceptability," reinforcing the idea that this is an important part of the humour.

"The edge," then, appears to be the point at which ambivalence is maximized in a postracialist society. It is as far as possible into the territory of racial controversy to titillate the antiblack libido, but also at the opposing limit that allows the denial of the humour's antiblackness. This ambivalence – this indeterminacy – becomes a source of humour. Anthony Farley (1997) elucidates how embodied racism, pleasure, and humour come together in this postracialist climate, where he observes:

To be black is to be available for humiliation, to be white is to partake of race-pleasure, and to be colorblind [or postracialist, in this instance] is to repress one's awareness of the entire enterprise. The colorline depends on all three aspects – humiliation, pleasure, and denial – for its power. (p. 481)

If Farley is correct, then blackface wearers do not linger at "the edge" solely because it is where one can avoid accusations of racism. Rather, denial works with embodied racism at "the edge" to produce and intensify racist humour. "The edge" is, therefore, the zenith of postracialist racist humour.

There is, of course, no requirement that any individual wearing blackface, or any audience enjoying blackface, be fully conscious of how their pleasure at this zenith is constituted. As we have seen, the humour of contemporary blackface in Canada goes largely unexamined. Indeed, the deniability that is possible at "the edge" can be turned inward, such that blackface wearers and their audiences do not have to resolve the "racist or funny" question, even for themselves. A white participant at University 2 speaks to the lack of a need for conscious awareness:

Near the edge is where you get the laughs. And even if they are not sure what's wrong with it, if they have a sense of "that's funny," people feel willing to go for it whether or not they are ignorant. It's always seen as worth going for the laugh because privilege laughs a lot in our culture. (U2FG1P4)

This participant's observations suggest that contemporary blackface in Canada combines the humour that confirms racial superiority with the pleasure of deniability that is possible through a lack of self-reflexivity (Billig, 2001, p. 286; Freud, 1960, p. 121). This is why questions about whether a blackface wearer intended to be racist or was ignorant of the racism inherent in blackface are largely irrelevant and misguided. The racial pleasure of blackface can be had independently of intentionality. As Farley (1997) again notes, "the suggestion that racism in today's post-civil rights era is unconscious is secondary if we think of race as a practice people enjoy, as a form of pleasure" (487).

Jamaicanizing Blackness

The ways in which the prevailing postracialist context and the specific modalities of antiblackness in Canada inform the ostensible humour of contemporary blackface in Canada are also evident in what I call the externalization and Jamaicanization of Blackness in blackface. Images of incidents of contemporary blackface in Canada demonstrate that they normally portray Black people as non-Canadians – that is, as originating from a place external to the nation state. For example, where not portraying African American celebrities such as Michael Jackson, Mr T, and telephone psychic Ms. Cleo, Canadian blackface incidents have portrayed an imaginary Ethiopian beauty queen and parodied a fictitious woman from Guadeloupe (Armstrong, 2013; Béland, 2012; Canadian Press, 2012; MacMillan, 2005; Prestwich, 2013). A significant number of incidents of contemporary blackface in Canada specifically portray Blackness as Jamaican. Among blackface portrayals reported in the media, there have been at least three incidents featuring Black weed-smokers and/or (dread)locks – stereotypical tropes of Jamaicanness for their associations with Rastafarianism (CBC News, 2014c; HueyFreeman222, 2007; Mahoney, 2009); two portrayals of Bob Marley (CBC News, 2014c; TVA Nouvelles, 2017) in addition to the one mentioned above; one incident at Hautes Études Commerciales Montréal portraying Jamaican sprinter Usain Bolt while wearing the Jamaican colours, carrying Jamaican flags, and chanting "smoke more weed, man" (Montpetit, 2011); and two portraying the Jamaican bobsled team as parodied in the film Cool Runnings (CBC News, 2014b; Mahoney, 2009). When these incidents are compared to blackface incidents in the United States where Blackness is most commonly represented in the "ghetto parties" register (C. M. Cole, 2012), the prevalence of this Jamaicanization of Blackness through contemporary blackface in Canada is conspicuous.

The logics behind the externalization and Jamaicanization of Blackness become clearer when we consider the popularity of blackface portrayals of the Jamaican bobsled team, as iconized in the parodic film
Cool Runnings. In this film, and therefore in the blackface portrayals that
repeat it, humour is produced by the alleged incongruence of Blackness
with the winter weather and winter sports often invoked as prototypi-
cally Canadian. The humour in these blackface portrayals is therefore
consistent with the racial logic whereby Canada limited Black migration to Canada by asserting that Black people were not suited to the
country's climate (Bashi, 2004, p. 587). Indeed, the discursive salience
of the idea that Black/Jamaican is foreign and out of place in Canada
figures poignantly in a University of Windsor blackface incident. In it,
to fulfil a course assignment, a student wore blackface and "spoke with
a fake Jamaican accent" to illustrate the experience of deportation. The
course instructor praised this presentation and awarded the student a
good grade (Canadian Federation of Students-Ontario, 2010, p. 7), suggesting they both found the portrayal apt.

We find further context for reading the Jamaicanization of Blackness
in blackface when we consider that the categories "Black," "Caribbean," and "Jamaican" have historically been conflated in dominant
Canadian discourse (Foster, 1996; Jackson, 2004; Walcott, 2001, p. 24,
2003b, p. 12). These conflations are not benign, but rather are instrumental in defining the boundaries of national belonging in racial terms.
They draw heavily on the ways in which Canadian antiblackness positions all Black people in Canada as recent immigrants, and the ways
in which multiculturalist discourse ascribes hyphenated identities to
Black and other racialized Canadians such that they are rendered as
never belonging in Canada – regardless of how long they and their families may have been here (Foster, 1996, p. 69). This makes possible a code
for speaking about Black people in racial terms without actually mentioning race. Black people, and particularly Jamaicans, are frequently
constructed in the Canadian media and popular discourse as criminals,
cheats, and troublemakers who ostensibly squander the opportunity to
become "responsible" Canadians, and who therefore merit deportation
(Benjamin, 2003; Greenhill, 1993, p. 89; Jackson, 2004; Walcott, 2003b,
p. 12). This discourse makes Black/Jamaican perpetually out of place
in Canada.

These trends played out quite specifically in the ways that Canadian
sprinter Ben Johnson's fall from favour is/was discussed in Canada –
significant to this argument because Johnson was born in Jamaica, was
the subject of Canadian racial humour, and because his troubles occurred
in the same year that the *Canadian Multiculturalism Act* was passed

(Jackson, 2004). Johnson won gold for Canada at the 1988 Olympics, but was later stripped of his medal after failing doping tests. Despite his status as a Canadian citizen throughout, Johnson was referred to in the media variously as Canadian, Jamaican-Canadian, or Jamaican depending on the degree of favour he held publicly at that moment (Greenhill, 1993; Jackson, 2004). The joke-work of the numerous Ben Johnson jokes that emerged after this incident similarly relied on racialized notions of Canadianness, and were a significant locus for public expression of the tensions between Canada's official stance on multiculturalism (as problematic as this is in itself) and more xenophobic public sentiment (Greenhill, 1993, p. 85).

Therefore, contemporary blackface in Canada and its preoccupation with portraying Blackness as non-Canadian/Jamaican draws its humour from this larger discourse of the incongruity of Blackness in/and Canada. Much as it did in the days of minstrelsy, contemporary blackface in Canada participates in the construction of racialized national identities, now by positioning Black people as foreign and unsuited to the racially constituted nation state and, by default, positioning white people as true, rightful, worthy Canadians.

Situated as it is within a postracialist context, this humour too takes place at "the edge" because of the ways in which it allows for multiple layers of ambiguity and denial: is it celebrating multiculturalism or rejecting it? Is it parodying Blackness/Jamaicanness or paying tribute? And given the coded language that racializes Jamaicanness, is it even about Blackness? As we have seen, the deniability around each of these unsettled questions would serve to intensify the racist humour of the already racist practice of blackface.

Both race and humour theorists have argued that racist humour is a means for mobilizing racist ideas where explicit racist discourse is nominally frowned upon (Goldberg, 2012; Howard, 2014a; Pérez, 2013, 2016). Further, as Thobani (2007, p. 79) points out, national belonging is rehearsed and celebrated through ritual – both those as widespread and formal as singing the national anthem and those as informal but pervasive as asking racialized people, "Where are you from?" In a postracialist climate where race is not supposed to be a factor, blackface in general, and the Jamaicanization of it in particular – identified as ritual by their iterative nature – allow the perpetuation of the logics that constitute dominant conceptions of Canadianness. By rehearsing the tropes of Canadian antiblackness, they help to teach and fix authorized views of the nation state, its origins, and its relationships to Blackness.

These logics often escape critique and deconstruction because the humour context is not supposed to warrant this kind of serious attention (Billig, 2001; Pérez, 2016). Yet these logics have real material impact. They take concrete form through the ways in which Black people encounter Canadian immigration policy and practice, quite often informing the ways in which immigration and deportation decisions are made (see, e.g., Calliste, 1994; Lawson, 2013). People who have lived or been raised in Canada but who for various, often structural, reasons have not become citizens, and especially those who have run-ins with law enforcement (itself an antiblack encounter), experience the precarity of their belonging here and the possibility of deportation (Barnes, 2009; Lawson, 2013). These racist ideas are further instantiated in the everyday antiblackness that organizes how Black people in Canada are regarded and the rights they are presumed to have in civil society. Contemporary blackface in Canada and its humour, then, are implicated in perpetuating the ideas that make these practices defensible in mainstream discourse.

Conclusion

Though, as we have seen, blackface is unselfconsciously considered humourous in the dominant imagination, humour is never automatic, and racist humour is never just given! It is woven of the complex meanings available in the times and spaces within which it occurs. Consequently, its interpretation, while contested, is also not infinitely open. Racist humour can only be understood by exploring how broader social meanings, particularly those that constitute racial and national subjectivities, converge to produce it. This is the task I have approached in this chapter. By focusing on antiblackness and the specific ways that embodied racism constructs and then targets the Black body, I have argued that embodied racism, which focuses on Black anatomy, is comprehensive and persists today much as it has for centuries. Founded upon an antiblack libidinal economy that makes Blackness hyper-corporeal, and makes the domination of Black bodies indistinguishable from white pleasure, this embodied racism produces modes of white humour. One of the myriad ways that it does so is reflected in contemporary blackface. By attending to how contemporary blackface in Canada presents visually, and how social subjects talk about it in Canada today, I have further argued that the humour of contemporary blackface in Canada is constituted by its engagement at multiple levels with extant social relations in Canada that are postracialist and antiblack, and without which the humour is impossible. As such, this ostensibly harmless humour is implicated in the dissemination and rehearsal of the ideas that circumscribe Black life and make it out of place in Canada.

Yet I reiterate here that there is no need to assume that those who enjoy blackface are fully conscious of how their pleasure is constituted and of its racist effects (though undoubtedly many *are* aware). Indeed, the possibility that non-Black Canadians participate unwittingly in an antiblack libidinal economy as they enjoy blackface is perhaps as or more disturbing than if Canadians were always conscious of the source of their humour. What might it mean that blackface participants and their appreciative audiences are, beyond their conscious attention, able to so seamlessly reproduce and deeply enjoy the tropes of Canadian antiblackness – both historical and current? The foregoing analysis makes the more comprehensive case that contemporary blackface in Canada humour is only legible through Canadian racial discourses and relations of antiblackness.

3 Defending Blackface: Performing the "Progressive," Postracialist Canadian

This chapter further examines mainstream blackface discourses, this time based on the study data from print and electronic articles reporting on Canadian blackface incidents in mainstream media outlets, relevant campus newspapers, and letters to the editor since 2005. It pays particular attention to the sometimes thoughtful, occasionally openly racist, and usually unguarded reader comments associated with online articles. The chapter is based on themes generated from the data about the various ways that blackface is justified in the articles and especially the reader comments. Here, I am interested in learning more about the discursive juxtaposition of these defences of blackface with hegemonic understandings of what it means to be Canadian, and in particular the claim to Canadian progressiveness – all of which typically attend public debates about blackface in Canada. I use the term "progressive" here to refer to the claim to Canadian racial egalitarianism that is actually quite a conservative discursive position because of its relationship to Canadian postracialism, which will be discussed further below. I also use the term "subjectivity" (rather than, say, "identity") to indicate the ongoing constructed, always unfinished, nature of subject positions – the ways in which social subjects continually struggle to establish and re-establish themselves as particular kinds of persons.

In the chapter, then, I demonstrate that the presumption of Canadian racial egalitarianism frames debates about blackface in Canada, but that it is largely mobilized in defence of blackface rather than in opposition to it. I argue that blackface and the logics undergirding its

An earlier version of this chapter appears in Howard, P.S.S. (2018). On the back of Blackness: Contemporary Canadian blackface and the consumptive production of post-racialist, white Canadian subjects. *Social Identities*, 24(1), 87–103. https://doi.org/10.1080/13504630.2017.1281113.

defence are forms of racial consumption through which ostensibly progressive Canadian subjectivities are secured. This progressiveness is
a claim to a racial transcendence that feels it therefore need not care
about causing racial offence to Black people, and thereby signals the
ways that Canadian progressiveness is constituted by antiblackness.
Contemporary blackface discourses in Canada are therefore postracialist in their ability to juxtapose racist expression, generated within racist structures, with claims to having overcome racism (e.g., Cho, 2008;
Goldberg, 2009, 2012, 2015). Postracialism is a long-standing feature
of Canadian national mythologies that are partly constructed through
revisionist understandings of the nation's relationship to Blackness,
and against an ostensibly more virile racism in the United States. This
Canadian self-concept requires a collective national amnesia not only
around Canada's history of blackface minstrelsy, but also around the
broader constitutive antiblackness of the Canadian settler-colonial project. Overall, by analysing blackface in the context of nationalist postracialism, this chapter clarifies what is at stake for Canadians who participate in defending contemporary blackface, and helps us to understand
how both blackface and unexamined Canadian claims to an inherent
egalitarianism are trotted out against Black critique, and thus perpetuate antiblackness in Canada.

Blackface, Racial Consumption, and the Production of White Subjectivities

In the previous chapters, we saw that blackface is an appropriation of
the Black body, and that its humour depends upon notions of Blackness as ontological Otherness and a problematic association of Black
people's bodies with white pleasure. This humour dynamic is only one
form of a broader phenomenon of racial consumption – which has been
defined as interacting with race through consumerism – "a wide variety
of practices that involve our engagement with a range of objects, products, services, stories, images, texts, styles, spaces and places" to "make
and remake meanings" (Pitcher, 2014, p. 3). According to Pitcher, racial
consumption is always a means to "'say' something about ourselves
and others" (p. 5).

Two examples might demonstrate how contemporary blackface in
Canada does this consumptive work of telling us "something about
ourselves and others." In an incident portraying characters from the
film *Cool Runnings,* the blackface wearers reported: "This movie played
a large part in our childhoods, and we simply wanted to express our
feelings towards it with realistic costumes, which in this case included

skin color" (Mahoney, 2009). Here, Blackness, signified through altered skin colour, is central to, and sufficient for, expressing nostalgia and memorial.

Likewise, in a blackface incident that Patrick at University 7 describes, we see this generative consumptive dynamic at work as the blackface wearer explains his motives:

> [The blackface wearer] has kind of like a higher voice and … the [party] theme was "What I would like to be." He would like to have a deeper voice, so when he thought of someone, he thought of Barry White. … And again, word for word … this is what he would say [to me]: "I wanted to be Barry White and the only way I can show people that I am Barry White is to show that I am Black." (U7S1)

For this blackface wearer, the fantasy of having a deeper voice could be realized without singing, without a microphone, without a piano, music, or lyrics to Barry White's songs – none of which he employed – but rather through appropriating Blackness through blackface. Similar to the *Cool Runnings* incident above, and as with the impersonation of Bob Marley in the previous chapter, darkening the skin is integral to accomplishing the meanings the wearers desired.

Of course, the "something" that is said is always a racial "something." Contemporary blackface consumes Otherness – in this case Blackness – to achieve ends for which the mobilization of Blackness is indispensable.

Racial consumption is historically informed by a colonial ambivalence that makes Blackness both abject and object of desire (hooks, 1992a; Roediger, 1999). It is also informed historically by journeys across racial boundaries into racial space, and accounts of these journeys, whereby white subjectivities are constructed – for both travellers and their audiences (Kirby, 1998, p. 49; Phillips, 1997, p. 59). Thus, here I further define the notion of racial consumption to refer more specifically to the phenomenon whereby white subjects fetishistically engage Blackness (as they imagine it to be) to do the work of self-making – that is, to discursively construct their subjectivities (hooks, 1992a; Watts, 1997; Yousman, 2003). hooks (1992a) refers to this as "eating the Other." As we saw in the previous chapters, wearing blackface, its transitory "touristic" nature, and the minimal effort to appear authentic all make the blackface wearer feel more white (where white is taken to be synonymous with Human), and contemporary blackface wearers, like nineteenth-century minstrels (Roediger, 1999, p. 117), secure their subjectivities by making it clear that they are not really to be mistaken for Black.

It is not only those who wear blackface who reinforce their subjectivities through blackface performances. Blackface enjoys the approval and complicity of others who are not directly involved, but who repost pictures on organizational websites (e.g., Benedictson, 2013; McGill Daily, 2012), vote and award (sometimes monetary) prizes for "best costume" (e.g., Benedictson, 2013; Dempsey & Allen, 2010; Mahoney, 2009), and vociferously defend blackface and its perpetrators in the myriad subsequent discussions taking place in person and in the media. This broad-based participation, involving those wearing blackface and those who do not, has historically attended blackface minstrelsy and its identity-making potential. Many minstrel troupes consisted of the "endmen" and the master of ceremonies, "Mr. Interlocutor." The endmen (armed with blackface, garish attire, and malapropisms) along with Mr. Interlocutor (sometimes *not* in blackface, wearing formal coat and tails, and speaking with "genteel" dialect) (Lott, 1993, pp. 140, 264), worked together to provide the contrasts through which they and their audiences could know themselves. Participants in discussions about contemporary blackface in Canada are similarly able to construct progressive Canadian subjectivities without wearing blackface, as I shall argue. Signalling this, I refer to discussants who justify contemporary blackface as "interlocutors" to highlight both the discursive aspect of identity-making through blackface and their complicity in co-constructing white subjectivities through Blackness in a manner analogous to the role of the historical Mr. Interlocutor.

Constructing Progressive White Selves

Theories of whiteness, rooted in Black scholarship (e.g., Baldwin, 1966, 1984; Du Bois, 1920; hooks, 1992b; Morrison, 1992), have established the ways in which white subjectivities are crafted in opposition to Blackness. More recent scholarship on whiteness has critiqued the ways in which this process is still at work even when the attempt is ostensibly to construct non-racist white subjectivities (Frankenberg, 1993; Howard, 2004, 2006; Lomax, 1966; Moon, 1999).

While the subjectivities secured through historical blackface minstrelsy were more overtly white supremacist (Lott, 1993; Roediger, 1999, p. 118), more recent forms of racial consumption often engage Blackness with a view towards reinventing whiteness as progressive, as critiqued by several scholars (hooks, 1992a; Tate, 2003; Yousman, 2003). For example, since the popularization of hip-hop beyond Black communities in the 1980s, racial consumption has been discussed largely with respect to white youth's engagement with Black popular culture. In this context, while not ruling out the possibility of a patent will to dominate in some instances, and while indicating the always already deeply colonially informed motivations involved in racial consumption, bell hooks (1992a) suggests that white youth at the time of her writing sought out consumptive racial experiences in an effort to forge trendy, non-oppressive, white subjectivities. Ostensibly dissatisfied with the social relations of racial neoliberalism, they saw these experiences as acts through which they might dissociate themselves from the racism of their forbears and the implicit norms against social interaction across colour lines. They came to know themselves as racially progressive white people, even while there was no actual social transformation or commitment to contest antiblack social structures (hooks, 1992a, p. 24; Tate, 2003, p. 5; Yousman, 2003).

Similarly, while they act out of the socially embedded association of the Black body with humour (as argued in the previous chapter), it appears that those who participate in contemporary blackface in Canada may not always deliberately set out to cause racial offence (though undoubtedly some do!). Instead, they act upon a naive assumption of racial camaraderie, in a context where race ostensibly no longer matters. This is suggested by the warm feelings towards Black celebrities claimed in the name of tribute, and through their involving Black and other non-white participants[1] in their blackface performances (CBC News, 2014b, 2019; Mahoney, 2009). Of course, to say this is not to deny the normalized antiblackness (sometimes rendered unrecognizable as such to the wearers) at the heart of contemporary blackface and the social order that produces it. Thus, more salient than the intentions of blackface wearers are the ways that they and other Canadians make sense of blackface incidents *after the fact* such that notions of colourblind Canadian progressiveness and antiblackness coincide, leaving in place a logic that justifies blackface and that ignores Black objections.

Egalitarian Blackface?

The presumption of friendly, even-handed, interracial humour occurs in defences of blackface, as, for example, where the following online interlocutor suggests that racial cross-dressing occurs equally in all directions, and on equal terms, for the sake of fun:

> What these guys did was NOT stupid, was NOT insensitive and was NOT a racial statement of any type. How many white people used a Barac [*sic*]

---

1 The involvement of non-white persons in blackface is a complex phenomenon that I analyse further in Chapter 8.

Obama mask this year? How many people dressed as Mexican's [sic] and made their skin darker to legitimize the character they portrayed? How many Black people used a George W. Bush mask? It's 2009 and this is behind us (as a society). What these guys did was try to have fun and portray characters from a funny movie. (User *Rob*, Comment on Urback, 2009)

As we begin to see in this repeated insistence upon what blackface is not, the progressiveness ("this is behind us as a society") claimed in relation to contemporary blackface in Canada is simultaneously strikingly impudent and unapologetic. Consider, again, this even more impudent comment from a blackface wearer: "So is it now offensive for a white person to dress up as a Black person? I dress up as jimi hendrix every halloween, ... you mor(on)s[2] are taking this race garbage way too far. DUMMY-UP!" (User *Pink*, Comment on Myles, 2014). This white blackface wearer asserts their ostensible right to do so, while simultaneously insulting the intelligence of those who understand blackface as racist. Interlocutors also adopt this insolent tone, which is directed primarily at Black objectors, as in this instance:

And why can't Black people look at this with some objectivity and common sense? ... Can a white guy wear a LeBron James jersey or better yet FUBU? Can a white guy buy a Lil Wayne album AND sing along to it in his car? (User *Andre*, Comment on Urback, 2009, emphatic caps in original)

Unable to critically assess the way that their not being Black informs their own opinions about blackface, this interlocutor unselfconsciously accuses Black people who object to blackface of being blinded by their Blackness. Equating blackface with engagements with Black popular culture, and levelling all forms of racial consumption without regard to historical context, they forcefully defend white people's prerogative to wear blackface as they see fit.

Similarly, dismissing objections to blackface as much ado about nothing, another interlocutor defends the right to blackface and racial costuming while suggesting that blackface provides an opportunity to educate ostensibly ignorant Canadians:

This sniffle offense is overblown bigtime, slow news day on a campus that has lost its voice in free expression. I suppose we aren't supposed to ever

---

2 It is unclear what this commenter means by the unusual punctuation of the term "mor(on)s."

see a geisha either. Instead of creating controversy, this was a great opportunity to share some sensitive history to a largely uninformed Canadian
public. (User *In Vancouver*, Comment on Urback, 2009)

Finally, in a response to a blackface portrayal of PK Subban, another
interlocutor insults those who object to blackface and writes their objections off as political correctness:

> Oh please. Get over yourselves, you losers. I'm sure the fan meant no
> harm, and in fact cares more about PK than any of you politically correct
> posers. I know PK personally. The fan did nothing wrong. I am offended
> by PC. blackface? Not so much. (User *Svg*, Comment on Myles, 2014)

These responses, then, reflect an impunity associated with contemporary blackface in Canada. Both participants and interlocutors impu-
dently and unapologetically reject objections to blackface, particularly
where mounted by Black persons. What stands out here is the contrast
between this impunity – promoting an insolent, cocky whiteness – and
the more tentative and deferential subjectivities of the racial consumers
of whom hooks wrote in 1992, whom hooks and others writing in that
decade (e.g., Giroux, 1997; Kincheloe & Steinberg, 1998) argued acted
out of a self-conscious whiteness in an effort to rearticulate hegemonic
whiteness.

Yet I reiterate here that this unapologetic impudence coincides with
a performance of racially progressive Canadianness. Thus, while one
interlocutor defended blackface, he also presumed an ostensible racial
awareness that would have allowed him to "share sensitive history
to a largely uninformed Canadian public" that, evidently, does not
include him (though to what end is not clear, given his defence of
blackface). Similarly, in another excerpt we are exhorted to accept a
"fan's" presumed regard for Subban (exhibited through a blackface
"tribute"), along with the interlocutor's professed personal relationship to Subban, as evidence of interracial amicability and the impossibility not only of racial intent but also of racial harm. In both cases,
the interlocutors are claiming to be politically savvy and racially progressive, but here being racially progressive is not concerned with dis-
sociating from dominant whiteness or from racist expression. Instead,
in the context of contemporary blackface in Canada, progressiveness
is understood as being so beyond the race question that one is now
freed from worrying about causing racial offence, from any need to
consider the salience of racial location to social perspective, and from
the need to take seriously the objections of Black people. In fact, this

racial progressiveness can even insult and ridicule Black people and their perspectives. Canadian racial progressiveness claims interracial friendship on terms that ignore history, insist that the racist tropes it bandies about have no racial meaning, and thus reveal its constitutive antiblackness.

Canadian Postracialism

This suturing together of unapologetic racial/racist expression with a sense of having transcended race is a key feature of postracial-ist discourse (Goldberg, 2015, p. 72; Howard, 2014a), which I argue defines performances of, and debates about, contemporary blackface in Canada. Not to be misunderstood as being truly beyond race, post-racialism is "a certain way of thinking about race, and implicitly of racist expression ... [that] has been giving way to novel understand-ings, orders, and arrangements ... The postracial ... is a neo-raciality, racisms' extension if not resurrection" (Goldberg, 2015, p. 24). Post-racialism acts from the presumption that race is no longer socially significant, that racism has been overcome, and that anti-racism is gauche. Cho (2008) distinguishes postracialism from colour-blind ideology, which works by setting up behavioural ideals appropriate for a utopian moment of racial transcendence yet to come. Colour blindness claims not to see colour (i.e., race), and fails to account for the histories and extant conditions that differently locate vari-ably racialized social actors in the present. In contrast, postracialist ideology makes the claim that the moment of racial transcendence is upon us – already manifest and fully established – precipitated by a specific watershed event (Cho, 2008, pp. 1597–8). Postracialism enjoins us to

> give up on race before and without addressing the legacy, the roots, the scars of racisms' histories, the weights of race. We are being asked to give up on the word, the concept, the category, at most the categorizing. But not, pointedly not, the conditions for which those terms stand. (Goldberg, 2009, p. 21)

This silencing of race while racial arrangements endure is, then, a tech-nology of whiteness engineered to do away with race on the basis of its spuriousness, with the intention of casting racism as similarly spuri-ous, and thereby doing away with the bothersome task of addressing it (Cho, 2008, p. 1596; Goldberg, 2009, p. 22). Postracialism "levels the discursive playing field" for white people, no longer recognizing the salience of the experience of racial oppression for defining and identifying racism (Cho, 2008, pp. 1594–6), and thus necessarily rejecting Black critique.

As Goldberg (2012) argues, postracialist conditions where race becomes unnameable (that is, where race has disappeared) produce the "dis-appearance of race," whereby racist incidents erupt in unanticipated and sometimes ambiguous but usually crude and objectionable ways (p. 125). Goldberg writes:

> Racial disappearance … signals both the conceptual evaporation and the material unrecognizability of racial matters … racial *dis-appearance* speaks to the ways in which racialities re-appear in sometimes unexpected, perhaps unpredictable and less noticeable ways once race conceptually disappears. (p. 125, emphasis in original)

The lean towards unapologetic, "progressive" postracialism in Canada is partly attributable to temporal context. hooks's (1992a) article was written prior to the post-9/11 debates that crowned a snowballing conservative backlash, and prompted a more bold assertion of whiteness in North America. Certainly, there was a revision of Canadian identity post-9/11, at which time, in mainstream discourse, "Canadianness" was redefined in civilizational terms, highlighting solidarity between "Western" nations and asserting a transnational whiteness (Arat-Koc, 2005). Thus, the aggressive defence of contemporary blackface in Canada may be a part of dominant whiteness globally asserting itself self-righteously against race-conscious analyses and social correctives.

Yet I suggest that the Canadian relationship to postracialism and the consequent impudent whiteness in the discourses of contemporary blackface in Canada are more complex than can be properly understood through a solely temporal analysis. I argue here that Canadian postracialism is characterized by its roots in a national claim to egalitarianism that is partly forged through an ostensible contrast to American racism, as well as through its professed relationship to Blackness. I contend that it is this Canadian subjectivity that is at stake in the defence of blackface.

The claim to Canadian racial transcendence is a recurring feature in discourses of contemporary blackface in Canada. For example, one online interlocutor writes:

> The whole race issue needs to be put to bed. We are all people just trying to make it in the world. Both sides make fun of the other. The US has a Black

president. Things have changed. Look at all of the interracial relationships these days. One day we are all going to be the same color. (User *Halloween Costumes*, Comment on Urback, 2009)

According to this interlocutor, "we" can retire race (that is, anti-racist critique) and accept blackface as harmless fun to lighten a life that is (equally) difficult for everyone, all because "things have changed." This comment is postracialist because even as it defends racist expression, it claims to inhabit a moment after which social transformation has occurred and in which Canadians are no longer differentially located through processes of racialization; where Blackness no longer marks one for dehumanization. This interlocutor asserts an unproblematic "we" – the universal, non-raced (but implicitly white) liberal Canadian subject – whose knowledge and experience is not informed by power differentials, but who rather is a good-natured egalitarian "just trying to make it in the world." The same claim to racial transcendence is made in the following, with specific reference to Canada:

This [blackface] debate is just outdated. ... Most kids in Canada are now growing up in increasingly multi-cultural environments which just forces them to throw out the entire notion of "the other" because they are forced to see past race. Also it is worth to mention [*sic*] that so many Canadians are a mixture of different racial/ethic groups and this blurs the definition of "race." ... This is not 1960 ... We need to stop mentioning "race" in order to make it what it is: irrelevant. (User *Jess*, Comment on Urback, 2009)

Here, it is explicitly Canadianness, and the racial/cultural mixing that ostensibly characterizes it, that make race and anti-racist critique irrelevant.

To be sure, these claims are temporal in part. One interlocutor refers to being beyond 1960, the other to being in the Obama era. Nevertheless, the way that postracialism is mobilized precisely through Canadianness – explicitly in the latter comment, and implicitly in contrast to the United States in the former – is conspicuous. Though the first interlocutor seems to offer the election of President Obama as a postracialist watershed event, Canadian national narratives generally claim much earlier watershed events, naming variously the declaration of a state policy of multiculturalism (Alvarez & Johnson, 2011) as implied by the second interlocutor, but more poignantly for the present discussion, the abolition of slavery in pre-Canadian British North America prior to its abolition in the United States so that the Underground Railroad had destinations here. We see this in the cautionary remarks of a blackface participant who now comments under photos of the event on YouTube:

> Many people do not realize that Canada was one of the first nations to abolish slavery, in fact many proud Canadian families escaped the United states for that very reason … I cant [sic] say we haven't had our own problems with such racism, but historically speaking. We were a safe haven during the civil war and many many years before that. If you find this hard to believe i recommend you look into "The Underground Railroad." (User *DeltaImmortal*, Comment on HueyFreeman222, 2007)

Post-race discourse in the United States in the Obama era, therefore, perhaps influences but certainly does not initiate Canadian postracialism. In fact, through the identification of a watershed event that occurred even before Canadian confederation, postracialism and Canadianness merge, and Canada becomes synonymous with the transcendence of antiblackness. According to this comment, the fugitives' resistance to American slavery secures their "proud Canadianness" even before arrival, and implies further that upon arriving in the space that is now Canada, they joined a pre-existing community of (white) Canadians who also abhorred slavery. Canadianness and racial progressiveness are thus fused. This narrative forgets the inconvenient facts of the short duration of the Underground Railroad, that emancipation throughout the British empire was based in expedience rather than moral epiphany, and that the racist conditions fugitives from slavery experienced in Canada provoked many Black "proud Canadians" to return to the United States after 1865. Instead, the story is spun so as to turn the pragmatic motives of the developing ruling class in pre-Canada into anti-slavery. By their appropriation and revisionist narration, then, Blackness and Black experience are vehicles *through* which Canada claims its postracialism. This is part of a broader Canadian tendency. As Cooper (2006) writes:

> Black history [in Canada] has less to do with Black people and more with white pride. If Black history narratives make whites feel good, [they are] allowed to surface; if not [they are] suppressed or buried. (p. 8)

Thus, unlike in the United States, what is at stake in Canadian blackface debates, and Canadian postracialism more generally, is not simply personal integrity and moral character but, in fact, the entire weight of national identification and consciousness. The anger and impudence towards Black objectors that shows up in blackface discussions is animated by an entrenched presumption that Canada is a refuge from antiblackness. Continuing to feel good about being Canadian depends on it.

Blackface, Canadian Postracialism, and Knowledge Production

The knowledge-producing implications of Canadian postracialism in this context are twofold. First, blackface must be ahistorically known as anything but racism. For example, consider a comment after a black-face incident portraying Olympian Usain Bolt from an interlocutor who claims to be of mixed race. For them, blackface is simply a harbinger of a happy, mixed-race future – a positive sign that Canadian youth have "moved on," racially innocent in a world that is not yet ready for their forward thinking:

> I would like to hear from the students involved, it would be no surprise if they already assumed solidarity of all this planets [*sic*] people and were stunned and horrified to have hurt the very track star they admire. I bet they are remorseful for the hurts they caused inadvertently – unlike [the Black whistleblower] who likely won't get the hurt he is causing until his own pale grandson climbs on his knee painted up with dark make up and says "I love you Grandpa. I wish I looked more like you" ... Mockery in the spirit of fun and cross cultural solidarity for all Canadians regardless of colour(s). (User *beigeface*, Comment on Hannaford, 2011)

Here, instead of steering clear of blackface in light of its disreputable historical roots and manifest potential to racially retraumatize, Canadian nationalistic progressivism rather *authorizes* blackface, transforming antiblack mockery into racial egalitarianism where not a positively regarded historical ignorance taken as innocence. Black critiques that suggest the existence of antiblackness in Canada strike at the heart of hegemonic ways of knowing the Canadian self[3] and therefore cannot be heard because the national progressive identity depends at least partially upon a particular narration of Canada's relationship to Blackness.

Second, given the miscegenation theme in this comment, and the typical postracialist reversal whereby the "real racist" is the person who objects to blackface (Cho, 2008, p. 1595; Goldberg, 2009, p. 79), Canadian

---

3 Importantly, these dominant constructions of Canadianness are bought into largely by white Canadians, but also by many racialized Canadians who respond with just as much indignation.

postracialism accomplishes its exclusions and helps the nation to know who can really be Canadian. If Canadianness is synonymous with good-natured naivete, then those, like the Black whistleblower above, who interrogate Canadian blackface's antiblackness are, by implication, ingrates whose Black consciousness makes them not quite Canadian. Ultimately, to be recognized as Canadian requires giving up on a critique of antiblackness, and eventually giving up on Blackness altogether through an apparently inevitable racial mixing that will nevertheless always regard Blackness as the butt of the joke. Here it becomes clear, again, how Canadianness is constituted in opposition to Blackness, in ways that always already make its belonging in Canada impossible.

Denying Canadian Blackface History

I have argued above that discourses of contemporary blackface in Canada reveal a Canadian postracialism that juxtaposes racist expression and racial transcendence. It is worth noting that in many contemporary national contexts, postracialism displays no need to argue away such stark contradictions; their racist logics and racial injustice proliferate while the irrelevance of race is simply stubbornly insisted upon (Goldberg, 2015). While racist logic and racial injustice certainly proliferate through Canadian postracialism also, its entanglement with a progressive national subjectivity comes with unique contradictions that must continually be managed at the risk of falling out of Canadianness. Here, I look at the ways that defending Canadian progressiveness vis-à-vis the United States in blackface discussions requires a national amnesia around Canadian blackface history.

As a "middle power" located just north of the American "superpower," Canada struggles to define itself as different from the United States. Canadian identity has therefore long been conceived through hyperbolic binaries that produce it as not-American (Seiler, 2002, p. 53) even while claiming the United States as its closest ally, and while participating with it in transnational whiteness. One of these binaries has to do with how Canada purportedly deals with race. Canada understands itself in its national mythologies as having always been more accepting of Black people and of cultural and racial diversity, enshrined finally in its federal multiculturalism policy, and contrasts itself to America's supposed emphasis on assimilation (Seiler, 2002, p. 55) if not outright racism.

Yet Canada and the United States are both white settler colonies embroiled in ongoing colonial relations that include an intractable antiblackness (Day, 2015; J.S. Simpson et al., 2011). In practical terms, then, and in the ways that Blackness is lived day to day, the race-based distinction between Canada and the United States proves to be grossly exaggerated – Canada, for example, demonstrating disproportionate rates of Black (and Indigenous) death at the hands of unaccountable law enforcement like the United States (D. Cole, 2020; Nangwaya, 2013; N. Simpson, 2020). Nevertheless, Canadian progressiveness is famously constructed vis-à-vis American racism, and the Canada-US border ostensibly represents the frontier of racial tolerance. Given this Canadian fantasy, postracialist statements such as that of an interlocutor quoted earlier saying that "the US has a Black president" take on new meaning. Such a statement does not position the United States as a leader in racial egalitarianism, but rather serves to intensify Canada's always already incontestable racial transcendence by indicating that racial egalitarianism has now *finally* spread *even to* the United States.

However, the Canadianness produced through this fabled relationship to the United States (and Canada's mythical relationship to Blackness) is necessarily in tension with Canadian blackface and the whiteness secured through impudent blackface discourse. This tension must be negotiated carefully so as to hold on to both aspects of Canadianness, hence the constant need to juxtapose defensive impudence with performances of racial progressiveness. We see this strategy again in the following interlocutor's remarks:

> I question if people have gone too far with this issue. I understand where the BSU [Black Student's Union] is coming from. At the same time, I saw enough white males dressed as Tiger Woods/The Jamaican Bobsled Team. I personally didn't find it offensive. At the same time I'm a white male, who considers himself politically uncorrect. I think this has become more of a cultural issue than anything. It seems the right to parody an ethnic or minority group has become a cultural norm within today's society. Is this right? No. Does racism still exist[?] It seems to have transcended to a new form thanks to North American media and youth culture. (User *Alex*, Comment on Urback, 2009)

The ambivalence in this response is striking. The interlocutor performs a progressive awareness of racism ("I understand where the BSU is coming from") while, in typical postracialist fashion, supplanting this embodied Black critique with his own embodied white perspective ("I personally didn't find it offensive"). He lays proud claim to being "politically uncorrect," defends blackface, and sees those who challenge it as overreacting ("I question if people have gone too far with this issue"); and yet he seems unsure whether we are seeing racism in a "new form."

These tensions are nowhere more evident in blackface discussions than where they involve the history of blackface itself. Hegemonic Canadian blackface discourse consistently locates blackface minstrelsy historically in the United States rather than Canada. Thus, in the wake of a blackface incident, a McGill campus newspaper article states that "blackface was a form of theatrical makeup popularly used by minstrel performers *in 19th century America* to popularize cruel stereotypes of Black people" (McGill Daily, 2012, emphasis added; see also Lightstone, 2014). However, minstrelsy was very common throughout Canada into the 1970s (Le Camp, 2005). Travelling American minstrel troupes were welcomed in Canada, revealing the Canada-US border to be, in fact, quite porous to US-style antiblackness. Moreover, several home-grown professional Canadian blackface troupes such as the Saskatoon Minstrels and the Ardrossan Snowflake Amateur Minstrels (Le Camp, 2005, pp. 371–2) existed. Blackface was a favourite form of Canadian entertainment for local amateurs at fundraisers, and state institutions such as schools and police forces, and community groups such as churches and charitable organizations, all regularly staged minstrel shows (Le Camp, 2005, pp. 327–9).

The Canadian tendency to deny Canadian minstrelsy is particularly pronounced in Quebec (Canada's francophone province), where interlocutors use the politics of Quebecois identity vis-à-vis English-speaking Canada to distance themselves even further from racial culpability. As an online interlocutor states unequivocally, as though fact: "The blackface taboo is not historically rooted in Québec. Québec didn't have minstrel shows or the like" (Montpetit, 2011). Invoking cultural unfamiliarity, a student at a Quebec university struggles to understand the objection to blackface in this response to an incident on her campus:

> I wasn't aware of anything. You know, in my head, it's so innocent, you know. It is not a part of my culture ... I do not have this baggage, so I try to translate how I'd feel. (translated from French by author[4])

These denials also do not hold up to scrutiny. Blackface was a part of popular culture in Quebec, featuring such shows as "Belle Davis et

---

4 Some of the interviews I conducted were at francophone universities and/or with francophone participants. In some instances (as here), I indicate a translation but do not indicate the university; in others I indicate the university but do not indicate that the excerpt has been translated. These measures are taken to preserve participant anonymity as much as possible.

ses negrillons" (Le Camp, 2005, p. 358); and the composer of Canada's national anthem, the Quebec-born Calixa Lavallee, toured the United States and Canada as a blackface minstrel (Thompson, 2015).

In order to maintain the pivotal notion of Canadian racial progressiveness, these claims about blackface in Quebec and Canada are presumed, and asserted confidently without any appeal to evidence or any sense of a need to do so. In this, discourses of contemporary blackface in Canada demonstrate yet another characteristic of postracialism – the "denial of denial" (Goldberg, 2015, p. 75). As Goldberg writes of the postracialist:

> I assert my (non)racial, my postracial innocence not just by denying that I any longer, or ever, make (or made) racial reference or mobilized racist exclusion; I now further deny that I am in denial. I can't possibly be racist now because I never was then … I can't be in denial because – tolerant then, as now – denial was never an issue. (pp. 74–5)

In efforts to balance the aspects of Canadianness that are in tension, hegemonic Canadian blackface discourse both denies the history of blackface and glibly denies that there is anything to deny.

These contradictions are further heightened to the extent that Canadian blackface discourse does not unconditionally absolve all blackface. Canadian racial progressiveness is produced through the assumption that minstrelsy was not an issue *here*. The implicit suggestion is that, by contrast, where blackface occurs in the United States it is intolerable given the history of minstrelsy *there*. Ultimately, the Canadian denial of the denial allows it to unselfconsciously indict contemporary blackface in the United States while celebrating the contemporary Canadian version in order to recuperate progressive Canadianness (vis-à-vis the United States) that is threatened by critiques of Canadian blackface. This tortured self-congratulatory but self-incriminating logic demonstrates the profound pedagogical effects of postracialism operating at the level of national consciousness, through which being Canadian makes it impossible to know national racial history and the history of antiblackness in Canada.

Nevertheless, the denied history of Canadian minstrelsy has much to offer for understanding its contemporary counterpart. Minstrelsy in the United States was of two strains: first, that perpetrated by immigrant and working-class whites attempting to work out their place within a racial hierarchy (Lott, 1993; Roediger, 1999), and second, that performed by elite whites to discipline Black people whose social mobility marked them as "out of place" (Breaux, 2012). Historically, Canadian blackface most resembles this second strain, while the smaller proportion of Black people in Canada made the imperative to put Black people back in their place less of a factor. Lorraine Le Camp's (2005) study of Canadian minstrelsy demonstrates that blackface was well entrenched among the Canadian elite, and that watching and participating in minstrelsy was a way for white families and communities to bond across the social spectrum (p. 314). Blackface performances were defended as a nostalgic tradition at such educational institutions as Upper Canada College in Toronto in 1888 (p. 302) and Waterloo College (currently Wilfrid Laurier University) in 1949. Blackface also aired annually on state-run Canadian Broadcasting Corporation television (p. 307).

Blackface later became less publicly acceptable only in response to sustained resistance from Black Canadians, and even then was only reluctantly attenuated in the public sphere (Johnson, 2017; Le Camp, 2005, pp. 309–13) as a "generous" concession to Black people that included expressions of regret that people just don't seem to understand the ostensible non-racist roots of the practice (Le Camp, 2005, p. 308). Thus, what was recognized in the United States as an effective means of reminding Black people of their place (Breaux, 2012) was defended historically in Canada simply as innocuous, non-racist entertainment.

Contemporary blackface incidents and debates in Canada are remarkably similar to those of the early twentieth century when we recall that contemporary blackface in Canada is also popular at educational sites (often elite) and in official entertainment channels, and is justified as harmless fun and interracial camaraderie despite Black objection (CBC News, 2014d, 2019; Dunlevy, 2016; Mahoney, 2009; McGill Daily, 2012; Montpetit, 2011). This blackface history, which is reproduced in contemporary times, further highlights the well-established relationship between white Canadian subjectivities and the problematic terms upon which Black people find themselves included in Canada, despite claims to the contrary.

Conclusions and Implications

Analysing Canadian blackface and progressive white Canadian subjectivities as postracialist reminds us of the symbiotic colonial relationship between racial fetishization/fascination as found in contemporary blackface and the foundational white supremacy of the Canadian settler-colonial context. It helps us better understand the ways in which these Canadian subjectivities act as significant barriers to what can be known about antiblackness in Canada. In Canadian blackface discourse, the fantasy of racial transcendence, especially vis-à-vis the United States, occludes any careful, historically informed analysis and enables the ongoing racial-colonial project here – one that includes a pointed antiblackness.

This analysis can also help us to rethink the effects of this contra-dictory dynamic on knowledge production around social justice. The contradictions within white subjectivities, and specifically in blackface, have often been regarded as at least potential sites of anti-racist promise (e.g., C.M. Cole, 2012; Lensmire & Snaza, 2010; Lhamon, 2012). What-ever the (dubious) merits of such arguments, it seems that these con-tradictions have not so far produced anti-racist results on a broad scale; instead, contradictions have largely been resolved in ways that sustain white supremacy. An analysis of these contradictions as postracialist suggests that they are not slippages in racist discourse, but rather a constitutive part. Further, in terms of promoting anti-racist change in whites, it is worth noting that the impudent responses in blackface dis-cussions are characteristic of anonymous online comments and discus-sions taking place in largely white spaces. They are quite different from the rare but more apologetic responses made by blackface wearers in instances where Black communities have mobilized to hold them pub-licly accountable (e.g., Mahoney, 2009), affirming that effective Black resistance is more pedagogically promising and socially transformative than white contradiction. Thus, I am more inclined to regard the con-tradictions of blackface and Canadian ostensibly egalitarian whiteness pedagogically not as anti-racist openings, but rather as red flags calling Black communities and our allies to sustained or enhanced challenges to the antiblack terms upon which Canada discursively establishes its progressiveness. The struggle crucially continues!

4 Pornotroping Performances: Overt Violence, Un/Gendering, and Sex in Contemporary Blackface

As I have argued in Chapter 1, blackface is experienced by many Black people as antiblackness. For them, the offence of blackface is primarily rooted in the ways in which it re-presents the dissection and appropriation of the Black body – that is, represents the enfleshment processes that seek to transform Black people into fungible flesh, the violence that characterizes slavery and its afterlife (Hartman, 1997; Spillers, 1987). I remind the reader here that enfleshment names the mechanism within which gratuitous violence and the reduction of the Black person to property (mere flesh) are mutually constitutive, producing each other (Spillers, 1987, p. 67).

This chapter takes up two further interventions to complement the findings of Chapter 1. First, the representational aspect of contemporary blackface positions it interestingly as an object of analysis. This disparaging representational practice would be enough for most reasonable persons to denounce the practice of contemporary blackface. However, as we saw in Chapter 1, the problem with blackface is not simply that it is "insensitive" by making black enfleshment that which can be re-presented for pleasure. Certainly, one has to be analytically cautious about the slippage between the re-presentation of enfleshment through a blackface performance on one hand, and the actual social processes of enfleshment on the other. Nevertheless, the argument that I pursue further in this chapter is that they are, in fact, inseparable.

The chapter's second intervention is to undertake a gender analysis of contemporary blackface in Canada that is grounded in the research study. As I pored over the participants' words, the forms that blackface incidents have taken, and the online comments in popular media, it appeared to me that gender was implicated peculiarly in contemporary Canadian blackface. Gender appeared to organize who became involved in blackface (overwhelmingly white men) while at the same time seeming less significant in the organization of the portrayals. Further, while it is certainly possible that I may not have asked all the right questions, I found no evidence that the Black students who participated in focus groups for the study experienced the blackface they encountered differently based on their gender identification. As we saw in Chapter 1, what was of overwhelming and almost singular significance to Black participants was the way that blackface appropriated aspects of their bodies that identified them as Black.

As is my general approach throughout this book, I work up from data towards an exploration of theoretical literature that seems relevant to the main preoccupations of the data. Thus, as I pursued these analyses, I was led to Hortense Spillers's (1987, p. 67) formulation of the pornotrope, and Alexander Weheliye's (2008, 2014a) elaborations of it, for their utility in tracing how antiblack violence, (hyper)sexualization, (un)gendering, and the scopic/visual come together in the will to transmute Black people into bare flesh. With respect to my first argument in this chapter, and resisting, for a moment, Hartman's (1997, p. 3) methodological injunction against being preoccupied by that which is most spectacular in antiblack relations, I explore instances of blackface that explicitly portray antiblack violence, in order to, like Hartman, make a more general claim about the implication of all blackface in processes of enfleshment. Consistent with Moten (1999) who rightly asks "whether performance in general is ever outside the economy of reproduction" (p. 70), I insist that blackface plays a crucial role in (re)producing the enfleshment processes that it portrays. Put differently, I argue that contemporary blackface perform*ance* is perform*ative*.

On the second point, by tracing both white women's participation in contemporary blackface as well as blackface portrayals of Black women, I argue that they are, together, informed by the simultaneous, sometimes contradictory, sexualizing and ungendering moments of the pornotrope.

By understanding the ways in which seemingly disparate incidents of blackface are bound together by the pornotrope, we can come to appreciate the seamless relationships among blackface humour, antiblack violence, and the performance of the spectacular that together constitute contemporary blackface's enfleshing desires. I conclude that any engagement with blackface is an engagement with all these violent relations.

Blackface Depictions of Antiblack Violence

On the evening of 30 October 2010, Mark Andrade, a Black man, watched as two white men in costume entered the hall of the Royal Canadian Legion in Campbellford, Ontario, for a Halloween party and paraded around the room. One wore a hastily constructed Ku Klux Klan costume, and was draped in the US Confederate battle flag that has, for many, come to represent the values of slaveholding states of America prior to the American Civil War. In his hand, he held one end of a rope, the other end of which was tied around the neck of his friend, a retired Toronto Police Services officer, in blackface. Andrade left the hall outraged, and began making photos of the incident public, while back at the party the men were awarded first prize in the Legion's costume competition that took place that evening (Allen, 2010; CTV News, 2010; Dempsey & Allen, 2010). Notably, yet unsurprisingly, the perpetrators later claimed that they were not in any way racists, and that "it was a stupid thing. In hindsight now, we should have never done it ... I should have realized that maybe somebody might have been offended" (CTV News, 2010).

The costumes' reference to deadly antiblack violence could not have been clearer. This incident constituted a very stark visual depiction that drew on two unambiguous symbols of antiblack violence: lynching, the iconic gendered violence used to negate Black freedom in the Jim Crow period in the United States, and the Ku Klux Klan, an explicitly white supremacist, terrorist organization committed to Black death. The confederate flag only intensified this signification. Yet the depiction of Black violence was one over which white racial bonding was able to occur, as made clear through the crowd's approval and subsequent award. We see here that what the perpetrators and their white audience understood as non-racist blackface fun is not only not incompatible with racial violence, but also underwritten by indifference to Black suffering and therefore contempt of Black people. I draw our attention to the fact that, with the obvious exception of Andrade, the entire room seemed oblivious to what might structure who could enjoy such a performance and who would be repelled by it, demonstrating an inability to foresee or at least care about Black outrage at a depiction of Black death. This performance had the effect of drawing a racial boundary and confirming the space as one in which Black humanity is not recognized, and where Black suffering causes no outrage.

This incident is similar in many respects to another blackface incident that took place at the 1995 installment of the Good Ol' Boys Roundup in Ocoee, Tennessee – relevant to this study because allegedly several Royal Canadian Mounted Police (RCMP) officers were in attendance, proudly declaring their Canadianness and announcing their presence with a large Canadian flag draped over their camper (Eggerston, 1995). The Roundup was an annual, private, camp-style recreational gathering initiated in 1980 by law enforcement officers of the former US Bureau of Alcohol, Tobacco and Firearms. It was originally intended for other law enforcers, but later grew to include a majority of people who were not law enforcers (US Department of Justice, 1996). Many persons in attendance at the 1995 event reported that, among other forms of antiblackness, a skit was performed in which a white man in Ku Klux Klan attire simulated sodomizing another white man wearing blackface to portray a Black man (Eggerston, 1995). This prompted an investigation by the US Senate Judiciary Committee (ABC News, 1995; US Department of Justice, 1996). While the hearing found insufficient evidence to conclusively confirm that this skit took place in 1995 (which does not mean that it did not take place), it did confirm a racist climate since the inception of the event, and that a similar skit *had* occurred in the 1990 event in which a man in blackface was traded for a dog, and then simulated oral sex on his "buyer" costumed as a Klansman.

The same themes of portraying, celebrating, and bonding over antiblack violence are present in these Good Ol' Boys blackface skits, here including a layer of sexualized racist violence. They had the same effect of exclusion and marking off antiblack territory that the Campbellford incident did. Though the Senate investigation found that ostensibly "the organizers did not specifically intend for the Roundup to be a 'whites-only' racist gathering," it also found that in its history, only four Black people had ever attended, though several had been invited but declined to attend because they felt "they would not be welcome" (US Department of Justice, 1996). Notably for this study, the numerous symbols that had become associated with the event by 1995, causing Black people to avoid it, clearly did not deter the Canadians who were ostensibly in attendance.

Blackface depictions of racist violence as humourous are not infrequent. Falling into the same category, in May 2019, a white student at a high school in Halifax, Nova Scotia, posted pictures on social media of herself in blackface with a whip crudely drawn into one of the images and labelled so that viewers would be sure to know what it was. The photos had two captions; one read: "Since I'm in ACS [African Canadian Studies], I'm trying to really see get [*sic*] into an Africans [*sic*] skin to see things from their perspective better :)"; the other read: "Ow it hurts" (CTV Atlantic, 2019, see videoclip). The smiling emoticon in the first caption serves to add a veneer of humour to an otherwise clear depiction of racist violence, which the second caption demonstrates the student intends. On one level, the perpetrator sees fit to represent her feigned empathy (repudiated in the same moment) by placing her own white body (in blackface) under the whip. This choice demonstrates the classical self-referential nature of white "empathy" that puts Blackness under erasure (Hartman, 1997, p. 21; Sexton, 2010). On this level, the act already underscores the student's inability to comprehend the suffering of Black people on its own terms without inserting her white self in their place. Yet the expression of empathy is itself a parody, as the student is, quite transparently, the one responsible for cracking the whip. Through this layered performance of antiblackness, the student actively resists the stated intent of African Canadian Studies in Nova Scotia, which is to "contribute ... to the improvement of race relations, cross-cultural understanding and to students' understanding of human rights" (Nova Scotia Department of Education, 2009, p. 1) – an objective that one could argue is itself a liberal objective written with primarily non-Black rather than Black students in mind. Through this blackface performance – one associated with the prototypical violence of slavery – the student decisively distances herself from Blackness and firmly (re)constitutes her identity as white by displaying indifference towards antiblack violence and, indeed, a will to inflict it. ACS is an optional course, so the student would have to have chosen to take it. Yet, knowing the vagaries of high school course selection and scheduling, it could well be that ACS was the only option to fulfil the mandatory Canadian history requirement that fit this student's timetable. Whatever the case, this blackface act served to announce the student's clear rejection of the empathetic white subjectivity that the writers of such a course might have imagined it would produce in/of her. The performance recuperated a dominant white subjectivity by redrawing, with blackface and racial violence, the racial boundaries that the ACS course had hoped to dissolve. Additionally, the humour that the student writes into the act works both to express her complete disdain for this objective and to inoculate her (to herself and others) from owning the seriousness of her antiblack intentions and her now reconstituted white racial identity.

Just a few years before, in a 2013 instance in Dartmouth, Nova Scotia, a delivery driver for a furniture store, Elsworth Bottomley, who is Black, encountered the statue of a Black man from the store's stock which had been hung by the neck in the store window with a noose constructed from tape. The eyes of the statue were painted white, "blackface style" according to a human rights lawyer brought onto the case, thus layering a blackface motif onto this representation of a lynching (CBC News, 2013a). Two employees responsible for the incident were immediately fired. However, Bottomley reports that this occurrence was the culmination of many incidents of racist harassment – interpersonal and institutional – that he had experienced on the job. Specifically, he had been called racist epithets, received a text message from a co-worker insulting Black people's intelligence, and had been told by a manager that "he worried about sending two black delivery drivers to a job because that would intimidate customers" (CBC News, 2013a). Indeed, the store was later found guilty of racial discrimination in a separate human rights case that had been filed earlier by another employee, further substantiating his claim to a broad climate of antiblackness at the store (CBC News, 2014a; Saltwire Network, 2014).

The way that this incident marked off antiblack territory was extended geographically and perpetuated systemically in the response of the Halifax police department, which in the face of this clearly racist act suggested, "It could be *anything*, it could be threats, it could be harassment. That sort of thing. But until we are able to look at all of the information in a totality, we can't really make a call at this point" (CBC News, 2013b, emphasis added). In response to this reluctance to name the incident as racist, Bottomley expressed his feelings of abandonment, saying, "You just feel like there's no one there right now to fight for me. I mean where do you turn to? It doesn't feel like there's any hope" (CBC News, 2013b). Therefore, the portrayal of a lynching served to instantiate the message of Bromley's unbelonging in concrete terms that he would not miss, and that were ultimately successful, as Bottomley subsequently felt compelled to leave the job. Important to my analysis here is that in the perpetrators' estimation the blackface motif seemed an entirely fitting addition to this lynching in effigy, serving to intensify its message.

Crucially, the incidents of contemporary blackface in Canada I refer to here demonstrate that it is not only Black people (like the Black participants in my study) nor only Americans (as postracialist Canadian mythologies would suggest) who understand the congruities between blackface, slavery, and its afterlife. Clearly, the violent relations of slavery and Jim Crow are also a significant preoccupation for many Canadian blackface perpetrators who easily discern these connections, and draw on them to varying degrees in their blackface performances to shore up white identities and define antiblack geographies. Furthermore, national boundaries prove as irrelevant to the geographies of antiblackness for these white perpetrators as they do for the Black participants in Chapter 1. Canadians draw on American motifs such as the confederate flag, they cross nation-state boundaries to participate in antiblackness (as at the Good Ol' Boy Roundup), and they are captivated by the trope of lynching though on official record no post-slavery extrajudicial hangings of Black people occurred in what is now Canada.[1] Clearly, though it might claim otherwise, white political life in Canada is as deeply embroiled in, and as profoundly preoccupied with, the afterlife of slavery as Hartman (2007, p. 6) asserts Black political life is.

Gender and Contemporary Blackface in Canada

The gendered aspects of contemporary blackface in Canada are intriguing. Much like historical minstrelsy, contemporary blackface in Canada is overwhelmingly a white man's game in which white men portray Black men. Of thirty-three incidents of contemporary blackface in Canada since 1990 (most of them since 2005) for which I have found readily available images, twenty-eight, or 85%, involve white men as perpetrator, portraying Black men in twenty-five instances, or in 75% of the thirty-three incidents. In the other three instances, white men were portraying Black women. Nevertheless, white women are involved in Canadian blackface instances in multiple ways. In many cases white women, if not in blackface, appear smiling in photographs alongside white men in blackface, not infrequently with the perpetrator's arm draped around them (e.g., see images in Benedictson, 2013; Kambhampaty, Carlisle, & Chan, 2019; Karstens-Smith & Rushowy, 2013). Given the popularity of this specific pose in blackface photographs, it could be said that these particular performances reference the historical crisis of white masculinity posed ostensibly by Black men's sexuality and the threat of interracial relationships between Black men and white women. These anxieties, which have long been a subtext of minstrel performances, have often been the excuse for deadly, ritualistic, racist and sexualized violence against Black men, (Harris, 1984, p. 15; Lott, 1993, p. 25, drawing on Ellison 1958) and, as we have seen, are sometimes the subject of contemporary blackface performances. This blackface pose in contemporary Canada, then, perhaps attempts to perform an ease with these historically taboo interracial relationships, all the while attesting to their looming salience, and allowing white men to embody and thereby momentarily neutralize these anxieties. The white women in these poses prop up these blackface performances of whiteness, specifically white masculinity.

---

1 There is only one account of a lynching in Canada that I am aware of, and tragically, yet unsurprisingly, it involves an Indigenous person. In it, a Sto:lo man was taken from the custody of British Columbia by an American mob and hung near the US border. See https://thewalrus.ca/the-lynching-of-louie-sam/.

White Women in Blackface

Yet there are instances in which white women are more directly involved in blackface as perpetrators (25% of incidents in the sample of thirty-three cited above).[2] In the majority (three-quarters) of these, there is no particular attention to giving an explicitly gendered performance – by which I mean to say that gender is not spectacularized. In fact, in many of these instances the women in blackface are co-perpetrators with men in blackface, and there are no clear gender distinctions between the portrayals apart from what might be inferred from the sexed/gendered bodies of the perpetrators themselves. The male and female perpetrators in these instances wear almost identical clothing that is largely ungendered (see photographs in HueyFreeman222, 2007; J. Roberts, 2011), though in one instance the perpetrators all wear matching traditionally men's attire (see student protest photograph in Archemdis, 2013). The point of note here is that in the majority of incidents involving white women in blackface, the emphasis appears to be on spectacularizing race while gender remains at best a background consideration. It is certainly curious that the performance of gender by white women in Canadian blackface in these instances is not exaggerated in the ways that we might otherwise expect in carnivalesque contexts, particularly given the ways in which Black women's bodies have been routinely spectacularized historically and in the present. One might suggest that this speaks to a kind of sensitivity to gender issues (though not race issues) fostered in a climate of white liberal feminism. However, the dire consequences of liberal feminism for Black women and Black people in general, as clearly articulated by Black and other people-of-colour feminisms, make such a conclusion suspect. I suggest a more likely explanation later in this chapter.

A few instances of white women in blackface do explicitly attempt to portray Black women, with gendered racist implications. For example, for Halloween in 2005, a student at Queen's University in Kingston, Ontario, wore blackface and a gown to portray a beauty queen whose sash read "Miss Ethiopia." The student subsequently posted a photograph of herself in costume to social media (MacMillan, 2005).

Why a beauty queen, and why Ethiopia? We have no way of knowing what this student's actual intentions were, as there is no record

---

2 Some of these instances involve both white men and white women in blackface, accounting for why the 25% of incidents involving white women in blackface cited here and the 85% cited above for incidents involving white men in blackface add up to more than 100%.

of her having shared them. We can only speculate as to the logic that might have informed this particular choice of costume. We do know that in 2003, less than two years before this incident, Ethiopia was represented for the first time in a Miss World pageant, and Hayat Ahmed, Miss Ethiopia, placed among the top twenty contestants as a semi-finalist (Miss World 2003, 2019). Perhaps the perpetrator had been enamoured of Ahmed, and/or wanted to celebrate Ethiopia's debut in the pageant. She could just as easily have been unaware of this context and chosen Ethiopia as the country of origin for her black-face beauty queen haphazardly. Yet human choices are never *just* random, and are always made within a broader context that imbues them with meaning. Among these contextual factors, we might consider the prevailing discourse at the time in the West about Ethiopia as site of human rights abuses and abject poverty (see, e.g., Human Rights Watch, 2005; Vidal, 2003). Given what I have argued about the incongruency that underlies the humour and entertainment value of contemporary blackface in Canada, this costume, with its insistence on darkening the skin, juxtaposes, and might be read as a caricature of, the idea of Ethiopianness/Blackness and that of the pageant queen as signifier of beauty. Should the perpetrator have been aware of the 2003 Ethiopian beauty queen, the costume comments on the noteworthiness (and therefore, the perceived quaintness) of an Ethiopian beauty queen. Should she not, then Ethiopia stands in as a broad signifier of exotic Black Otherness. In either case, the insistence on blackface in the portrayal points to the significance of Black skin within this nexus of meaning. The relationship between Blackness and beauty is made spectacle, if not parodied.

A much more exoticizing gender-marking blackface incident occurred for Halloween 2017 when members of a group describing themselves as "Law Enforcement Agencies in Newfoundland and Labrador raising awareness and funds for Special Olympics Newfoundland and Labrador" (Law Enforcement Torch Run Newfoundland and Labrador, n.d.) held a fundraising costume party in which, among other appropriative and derisive costumes, there were women and men in blackface. Photos of the party were posted to the organization's Facebook page. The blackface costumes were comprised of leopard print cloth, feathers, bows, shields with crude motifs perhaps intended to mimic African masks, and staffs with bones, teeth, and human skulls (see photograph in Kelland, 2017). The colonial trope of the mythical African cannibal is immediately apparent. The blackface together with these costumes served to make Black womanhood, and Blackness in general, synonymous with an exotic barbarity.

A similar instance caught media attention later in 2017 when, in London, Ontario, a police officer's sister posted, on Instagram photos taken in 2006[3] of the sisters wearing full-body blackface. Both women were dressed in a mash-up of what appears to be African and other non-Western attire with an assortment of costume accessories and accoutrements – including, again, feathers, a necklace of bones, and white markings superimposed over the blackface – together presumably intended to portray what they imagined traditional gendered African attire to be. The blackface photos are displayed along with a photo of the constable in uniform, and a laudatory note from the sister, "This WCW [Woman Crush Wednesday] shoutout goes to this beauty.... one of the strongest people I know!" (CBC News, 2018; London Free Press, 2017; Richmond, 2018). The constable comments on the post, expressing gratitude, but saying nothing about the blackface (Richmond, 2018).

The blackface photos are evidently a fun and happy memory for the sisters, a redoubled expression of their close relationship. They are bonding in the photos where they smile as they paint each other, and bond again over the fond recollection of it a decade later. The collection of photos and comments works together to identify the constable as a strong and beautiful woman worthy of a citation on Woman Crush Wednesday. The blackface photos, bones and all, portray Black/African womanhood as exotic, backward, and absurd. They implicitly serve as a contrastive background to highlight the ostensible beauty and strength of progressive white Western womanhood that the constable embodies, as signified by her photograph in uniform. The montage therefore casts Black womanhood as the essential antithesis of an idealized womanhood – that *against which* a white woman can come to know herself as such.

Overall, the explicitly gendered portrayals of Black women by white women in these three instances imagine Black women as coming short, in a racial historicist sense (Goldberg, 2002, p. 74), of the presumed full potential of (white) womanhood, or more nefariously, as its degenerate outside.

White Men in Blackface Drag

White men also use blackface to portray Black women, and it is perhaps not surprising that these are most wont to sexualize and focus disparagingly on Black women's physicality, much like their historical

---

3 This incident took place a decade before the officer was hired by the London Police Service.

counterparts in minstrelsy before them (see Lott, 1993, p. 26). For example, in June 2013, Daytona Bitch, a white Toronto drag queen, caught media attention with a blackface act in which he portrayed Miss Cleo, of 1990s Psychic Readers Network fame, a persona assumed by Youree Dell Harris, a Black woman. In an unconvincing defence of this act, and by his own admission, Daytona Bitch says, "The people I asked at [the club] thought it was hilarious that I was dressed as a big fat black woman" (Prestwich, 2013). The comment indicates that for both the perpetrator and the audience (as represented by Bitch) the "humour" of this act is in characteristic stereotypical conceptions of Black women's physicality – particularly striking in this instance as Harris, the original Miss Cleo, was not "fat."

Chuck Knipp, a Canadian-born comedian living and working in the United States, also dons blackface to play a Black woman. The character he plays, Shirley Q Liquor, is imagined to be on social assistance, is extremely fond of alcohol, is from the US South, and speaks with the kinds of malapropisms that are reminiscent of those used historically in minstrel shows. Drawing on well-worn stereotypes of the welfare queen and its accompanying racist imaginary of Black families and Black women's (and men's) sexuality, the Shirley Q Liquor character has nineteen children (whose outlandish names she often forgets and whom she would like to "get rid of") – each having a different father whose name she also cannot remember, who is not in the child's life, and whom she cannot match to a specific child (Holthouse, 2007; Schlueter, 2013). Here again, the Black woman's body is presented as absurd, for according to Knipp, though he performs at drag clubs, "I am not a drag queen ... No ... what do you call? Nail things. No eyelashes. I don't shave anything ... 400-pound bulk ... 'She's not glamour. She's not a pageant girl' ... It's just like: 'She shabby-ass drag'" (Schlueter, 2013, p. 174).

If the fact that Knipp performs in the United States would tempt some, in characteristic Canadian postracialist ways, to suggest this kind of portrayal would not happen in Canada, many similar tropes show up in Quebec comedian Réal Béland's blackface character Sandra Paul. The character is ostensibly a migrant to Quebec from Guadeloupe who speaks broken French. When playing Sandra Paul, Béland pads his chest, hips, and buttocks, and wears an Afro wig in an outlandish hairstyle with bows and ribbons reminiscent of the minstrel-esque Topsy character of Harriet Beecher Stowe's *Uncle Tom's Cabin*. Sandra Paul skits often revolve around the physical havoc she wreaks with her cumbersome body, her ludicrous frilly underwear always becoming exposed in the process (Béland, 2012; TheBctechGroup, 2012). In a 2004 blackface performance as Sandra Paul at Gala les Olivier, the annual Quebec humour awards ceremony broadcast on ICI Radio-Canada, Béland draws on multiple racist tropes – including cannibalism, innocent white people killed by African spears, and colonial notions of voodoo. Several sexualizing moments also occur during the skit. At one point, the character pulls out of her purse a hammer with string attached, identifying it as her IUD, and thereby suggesting an other-than-human sexuality/sexual anatomy. The skit, which is pretext for announcing the nominees and winner of an award, culminates with Béland telling the cameras to "zoom in" as he announces that he is about to "make a scandal." He then rips his dress open at the bosom to expose a padded brassiere through the dress, then proceeds to rip off a layer of the brassiere to reveal the name of the winner displayed on a label across what is supposed to be the nipple area of the protruding breast. The punchline of the skit, then, performs the pornographic exposure of the Black woman's body. The imagery is strikingly similar to that in Quebec painter François Malépart de Beaucourt's 1786 *Portrait of a Negro Slave* (later renamed *Portrait of a Haitian Woman*). Much as art history scholar Charmaine Nelson (2016) has noted about *Portrait of a Negro Slave*, Béland's 2004 blackface stunt "arguably served to entrench centuries-old, colonial racial ideals about black women as sexually lascivious and deviant" (p. 125) and "of Black women's intrinsic hypersexuality" (p. 126). It is also noteworthy that though this skit took place in February 2004, Béland posted a video of the performance on YouTube in April 2012, in what appears to be a show of impunity, barely six months after a widely publicized and controversial blackface incident at Hautes Études Commerciales (HEC) Montréal (Montpetit, 2011).

To summarize, so far in this chapter I have discussed the contemporary "Canadian" blackface incidents (though as we have seen, boundaries lose much of their meaning where it comes to this kind of antiblack display) that explicitly portray racial violence, as well as the ways in which contemporary "Canadian" blackface incidents engage with gender. In the former, we notice a confluence of racial violence, evident indifference to Black suffering and death, sexualization or a reference to it in some instances, and of course the visual presentation of Blackness. In the latter, there is an intriguing continuum of engagements with gender, from those that do not seem to engage gender in any significant way, to those that prop up white masculinity, to those that exoticize Black women and position them as the antithesis of white womanhood, and eventually to those that engage in an always dehumanizing sexualization. Of course, performance, the scopic, and the visual presentation of blackness through blackface take a central place in all the above. In order to understand the prevalence and convergence of these phenomena within and across these kinds of blackface incidents, I turn to the concept of the pornotrope.

Understanding the Pornotrope

In her 1987 essay "Mama's Baby, Papa's Maybe," Hortense Spillers uses the term *pornotroping* in a theoretical formulation of the modalities of domination in the context of the theft of the body and the violent processes that reduce Black people to indeterminate flesh. Identifying several moments in the enfleshment process, and the location of the pornotrope within it, Spillers (1987) writes:

> 1) the captive body becomes the source of an irresistible, destructive sensuality; 2) at the same time – in stunning contradiction – the captive body reduces to a thing, becoming being for the captor; 3) in this absence from a subject position, the captured sexualities provide a physical and biological expression of "otherness"; 4) as a category of "otherness," the captive body translates into a potential for pornotroping and embodies sheer physical powerlessness that slides into a more general "powerlessness," resonating through various centers of human and social meaning. (p. 67)

In its simplest terms, Spillers's formulation of the pornotrope theorizes the ways in which violence and sexuality are integrally co-constitutive of antiblack political domination producing "a simultaneous thingness and sensuality of the slave" (Weheliye, 2008, p. 71). The important insight here, as Alexander Weheliye (2008, 2014a) notes in his subsequent elaborations of the pornotrope, is that the political is not devoid of the sexual, and that where the sexual appears in contexts of domination, it is not somehow perversely misplaced, but rather generated by, and at home in, the dominative context (Weheliye, 2008, pp. 76–7).

Nevertheless, it is important not to understand pornotroping as an end in itself or to think of sex as the entirety, or even the fulcrum, of what is happening in the pornotrope. Pornotroping serves the end of enfleshment, to which the sexualization is just a means. The sexualizing dimension of the pornotrope is an epiphenomenon of the place of an antiblack libidinal economy at the centre of the relations of slavery and its afterlife. It marks the ways in which antiblack violence is animated in/through the desire and pleasure to be gained for non-Black subjects through the prostration of the Black non-subject. As Weheliye (2008) notes in an instructive play on words, the condition of enslavement subjects the enslaved to being "depraved" precisely because they have been "deprived" of freedom, and the "depravation" helps to produce the condition of unfreedom (p. 77). As Weheliye further elaborates, echoing Hartman:

> The violence inflicted upon the enslaved body becomes synonymous with the projected surplus pleasure that always moves in excess of the sovereign subject's jouissance; pleasure (rapture) and violence (bondage) deviate from and toward each other, setting in motion the historical happening of the slave *thing*: a potential for pornotroping. (p. 72, emphasis added)

Through an etymology of the term, Weheliye thus establishes that because of this dynamic relationship between white desire and antiblack violence, pornotroping constitutes a turning to/away from violence to/away from sexualization (p. 72). This dynamic oscillation in the pornotrope between brutalization and the sexual works to produce thingness or "the absence from a subject position" (Spillers, 1987, p. 67), *this* being the endgame of pornotroping.

Yet Weheliye (2008) argues that this oscillation also speaks to the fact that the brutalizing and depraving sexualization are so intertwined in the pornotrope that they do not always have to appear together. The presence of the one serves to remind us of the perpetual imminence of/ immanence in the other (p. 75). Thus, where both Spillers and Weheliye speak of a "*potential* for pornotroping" they indicate that the possibility of depraving sexualization always lurks but may not always explicitly announce itself in antiblack conditions. Weheliye notes that this is particularly the case in the state of unfreedom that constitutes the afterlife of slavery, under which conditions "pornotroping, having used up all its sovereign autonomy ... remains a potent *potential that lingers affixed to the black body*, even subsequent to 'emancipation'" (p. 77, emphasis added).

A crucial dimension of Spillers's (1987) original argument, to which Weheliye comes more fully in his 2014 chapter, is that enfleshment also results in what is really just another dimension of, the pornotrope: ungendering. Spillers teaches us that under the conditions of the "*theft of the body* ... we lose at least gender difference in the outcome, and the female body and the male body become a territory of cultural and political maneuver, not at all gender-related, gender-specific" (p. 67, emphasis in original). Spillers's insight is that within the processes that negate humanity, mangle the body, and produce the enslaved as property, hegemonic notions of gender lose their meaning. The gendered domestic expectations that hegemonically determine who is protector and protected (p. 68), who is positioned as desiring subject and who as desired object, do not hold in any consistent way for the subjects of antiblack violence, particularly Black women. Weheliye extends Spillers to argue that both Black women and men are subject to invasion[4] by female and male master subjects, and both Black women and men become ungendered through the prostration (Spillers, 1987, p. 77; Weheliye, 2014a, p. 96). Overall, where the Black body becomes a site of appropriation, possession, and invasion, hegemonic gendered norms become confounded. They largely lose their accustomed significance and signification for Black/African persons made flesh.

We can conclude, then, that the manner in which pornotroping is able to both ungender and (hyper)sexualize in blackface performance has to do with the fact that the ultimate objective of the pornotrope is not, we must remember, about sex, never mind reciprocal, consensual sexual relations, but rather about enfleshment (Weheliye, 2008, p. 67). It is about the processes through which Black humanity is transformed into instrumental (Black) flesh. Sexualized violence is both a mechanism of enfleshment and constitutes only one of flesh's uses once flesh is produced.

The scopic is another crucial dimension of the pornotrope. As a technique of enfleshment, the pornotrope is nothing if not for its manifestation as performance requiring an audience. To this end, Weheliye (2008) notes that pornotroping "focuses on the process through which slaves are transformed into flesh *and then subjected to the (un)pleasure of the viewing sovereign subject*"; that it is "the *enactment* of black suffering *for a shocked and titillated audience*" (p. 71, emphasis added). Weheliye thus asserts that the scopic dimension of the pornotrope is not a tangential, secondary moment in enfleshment, nor is it simply the publication in the visual realm of an enfleshment process that takes place independently of the voyeuristic. Rather, in the pornotrope the scopic and the spectacular are essential to producing the political relations of domination and the process of enfleshment (p. 110). Stated differently, the pornotrope produces enfleshment by producing a scene. Enfleshment requires a dynamic within which white subjects gaze and pleasurably experience their status reflected back to them through the visual display of the Black body's prostration. As Hartman (1997 notes in this context:

> The exercise of power was inseparable from its *display* because domination depended upon demonstration of the slaveholder's dominion and the captive's abasement. The owner's *display* of mastery was just as important as the legal title to slave property. In other words, *representing power* was essential to *reproducing domination*. (p. 7, emphasis added)

---

4 It goes without saying that Black women remain infinitely more subject to sexualized violence than, and often at the hands of, Black men. Neither I here nor Spillers and Weheliye on whom I draw make any claims to the contrary.

The Pornotropics of Contemporary Blackface

The Pornotrope in Overtly Violent and (Un)Gendered Blackface

We can now take this multifaceted formulation of the pornotrope as an analytical tool to understand the forms of blackface discussed earlier in the chapter. The pornotropic dimensions of those incidents are not hard to discern. First, the very clear scopic dimensions of blackface – the ways in which performance and the accompanying appreciative audience are indispensable to the work they do – signal the working of the pornotrope. The lynched statue, the Good Ol' Boys skits, the anti-ACS, Miss Ethiopia, and London sisters posts on social media, the Campbellford lynching act, the Béland, Knipp, and Daytona Bitch drag skits – none would have been of any effect did they not make a public spectacle or had there been no audience. Each incident drew on and re-produced a set of antiblack scopic relations, reminding us of who can be made flesh to be pornotropically displayed for the viewing pleasure of whom. It is in this sense that Bottomley could say that the lynched statue in blackface "was a display meant for me to see and everyone else to witness" (CBC News, 2013b).

Second, the pornotrope is signalled by the ways in which sexualizing blackface performances and those portraying antiblack violence generated obvious pleasure for both perpetrators and their audiences via the prostration of Black people. What was deemed "fun" if not "harmless, non-racist fun" in these incidents is not only compatible with racial violence, but is dependent on it. These incidents uncover the libidinal dimensions of the blackface performances as well as the racist violence they instantiate. These libidinous energies are *sometimes* expressed in overt sexualization and/or depictions of sexual violence, but as we have seen in Chapter 2, they always provide the foundation upon which blackface comes to be understood as funny in the first place.

Third, the odd, only peripheral engagement with gender in many blackface incidents such that both men and women's blackface portrayals are largely gender non-specific,[5] and the significant cross-dressing that occurs where gender is specified is also, I argue, a function of pornotroping. The phenomenon is odd and requires explanation because

---

5 Following Spillers here, I do not in this argument intend to advocate for extant hegemonic notions of gender. Rather, I simply point out the ungendering that takes place in blackface. It would be naive to think that blackface perpetrators intended, through their indeterminate portrayals, to advance some progressive notion of gender.

of the tendency under other carnivalesque circumstances to parody the Black woman's body.[6] Rather than cite an unlikely liberal feminist solidarity, I suggest that this phenomenon is informed by the ungendering dimensions of the pornotrope. These portrayals indicate that what is most salient to blackface perpetrators is the blackness of the Black body and the presumption of its availability, regardless of gender, for appropriation and invasion by both white men and women, while never ruling out the potential for its sexualization.

What I am arguing here, then, is that the claim, based on the Black participants' responses in Chapter 1, that blackface is enfleshment – the "theft of the body" – resonates strongly with the way in which blackface incidents engage the pornotrope, which is a technology of enfleshment. Stated differently, if blackface is a performance of the enfleshment process (the ways in which Black people are reduced to property that can be dissected, seized without permission, possessed, ogled, inhabited, and discarded) of which the pornotrope is an integral mechanism, then it is unsurprising that these (porno)tropes associated with enfleshment feature so clearly in many blackface performances.

Contemporary Blackface: Performative or Just Performance of Enfleshment?

But if blackface is a *performance of* enfleshment, how does it also itself *count as* a process of enfleshment? At the outset, let me be clear that it would be untenable to claim that blackface is violent in the same ways or to the same extent as the gratuitous physical violence and death that mark processes of enfleshment more generally. However, to concede this is not the same as suggesting that these forms of violence are unrelated. Indeed, it is impossible to draw clear boundaries separating racist performance and racist violence. How, then, might blackface itself constitute a process of enfleshment?

We have seen that blackface is highly compatible with the antiblack ends of overtly racist incidents. For example, the addition of the blackface motif to the Dartmouth lynching-in-effigy and to the Halifax student's portrayal of the violence of enslavement underscored

---

6 As a case in point, we might consider the frequent impersonation of Serena Williams's body by her tennis colleagues, ostensibly as fun and camaraderie (see, e.g., Arceneaux, 2012; Ram gopal, 2013). I would argue that these instances are also pornotropic but that, unlike in the blackface incidents, the sexualization is present without the overt display of race.

the perpetrators' already clear, callous, antiblack objectives. Blackface similarly enhanced Knipp's antiblack objectives. Knipp performed the Shirley Q Liquor act on radio for twelve years prior to taking it to stage. In transitioning the act to stage, Knipp considered blackface essential to achieve visually the racist effects that his radio act had long been achieving aurally (Schlueter, 2013, p. 166). Therefore, blackface serves to intensify antiblack performance.

One might retort that it is the representation of blackness that is central to these incidents, and that makes blackface common to them, rather than any particular congruity of blackface with the pornotropic enfleshment of Black people. However, to make this claim would be to miss the fact that blackface is required precisely because it would normally be difficult to get an actual Black person to participate in any of these portrayals. As such, blackface is a coercive mechanism for bringing the "Black body" unwillingly into the performance of enfleshment. This nefarious role of blackface does not absolve it, but rather confirms it as imbricated in the pornotrope, complementing the appropriation and instrumentalization of the Black body.

But more significant is the way in which blackface is crucial to reframing the otherwise repulsive matters of murder, human suffering, and sexual exploitation as "harmless fun." The overt depictions of antiblack violence discussed above are not only a restaging of the violence that transforms Black people into flesh, but served through the use of blackface and the humour it ostensibly invokes to make Black pain illegible and inconsequential. They remind us of Hartman's (1997) observation about the slave coffle and the ways that white subjects could re-present the vilest instances of antiblackness as mundane, even joyful, by requiring the enslaved to sing: "what is remarkable is the way violence becomes neutralized and the shocking readily assimilated to the normal, the everyday, the bearable" (p. 34). Blackface incidents portraying racial violence display the blackface mask's suitability to the very same ends. In none of them does antiblack violence seem out of place or remarkable to the white perpetrators and audiences who enjoy them. Rather, to them it is, simply, fun. We therefore come to see that blackface does not only *perform* enfleshment or enhance exclusionary objectives to which it might otherwise be considered peripheral, but that it is directly generative of enfleshment by reproducing the indifference or "obscene blindness" that necessarily attends it, such that "the flesh['s] ... severe disjunctures come to be hidden to the cultural seeing by skin color" (Spillers, 1987, pp. 70, 67). This is Spillers's "hieroglyphics of the flesh" (p. 67) whereby Black suffering is rendered illegible – in this case by the

literal painting on of black skin. Blackface, at least in these instances
where it performs overt violence, casts and reinforces an antiblack
scopic regime – specifically, here, a particular way of seeing that re/
establishes or confirms Blackness as insentient, and Black suffering as
humorous and nothing to be particularly concerned about. Far more
than simply an inadvertent performance of enfleshment, or an insensitive re-presentation of scenes of antiblack violence, then, blackface
is powerfully implicated in actually producing conditions that reduce
Black people to mere flesh.

All or Nothing

Invoking the pornotrope as analytical concept helps us to understand
that these multiple dimensions – the mimicry of the Black body, the
ungendering, the racist violence, the hypersexualization, the spectacle
and audience, the "obscene blindness" – are of a piece, all intricately
intertwined and fundamentally inextricable. Any one aspect of the
pornotrope, like the tip of an iceberg, does not stand on its own but
is the surfacing of only a part of a much larger phenomenon below
the surface, resulting in the erratic manner in which the violence and
sexualized dimensions of the pornotrope show up across blackface
incidents. As Weheliye (2008, p. 75) has claimed broadly for the pornotrope, the violent and the sexualized dimensions in blackface do not
have to, though they sometimes do, explicitly appear together in any
one incident. Depictions of overt violence may show up without sexualization, and racist sexualization sometimes shows up without depictions of other forms of physical violence. As parts of the pornotrope,
however, they both always imply the other as an absented presence. In
the Campbellford incident, for example, the depiction of a lynching did
not overtly display sexualization, yet it evokes it. Lynching is always
already haunted by the notion of Black men's subjection to a deadly
prostration and denuding in the context of a presumed exaggerated
and unruly sexuality requiring punishment. Thus the sexual is clearly
not very far off in the Campbellford incident. Likewise, the hammer
as IUD in Béland's sexualizing skit evokes the notion of a violent and
brutal invasion of the Black woman's body, even if that violation is not
performed in the skit.

This interdependence of the aspects that constitute the pornotrope
suggests, then, that though the racist violence and sexualization are
not equally evident or severe across the incidents, they appear to
always already be latent alongside the scopic and enfleshing dimensions always present in blackface. Indeed, I would argue that the ways

in which the tacit violence and sexualization hide and reveal themselves is only exacerbated in the Canadian postracialist climate since the white Canadian subjectivities that perform blackface have a particular investment in this ruse in order to remain Canadian (see Chapter 3). Under these conditions, it is unsurprising that the extent of the inclusion of, or allusions to, signs of racist and sexualized violence will be suppressed.

Here, Goldberg's (2012) analysis of the postracialist climate and the dis-appearance of race again becomes useful:

> Racial disappearance in this sense signals both the conceptual evaporation and the material unrecognizability of racial matters ... racial disappearance speaks to the ways in which racialities re-appear in sometimes unexpected, perhaps unpredictable and less noticeable ways once race conceptually disappears ... Racial reference is supposed to evaporate but derogatory references, jokes, and insults become more voluble ... So when race disappears, the racial dis-appears. Racial arrangements pop up elsewhere, less readily marked and so not so easily categorized or identifiable. (p. 125)

What Goldberg signals here is the futile postracialist effort to deny and suppress the workings of race and racism while hanging onto racial arrangements. Much like the air-filled balloon a child attempts to hold underwater, the very effort to control and suppress produces the force, the haphazardness, and the uncontrollability of its erupting to the surface. This Goldberg calls "dis-appearance." I argue that while all blackface is itself a dis-appearing raciality, the various pornotropic dimensions of blackface – particularly those most easily identified as objectionable – also dis-appear erratically within and across blackface incidents in postracial contexts. Therefore, contemporary blackface performance proves eminently performative – instantiating the processes of enfleshment in the moment that it represents them, though this function is both obscured and occasionally exposed by the postracialist context in which it occurs.

Implicating All Postracial Blackface

Understanding the dis-appearance of the violent and sexualizing aspects of the pornotrope in blackface allows us to go a step further to consider all blackface, whether it depicts over racist violence and sexualization or not, and clearly not all blackface incidents do. Frankly, many blackface incidents simply do not revolve around these violent or sexualizing elements – neither in the portrayals themselves nor in the conscious intentions of the perpetrators.

However, to the extent that these incidents contain other character-istics of the pornotrope – the appropriation of the Black body or parts thereof, the ungendering, and especially the scopic regime that presents Blackness as spectacle provoking sordid white pleasure – it seems to me appropriate to bring the entire blackface practice under scrutiny with respect to the pornotrope. Given the importance among white Cana-dians of performing postracialism (as we saw in Chapter 3), and the tendency for blackface humour to be produced "at the line" rather than "over the line" (as established in Chapter 2), it is entirely consistent that the overt portrayal of racist violence might be suppressed in Canadian blackface. Instead, then, of looking at blackface incidents that portray racist violence and sexualization as anomalies that cannot be used to understand other blackface incidents, we might instead look at them as instances in which the always lurking but suppressed violence and sexualization defy suppression and dis-appear. The pornotropics of Canadian blackface are always present, and are not always successful at hiding, but rather occasionally break forth to unveil the violent rela-tions of domination that undergird blackface.

We see this unevenly dis-appearing pornotrope quite clearly when we consider how sexualization shows up unpredictably across blackface incidents. Thus, there is clear and overt sexualization, though to varying degrees, present in the Good Ol' Boys, Chuck Knipp, and Réal Béland blackface skits. But it is also present less overtly in other instances such as in Tyler Bozack's blackface portrayal of Michael Jackson in which he is photographed holding his crotch (Staff, 2012). Similarly, in a video of Justin Trudeau wearing full-body blackface in the 1990s, released to the media in 2019, there was speculation as to whether Trudeau had stuffed his pants as part of the portrayal (e.g., Blatchford, 2019; The Post Millen-nial, 2018) as suggested by the camera's pan to a shot below the belt. In this case, whether Trudeau did in fact stuff his pants is not central to the point I am making, and may well underscore it. The ambiguity of the portrayal, the conversation it sparked about this particular sexualizing possibility, and the way it resonated with so many across the Internet in the context of a discussion about blackface all exemplify the haunting pornotrope and its sexualizing dimensions. Together these incidents indicate the uneven and erratic postracialist dis-appearance of sexual-ization across blackface incidents, and thus the pervasive "potential for pornotroping" (Spillers, 1987, p. 67).

A final point needs to be made about the haphazard pornotropic character of all blackface. The Campbellford blackface incident, such a repugnant depiction of racial violence, apparently began on a whim when one of the perpetrators "bought a plaid shirt and the black hairspray that he used on his face *only hours before*" the event (CTV News, 2010, emphasis added), while the other who originally had specific plans to attend with his wife as Raggedy Anne and Raggedy Andy, impulsively "'decided to roll up a piece of bristol board and throw on a sheet' *a half-hour before the party*" (Dempsey & Allen, 2010, emphasis added). We see here how the decision to enter into the realm of blackface quickly devolved into a pornotropic display of racial violence because of the always haunting potential for pornotroping. A similar spontaneous process appears to be afoot in some of the other incidents, such as the painting of blackface eyes in the Dartmouth incident, and the hastily drawn whip in the Halifax student's social media post.

The juxtaposition of this spontaneity with the ways in which blackface perpetrators deny intent to offend – a claim that we cannot always presume is consciously inauthentic – speaks to the dynamics of unruliness and unmanageability once one enters the realm of blackface. It reminds us of the libidinal economy attending political domination – a sphere of allure that "cannot be controlled by the forces that (re)produce it" (Weheliye, 2008, p. 72). It is explained by the cohesive totality of the pornotrope. To choose to do blackface at all is to choose to tap into this multidimensional, but unitary, pornotrope. In so doing, one relinquishes control of how it might manifest. To engage one part is to engage the entire pornotrope – any or all of its many faces. Thus, if the more clearly objectionable aspects emerge betimes it is not because there has been an aberration, but rather that there has been an overflow of the pornotrope that refuses to be disciplined and cannot easily or predictably be contained within the already dubious postracialist boundaries one might hope to set for it.

Conclusion

Referring to the multiple dimensions of the pornotrope, and analysing two films that portray the process of enfleshment, Weheliye (2014a) writes:

> Scenes of subjection in *Mandingo* and *Sankofa*, bearing witness to the processes of the black body becoming-flesh, stand as stark reminders of what covertly underpins modern political formations, namely visual instantiations of naked life or the hieroglyphics of flesh ... integral to the creation of the flesh. Both films also powerfully highlight the stubbornly scopic

nature of pornotroping as a racializing assemblage, because, on the one hand, the dysselection of the black subject as not-quite-human requires visible inscriptions on the flesh and in the field of vision ... while, on the other hand, desire must remain invisible. (pp. 110–11)

The analysis in this chapter suggests that Weheliye's observations about film and media apply as easily to blackface in the contemporary Canadian postracial climate. As with film, blackface "enables the production of bare life as a politico-sexual form of life, wherein the remainder that is effected but cannot be contained by the legal order is disseminated in the visual realm" (Weheliye, 2014a, p. 98). In blackface, the "visible inscriptions" on/of (en)flesh(ment) that are always present are the dismembered parts of the black body – stolen and re-presented in the context of humour. The very public, performance-oriented manner in which blackface presents is not incidental – not just because of the necessarily visual nature of blackface, but because of the importance of the scopic to its pornotropic desires. In blackface, the pornotropic dimension is such that it remains "stubbornly scopic." The antiblack libido is allowed to portray itself as a desire for Black "flesh that they as selected master subjects, supposedly transcend and can therefore not inhabit" (Weheliye, 2014a, p. 111). They therefore pretend to inhabit it through the boundary-crossing, embodied fantasies of blackface. Magnifying the ambivalence of this libido is the way in which pornotropic blackface is used as a vehicle of white backlash, as in its resurgence in the Obama era, and in the context of the Black Lives Matter movement and protests against Black death caused by law enforcers (D'Sa, 2020; see also CBC News, 2013c).

While there is perhaps not sufficient basis to do more here than raise questions, the recurring involvement of law enforcement officers in contemporary blackface in Canada is also worth considering. Law enforcement officers, current, retired, or prospective, were involved as perpetrators in the Campbellford and Good Ol' Boys blackface incidents as well as the Newfoundland and London, Ontario, incidents – a remarkably high representation among the most troubling blackface incidents. This is noteworthy given the fraught relationships between law enforcement and Black people, and the ways in which law enforcement is an institution in and through which antiblackness is made violently material. We might wonder, then, how the attraction to blackface, an enfleshing phenomenon, is related to policing with its enfleshing desires in a racial state?

Overall, it is evident that the scopic/spectacular and ritualistic nature of blackface is a "hieroglyphics of the flesh" (Spillers, 1987, p. 67) – not just a reminder of some past domination no longer relevant and to be forgotten, but rather an instantiation of the dominant presumption of Black non-humanness that makes Black suffering illegible through its performance. Where the Black body is taken up as a site of appropriation, possession, and invasion, it is made to drip with a potential for pornotroping.

PART TWO

Blackface in Education Contexts in Canada

5 Blackface at University: The Antiblack Logics of Canadian Academia

Any exploration of contemporary blackface in Canada leads to the striking observation that educational spaces – or more accurately, those spaces associated with hegemonic schooling – are particularly popular sites for the recurrence of blackface. Just in the past fifteen years or so at this writing, Canadian media have reported blackface incidents taking place at Queens University in 2005 (MacMillan, 2005); Wilfrid Laurier University in 2007 (HueyFreeman222, 2007); the University of Toronto in 2009 (Mahoney, 2009); Hautes Études Commerciales (HEC) Montréal of the Université de Montréal in 2011 (Montpetit, 2011); McGill University in 2012 (McGill Daily, 2012); Mayfield Secondary School in Caledon, Ontario, in 2013 (Karstens-Smith & Rushowy, 2013); Brock University in 2014 (CBC News, 2014b); and the private Collège de Montréal in 2017 (TVA Nouvelles, 2017). Also reported in the media are a blackface incident during the Montreal student protests of 2012 (Morgan, 2012) and one associated with a student at Citadel High School in Halifax, Nova Scotia, in 2019 (CTV Atlantic, 2019). The 2010 Report of the Task Force on Campus Racism of the Canadian Federation of Students reports a blackface incident at the University of Windsor (Canadian Federation of Students-Ontario, 2010, p. 7). Two of the three blackface incidents involving Justin Trudeau, reported by media in 2019, took place in school contexts: one in the 1980s while he was a student at Collège Jean-de-Brébeuf, a private high school in Montreal, and the other in 2001 at a teachers' function at West Point Grey Academy, a private high school in Vancouver (CBC News, 2019). Besides these, there are several other blackface incidents at schools and universities that participants in this study referred to but that had escaped mainstream media attention.

Yet despite this clear relationship between (often elite) schools and universities and blackface, there is also an intriguing aura of the unexpected that seems to attend blackface incidents at these sites in public discourse. Blackface perpetrators always declare they were not aware of other blackface incidents, claim wide-eyed ignorance of the racist history of blackface, and express bewilderment that their allegedly harmless antics caused racial offence. More significantly, schools and universities, as institutions, claim to be caught off-guard, and have been routinely unprepared (in the senses of being both ill equipped and unwilling) to comprehensively deal with blackface. Based on interviews with university administrators in this research, it seems clear that universities in particular largely consider blackface an unanticipated anomaly that conflicts with their institutions' values.

This chapter explores what can be known about the nature of antiblackness in Canadian universities through the lens of the blackface incidents and other negative experiences that Black students have there. Contrary to what universities claim, this chapter argues that where blackface occurs in schooling spaces it is a performance fostered *by* those spaces and the relations that constitute them. The chapter attempts to make sense of what it is about sites of dominant schooling that might be so conducive to blackface. Here, that universities and schools are antiblack is not what is at issue. I argue alongside a legion of Black scholars (see, e.g., hampton, 2020; Harney & Moten, 2015; Kelley, 2016b; Walcott, 2018; Wilder, 2014) who have long maintained that it stands to reason that universities, as microcosms and indeed crucial arms of the antiblack, settler-colonial state, are also antiblack. Instead, I demonstrate from interview data the ways that university administrators see blackface as surprising when it occurs on their campuses, and the ways that Black people experience being considered as surprise at university. I argue that this phenomenon of surprise is produced by the inability of the university to account for Blackness within itself because of its constitutive and mandatory antiblackness. This antiblackness, in turn, is constituted by the university's function as a site for producing rationality and rational Canadian subjectivities precisely through making Black people its outside. Having laid this foundation, I then examine the work that blackface does, especially at universities, and how it is that blackface as an ostensibly individual but recurring and therefore ritual performance, comes to be such an apposite expression of antiblackness at school, yet so predictably unpredictable. Ultimately, I assert that the stubbornly postracialist claims of the university to be a site of progressive rationality, as well as its attempts to reconstitute itself as such against the Black insurgency that also occurs there, continually reproduce the motivations for blackface in all its antiblack meanings, as well as why it must always be considered surprise. Throughout, I draw on Katherine McKittrick's (2006) articulation of

Blackness as surprise in Canada and Sylvia Wynter's (1979) discussion of the Sambo figure.

Blackface as Surprise: "It's Not the School's Values!"

Sara Ahmed's (2012) important phenomenology of the university and the diversity work that takes place there points out that university administrators are often "shocked" that their institutions are perceived as bastions of whiteness. Despite the abundant evidence to support such a perception, administrators identify the problem to be that the perception is inaccurate rather than that the populations of faculty, staff, and students are, in fact, overwhelmingly white. As a result, they consider it their priority to set about *"changing perceptions of whiteness rather than changing the whiteness of* [*universities*]" (p. 34, emphasis in original). Here, a discourse of surprise functions to establish the university as racially egalitarian against the stark evidence to the contrary.

A similar but distinct dynamic of surprise seems to be at work with respect to the occurrence of blackface and other occurrences of antiblackness at the university. Seldom do university administrators' reflections seem to turn inward to consider how these occurrences might indicate a constitutive antiblackness of the university. Schools and universities, through the administrators to whom it falls to deal with blackface incidents, generally insist on seeing blackface as a surprising anomaly when it occurs on their campuses. For example, when we asked an administrator at University 4:

> INTERVIEWER: In your opinion, is there anything present on your campus or on campuses in general that might influence students to wear blackface?
> ADMINISTRATOR: No. Not really. Honestly, not that more than anything else. Not that more than anything else. Obviously there are elements of ignorance. That is very present. But I wouldn't foresee [blackface]. (U4A2)

Not only is blackface unforeseen from their perspectives, but university administrators and spokespersons we interviewed repeatedly spoke of blackface as contrary to their institutions' values. In this vein, the University 4 administrator goes on to say:

> If we had an incident of this magnitude in third year – that is, after having had these students for two, two-and-a-half years – I would have been surprised and terribly disappointed, and obviously our reaction would

have really been different. In this case, what was distinctive was that these students had not spent – When it happened, you have to understand that the students hadn't yet spent even a half-hour in class. (U4A2)

According to this administrator and others we spoke to, blackface incidents are perpetrated by new students who hold values that are alien to those of the university. They only occur when the students have not yet had the opportunity to be taught to conform to the university's values. For this administrator, had the students been at the university longer, they never would have engaged in blackface. Though this administrator is indeed referring to a blackface incident that occurred during a frosh event, they fail to account for the more senior student leaders responsible for animating the event, who had been at the university for some time and who were present throughout the incident. Instead, by blaming new students for such incidents, the administrator discursively sets the university off as a space where the antiblackness that motivates blackface is not endemic. Using the same discursive strategy, an administrator at University 3 told us:

So I think about the kinds of attitudes and values that students come in with that have been ingrained in them for eighteen years. And then we try very hard in four years to help them question and reframe and rethink about them, and have greater success with some than others. But I don't know that you can ever assume full responsibility for totally aligning every single person who is part of your community to have thoughts that uphold the high standard of your inclusivity and respect for diversity. (U3A1)

As with the University 4 administrator, this administrator also considers their university to possess ingrained egalitarian values. They do not consider the possibility that the university may, in fact, be a site where exclusionary values might reside or that there might be any continuity between societal values within and outside of the university. Instead, these and other administrators we spoke to at several other institutions narrate the university as largely at risk from the students who enter it year after year with inexplicable values fostered by their unenlightened families and communities located beyond the university. The university must constantly stem the threat to its values coming from "out-there." It is ostensibly faced with the gargantuan challenge of ensuring that it inculcates the university's superior, more enlightened values in each new student. Indeed, another University 3 administrator repeatedly deployed a metaphor of things "percolating" beneath the surface, positioning universities in general as constantly playing whack-a-mole through educational interventions to try to prevent things from "boiling over" before students can be set straight:

> So we do get a lot of what I call the under-the-surface boiling things ... It's boiling and what are we doing to address it? So I think that's really where I would say the majority of campuses are. ... There are things that maybe we don't know about that just are percolating at the surface. ... Like the incidences [sic] that come out, we can address ... Albeit bad, it is an opportunity to correct the behaviour, and we hang our hat on that as saying as an institution we worked with these people. ... You know, we can sell that! I am more concerned about the people that we don't hear about, that are filled with hate. Because those people exist! But how do we find them before we've reached the boiling point? ... And this is my big fear. Like, every day when I wake up I am like, "Are we at a tipping point? Is it just all under the surface and things are just coming out?" Like, we do our best to educate, but again we go back to the beliefs and values that people have. (U3A2)

A hard-to-identify, boogeyman student who would perpetrate blackface is made out to be far different from the normative student who has been there longer and, having been educated, now properly represents the university and bears its values. However, the university never fully knows the extent of the invading-racism problem, and the success of its educational interventions is not guaranteed. In making this argument, this administrator broadens the university's ability to absolve itself of accountability for blackface and other student expressions of antiblackness on their campuses whether the perpetrators are new or not.

Overall, then, the ways in which university spokespersons discuss these incidents make blackface surprising where it occurs within the university community. Antiblackness and other structures that produce inequitable conditions are to be understood as located outside the university, though they constantly try to enter and overwhelm. The university, by contrast, is seen as an enlightened space committed to equity and diversity. For these administrators, nothing in the university's relations, practices, or structures could be implicated in the production of antiblackness.

Thus, a discourse of surprise functions in the context of blackface in the Canadian university to establish and recuperate an ostensible racial egalitarianism, much as Ahmed (2012) has identified in universities elsewhere. This egalitarianism is fundamental to the legitimacy of the contemporary liberal university. Yet I argue in the following sections that the discourse of surprise has a much broader reach, and accomplishes a great deal more in the Canadian university. Surprise is not only applied to blackface incidents, but to the presence of Black people at the university, and is used in this way to establish a characteristic far more fundamental to how universities are conceived – that is, the "Human" faculty of rationality and intellectualism, of which Blackness and Black people are considered the antithesis.

Black People as Surprise at the University

In contrast to these administrators' views, Black students, staff, and faculty we spoke to do not experience the university as constitutively egalitarian, and do not understand blackface or the antiblackness that drives it as being contrary to the university's values. Again, I do not suggest that the idea that Black people experience the university as antiblack is a new insight. Instead, my objective in this section is to highlight that the experiences they shared in the context of discussions about blackface were those in which they were positioned as out of place, and therefore as unexpected, at the university in much the same way that blackface is always a surprise. And rather than simply attributing these incidents to the behaviour of a few, or even many, ignorant individuals behaving independently of the university's values, the Black participants felt that the values that undergird them characterized the university context.

In our interviews with Black people about blackface, the conversation inevitably turned to what they considered to be this broader context of antiblackness at the university. Identifying how he does not find the university a welcoming place, Donovan, a student at University 2, says: "You mentioned [residence hall A] and the student union, and all these kinds of things and places: I don't really feel like that's a place that is warm and friendly" (U2FG2P1). Miremba, a student at University 1, goes further, pointing out the ways in which, to her, the university fails to foster the equity values it proclaims, making the university climate in fact perilous for Black students:

When I pay my school fees, they tell me, "You're coming to a safe space where it's a diverse university where your views will be appreciated, your identity will be respected." But then when they don't do that, how do you get them to become responsible for that? ... I do know Black students who have considered, on several occasions, leaving this campus because they didn't feel emotionally safe, mentally safe ["*absolutely*," *another participant whispers*], or just capable of handling the isolation on this campus as a Black student. (U1BSOFGP2)

Miremba's feeling of being pushed out despite the university's lip-service equity is echoed by other participants across the university sites at which we conducted interviews. Jacqueline, a professor at University 5, speaks to this Black experience from a faculty perspective:

> Most universities across Canada have some kind of equity or diversity policy. And most of them are unenforced. My university has a beautiful one that mentions race and religion and disability and all that stuff, but when it comes time to hire, who is looking over our shoulders to see that the people that are shortlisted and get flown in for the lecture actually are those diverse constituents? Nobody! ... People don't want to talk about this, but there is a Black brain drain where we go to the States because they want us down there. And then some of us never come back, because the job never opens up for us. Some of our best and brightest are not even in the country because we are not wanted in the country. So of course you're going to leave! (U5F3)

In different ways, Donovan's, Miremba's, and Jacqueline's assessments all communicate that they do not find the university egalitarian and welcoming for Black people, but instead hostile and exclusionary. It is a space where Black people cannot be at ease, characterized by barriers to their entry and by structures that push them out.

Other Black participants tell a more specific story of their exclusion that involves the ways in which white people at the university, both faculty and students, express astonishment at their presence. From them, we come to understand that it is not just blackface that is perpetually shocking at the university, but that Black people are also confronted by various levels of surprise. Sometimes this surprise is hostile, where white people at the university seem outright offended at Black people's presence. For example, Zawadi at University 2 tells us:

> When they were building University 2 they did not have anyone who looks like me in mind. So it's a space that I have had problems with. When I was doing my undergrad – talk about blackface – I went to the student union and there was this [white] guy who just looked at me glaringly with a friend of mine. It's almost like ... he was offended that I was in the student union working out. ... White supremacy works in different ways, and this is one of the ways that it works. (U2FG2P4)

In other cases, the sense of surprise is expressed much more matter-of-factly. So, for example, in the midst of a blackface event at Hautes Études Commerciales, the business school affiliated with the Université de Montréal, Anthony Morgan, a McGill student at the time who experienced this incident and brought it to media attention, reported that when the students in blackface noticed his presence they remarked in the midst of their gaiety, "Hey we have a real black person here" (Montpetit, 2011). As they pretended to be Black, it hadn't occurred to this almost exclusively white group of students that they might encounter someone who actually was Black. They were surprised, if thrilled, to have a "real Black person" walk by. In this instance, what is particularly interesting about this reaction of surprise is that in 2019 38% of the international students at HEC Montréal, or 1,590 students, were from Africa – representing a not insignificant 10% of a student body of 14,356[1] (HEC Montréal, 2020). It is unlikely that the numbers would have been drastically different in 2011. Therefore, the sense of surprise occurred despite the regularly visible presence of Black students.

Similarly expressing the matter-of-fact ways in which Black people are presumed not to have a legitimate place at the university, and therefore are considered surprising there, Franklin, a University 2 student, says in a focus group discussion that had turned to the topic of violence at the university:

> I feel I can say that [I have experienced violence]! Not particularly in my program, but there are certain areas where you may hang around where I've gotten, like, "Why are you here?" "What got you here in this university?" Definitely I got that when I was residence staff. You know, "Out of all the interviews, and all the people that applied for this" – it was never [my] skills. It was like, "how did you get this?" as if it was out of the realm, my getting this position, and [a question of] whether you got this because of your colour. And that was very violent! (U2S1)

Franklin's experience again indicates the presumed out-of-placeness of Black people at the university, despite a Black student population that can be estimated at around 5% at his university. The numbers of Black students at Canadian universities are usually disproportionately small

---

1 There are no existing statistics for 2011, the year that this event occurred. Of course, the group "African students" is not the same as "Black students," since there are certainly Black students who are not international students, and students from the continent of Africa who might not be Black. HEC Montréal, like other Montreal universities, does not gather race-based data, making it difficult to know much about Blackness at these institutions. Quoting this statistic here is not an attempt to carelessly participate in the erasure of Blackness (which I discuss later in the chapter), but gives us a crude sense of the proportion of one part of the overall student population at HEC that is visibly Black.

across the board. Nevertheless, Black people, whether students, staff, or faculty, have long been found at the Canadian university – certainly since at least the mid-nineteenth century (see, e.g., Queen's Encyclopedia, n.d.; SSMU University Affairs, n.d.). Our numbers, though low, are not negligible. Therefore, the repeated construction of Black people as surprise at the university requires explanation.

Franklin's experience also draws our attention to a very specific logic that informs how Black people are cast out of the university community and considered surprise there: Black people are often considered imposters at the university because they are presumed not to have the credentials or the intelligence that would qualify them to be there. This presumption is reflected in Shanna's experience at University 6:

> SHANNA: I have friends who are African like me ... Some of us experience situations that are really not pleasant in our classes. We feel that some teachers rank the students, and that they tend to consider Africans as, well, not excellent, not competent, and it shows in the grades. [A friend of mine] said that in her class she always stays at the same level ... She was in a group of five, with two foreigners, a Mexican and [herself], an African. And the ranking was first the Quebecois students, then the Mexican, then her. Even though there was a [white] Quebecoise who came to her all the time, and she helped her with her homework because they were friends. But whenever the teacher grades their work, she notices that the other person gets better grades than her. (U6FG1)

Shanna and her friends have a common experience of feeling that they are being graded on the basis of preconceived racist assessments rather than by the quality of their work. Even more clearly demonstrating the relationship between Black out-of-placeness, white surprise, and the presumption that Black people lack the intelligence to be at university, Achille, also in the University 6 focus group with Shanna, tells us:

> ACHILLE: The first day when we arrived for class, there were only white people. Basically, I was the only Black person. And the prof, when he came in, asked me if I wasn't mistaken. I told him that no, I wasn't mistaken, and I gave him the course number. And he said, "Yeah. OK," that he just thought that I was mistaken. Just like that! I don't know why, but it was me that he asked if I was in the wrong course, as if – But it was a computer course – computer mathematics, so perhaps he was thinking –
> SHANNA: (interrupting): – that you wouldn't have the ability to take that course!
> ACHILLE: There you go! So – (U6FG1)

The matter-of-fact way in which, on sight, Achille is considered out of place in this university classroom by his instructor, before they had had any chance to interact on any level, and the ways in which the instructor seemed to shy away from offering an explanation (though no explanation would make sense) again suggest the antiblack foundations of surprise. Drawing on their experience, both Shanna and Achille surmise that this instructor's response is likely caused by a presumption that Achille is not intelligent based on his bodily presentation as Black.

Achille's, Shanna's, and Franklin's stories reflect a presumption of Black incompetence in university that is a long-standing one in Canada. In fact, the suspicious type of student evaluation that Shanna experienced is strikingly similar to the grievance that sparked the 1969 Sir George Williams Affair at what is now Concordia University in Montreal, in which six Black students accused a biology professor, apparently not the most racist of his colleagues, of unjust grading (Butcher, 1971, p. 80; Forsythe, 1971, p. 7). LeRoi Butcher wrote in 1971 about the Sir George Affair that

> apparently a history of strained relations stemming from the differential treatment he meted out to the students on the basis of race was common knowledge to [students]. Moreover, the students reported that they themselves experienced a phenomenon which, in itself, could go a long way in substantiating the pristine theory of the intellectual inferiority of the Black race. (p. 87)

Shanna's experience gestures to how enduring and deeply embedded these foregone conclusions about Blackness are in the university setting in the present, and to the apparent willingness of certain white instructors to bear out these assumptions in their grading, regardless of students' actual performance.

Black scholars in Canada have written of the association of Black people with a lack of intelligence, speaking about how it extends to presumptions about Black faculty. Daniel (2019) discusses the ways in which faculty, university administrators, and students all challenge the legitimacy of Black faculty to hold the positions that they do. Daniel concludes that "within the broader social dialogue around constructions of Blackness, in the ivory towers of academia, Blacks are at best afforded the option to be a student. The union between Blackness and intellectualism remains an unlikely combination in the minds of many White faculty members" (p. 30, emphasis added).

Overall, then, for these participants, and Black people more generally as reflected in the higher education literature, the university is hardly a location that values equity and diversity, much less one that values them as Black people. Instead, through its practices, equity policies that are enforced casually if at all, and the common-sense behaviour of non-Black members of the university community, Black people are re-presented as belonging beyond, and not within, the space of the university. We see that White people at the university are surprised when they encounter Black people in student spaces despite the fact that Black people have long been a part of Canadian universities. Together, Zawadi's, Franklin's, Shanna's, and Achille's accounts narrate the ways in which the surprise at Blackness is routinely grounded in a matter-of-fact logic that concludes that they are not intelligent enough to properly be there.

Surprise and the Production of Blacklessness

In the chapter "Nothing's Shocking: Black Canada" in Katherine McKittrick's (2006) book, McKittrick argues that through the active erasure of evidence of Black people in Canada

> unseen black communities and spaces ... privilege a transparent Canada/ nation by rendering the landscape a "truthful" *visual* purveyor of past and present social patterns. Consequently, "truthful" visual knowledge regulates and normalizes how Canada is seen – as white, ... not black, not non-white, not Indigenous, but white. (pp. 96–7, emphasis in original)

The "truth," then, of a white Canada is produced by a "systemic black-lessness" (p. 93) and is necessary to recreate Canada as a white space. This "truth" can be achieved through a technique of surprise. Discussing the case of Marie-Joseph Angélique, the enslaved Black woman violently executed for allegedly burning down Old Montreal in 1734, McKittrick writes that biographies such as those of Angélique "invoke ... a number of surprises that are astonishing simply because they take place in Canada, a nation that has and is still defining its history as Euro-white, or nonblack" (pp. 91–2). McKittrick continues: "the element of surprise is contained in the material, political, and social landscape that presumes – and fundamentally requires – that subaltern populations have no relationship to the production of [Canadian] space" (p. 92). McKittrick argues that whether it is by the presumed absence from Canada that informs the moment prior to the "shocking" discovery, or by the "wonder" and "astonishment" produced in the moment subsequent to discovery, the politics of rendering Blackness as surprise make it constitutively and perpetually *not* properly a part of dominant

Canadian geographies (pp. 92–3). It is, therefore, Canada's "ceaseless outlawing of blackness" (p. 93) that makes the technique of surprise both necessary and possible.

I argue here, then, that the way in which Blackness is ritually rendered surprise at the university is related to a particular need to maintain a fiction of the university as constitutively Blackless. I shall argue that the construction of the university as Blackless, like the construction of Canada as Blackless, is an active (if deeply psychically embedded and not necessarily conscious) process that occurs because of what is at stake for white Western subjectivities, rather than as a result of casual Eurocentric oversight, or a benignly mistaken conviction that Black presence at the Canadian university is only recent. It happens even though and in fact especially because Black people *are* at the university, where our presence challenges the university's antiblack colonial desires. The normative functioning of the university depends upon its being Blackless.

The University as Producer of Antiblack Canadianness

Radical scholars have convincingly argued the inherent coloniality and antiblackness of the North American university (see, e.g., Grande, 2018; Harney & Moten, 2013; Kelley, 2016b; Wilder, 2014). Indeed, Western state schooling, and in this case specifically Canadian schooling, has always been antagonistic to Blackness. In rosalind hampton's careful genealogy of a Canadian university, hampton points out that Canadian state schooling efforts were initially established to convert free and enslaved Indigenous people as well as enslaved Black people to Christianity on the one hand, and to train those who would be engaged in these conversion efforts on the other (hampton, 2020, p. 15; see also Bramble, 2000, pp. 101–2). Where this evangelism occurred in the fledging colonies that became Canada it is impossible to divorce it from the broader (social, political, and economic) colonial relations that made it possible, and which it was intended to advance. Education at this time would necessarily draw lines of distinction between the locations of colonizer/settler, colonized, and enslaved.

As the Canadian settler-colonial project progressed, schooling took the form of increasingly violent efforts to assimilate or annihilate Indigenous people with a view towards their disappearance, and to define the nation as white over against Black and racialized populations in Canada (hampton, 2020, p. 16). Universities, first established in Canada in the nineteenth century, played a central role in producing ideas of Canadianness – geographical and political – and patriotic Canadian identity (Axelrod & Reid, 1989, p. xvii; hampton, 2020, p. 18). Much like all Western knowledge, these notions of Canadianness were developed in tandem with, and upon the foundation of, racial logics that delimited what it meant to be civil(ized), respectable, rational – indeed Human (hampton, 2020, p. 17; Wynter, 2003; see also Goldberg 1993).

In the mid-twentieth century, with the advent of global decolonization movements, but more importantly as the nation state's labour needs shifted, Canada began to narrate itself differently as egalitarian and multicultural (Thobani, 2007, p. 15). While not divesting from longer-standing liberal and Enlightenment discourses of rationality and respectability, the Canadian university made vital contributions to the construction of Canadianness as reasonable – that is, as above the logics that drove slavery and colonialism. Canadian academics, like politicians, sought to establish that Canada had not been involved, and certainly was not presently involved, in such unpalatable relations as colonialism, whether within or beyond its borders (Cooper, 2006, p. 8; hampton, 2020, p. 62; Hudson, 2010; S. Razack, 2002, p. 2; Walcott & Abdillahi, 2019, p. 54). With specific reference to Black people, as Carmen Poole (2012) has shown, academic historians and authors of Canadian history texts systematically erased pre-Confederation Black experience and Canada's involvement in slavery and the slave economy of the Atlantic world from dominant historical narratives in order to advance the mythology of an egalitarian, multicultural Canada. One effect of this historiography has been to mystify the concept of Blackness with/in Canada. It erases Black people from the story of the making of Canada, and repositions Blackness as outside the nation, only legible as recently arrived (Poole, 2012; Walcott, 2001).

Hand in hand with this erasure, the Canadian university has actively resisted the study of Black life qua Black in Canada, as Peter Hudson and Aaron Kamugisha (2014), Rinaldo Walcott (2014a), and Walcott and Idil Abdillahi (2019) have all most recently forcefully demonstrated. Universities in Canada have by and large opposed Black people's calls for the creation of Black Studies departments, even in the wake of global decolonization and civil rights struggles when universities in other parts of the world, such as the United States, were doing so (see, e.g., hampton, 2020, pp. 24, 148). Canadian universities have since not made the kinds of infrastructural investments that would support Black Studies, and specifically Black Studies in/of Canada (Walcott, 2014a, p. 279). It is only within the last few years that initiatives of this sort have been achieved at Dalhousie University (a Black African Diaspora minor in 2018), York University (Black Canadian Studies certificate, in 2018), and Queen's University (a minor program in Black Studies, launched in 2021). Outside of these academic structures, Black scholars who take up Black Studies in Canada are scattered across departments and disciplines, while the study of Black life in Canada is taken up in traditional departments, if at all, solely through such filters as area studies (African and Caribbean Studies) or migration studies (Hudson & Kamugisha, 2014, pp. 6–7; Walcott, 2014a, p. 276), reinforcing the non-recognition of Black people as Black, and locating Black people as properly from outside of Canada. National as well as disciplinary boundaries are imposed in such a way as to stymie the ability to make sense of Blackness in Canada and its expansiveness beyond such boundaries. Disciplinary boundaries further resist the transformation that Black Studies might bring to the ways in which these disciplines are dominantly conceived (Hudson & Kamugisha, 2014, p. 7; Walcott & Abdillahi, 2019, p. 56), instead reducing Black Studies to identity politics. Black Studies is cast out of the realm of the social sciences and humanities through an academic antiblackness whereby Black people's experience loses its specificity and is both used as analogy (Sexton, 2010, 2016) and reduced to an inconsequential shade (if not shadow) of an ostensibly universal human experience (always already white). The message is constantly that knowledge of Black people in Canada, and Black people's knowledge more generally, is not worthwhile knowledge and does not contribute anything unique to existing understandings of the human condition in Canada or beyond (Hudson & Kamugisha, 2014; Walcott, 2014a).

Therefore, the ways in which the university locates Black people outside of the university both physically and conceptually are in symbiotic relationship with its roles of negating Black knowledge and producing antiblack knowledge that secure Canadian innocence and places Black people outside of Canada and outside of the Human. The investment in a Blackless university through surprise is therefore not a casual one. Black people and the scholarly knowledge our lives make possible threaten to undo not only racial ideologies, but also dearly and deeply held notions of the reasonable postracial Canadian state, what it might mean to be a good, respectable Canadian, and indeed what it might mean to be Human in Canada.

The University as Producer of Rational Subjectivity

Given the role of the university as described here, Black people and Black knowledge at the university create all kinds of trouble for those who would engage the university transactionally for what it can offer them in terms of identity. For ultimately, universities are not simply learning and credentializing spaces in any simplistic understandings of those terms. Rather, they are also spaces through which social subjects craft their identities, and wherein identifications such as "Canadian," "learned," and "qualified" are always already racialized.

In a chapter titled "Keeping the Ivory Tower White," Carol Schick (2002) highlights the ways in which students at a Canadian university use their affiliation with the space of the university to establish a toehold on bourgeois, white Canadian respectability. Students construct themselves as respectable white citizens by contrasting themselves with the racialized "Other" who is seen as belonging outside the walls of the university. Schick writes that the discourses upon which students rely to bolster these respectable, rational identities

> rely on the university as the home of official white rationality and knowledge – the markers by which a taxonomy of difference may be established and where "difference from" means "unequal to." Here is the mythological, safe, and pure place of abstraction and objectivity; the world of knowledge and theory; a place for the "disembodied" mind ... the real-world politics of gender, culture, ... are strongly resisted. ... this space must be maintained; the identities – those who are in control and those who are not – cannot be confused. (pp. 109–10)

Here, being understood as white and respectable fundamentally requires being understood as "rational," and the university is a crucial space through which this rationality may be claimed. Indeed, Western universities are famously reliant on a fiction of the university as a self-governed community of rational persons (read: elite white men) who resolve any conflicting interests among them through scholarly debate on ostensibly neutral ground that is presumed not to be shot through with racialized and other inequitable social relations. Those persons whose experience would suggest that the university is otherwise, who insist that our bodies cannot be separated from who we are and how we know, and who point out that the university's structures are not neutral but rather raced, classed, and gendered, are thought to bring "irratio-nality" into the space of the university. Therefore, if the white rational identities that these students invest so much into establishing are to stand, Indigenous, Black, and other racialized people along with their politics must be located definitively beyond the space of the university, and the boundaries between inside and outside must be reinforced. For these students, discourses of belonging and unbelonging (which are inextricable from discourses of race) are crucial to the success of their identity formation as rational, bourgeois white (or almost white) Cana-dians (Schick, 2002, p. 116). Schick points out that a majority of the participants interviewed for her study were of working-class, non-British,

European ethnic backgrounds (p. 103), an insecure and unstable white identity in the context of Canada to be sure. These students use the university to establish themselves as rational and reasonable (p. 108) even as they also use it to appropriate the currency of the more highly valued and secure social location of respectable, bourgeois, (white) British settlers (p. 106). It is therefore particularly salient that it is mostly Indigenous persons over against whom the students in Schick's study crafted their dominant identities in this instance (p. 106).

Schick's analysis of the Canadian university echoes the more specific arguments that Sylvia Wynter has long made with regard to schooling, the university, and academic knowledge. Wynter has resolutely and repeatedly argued that academics, particularly (but not exclusively) those in the social sciences and humanities, are responsible for perpetuating racist understandings of the Human. These ideas first emerged in Renaissance humanism, were extended through Darwinian thought, and are continually mobilized through various academic discourses specifically to appoint blackness to a space of negation beyond the category of Human (e.g., Wynter, 1994a, 1994b, 1995, 1996, 2006).

We see how the space of the university affords a similar and related process of identity formation against Blackness in rosalind hampton's study of McGill University. Hampton identifies the ways in which the study's Black participants experience the university as a bounded bubble, deeply invested in the production of Anglophone/British, elite whiteness (hampton, 2020, p. 75). In this case, it is also Black people who are placed beyond the Canadian university's boundaries through its social relations, enabling others to use the space of the university to be created or reconfirmed as white (see p. 110).

However, as discussed in the previous section, it is not only whiteness that the university produces through its relationship to Blackness. The words of one of hampton's participants, CH, make this rather obvious. CH says (without melancholy, to be clear): "I just don't feel that I am a reflection of what McGill is. At all. I feel like I am its antithesis. I feel like I am its, its darkness. And I like that" (hampton, 2020, p. 134). In CH's experience at the university, her existence as a Black woman is not simply a foil against which others can know themselves as white. Rather, she becomes aware that she is understood to be the embodiment of everything that a respectable "McGill person" is not, or ought not to be. One can know oneself as of/from McGill simply by *not* being who CH is. Of course, CH's experience is not unique, nor is it limited to this one university. The Black people I spoke to in my blackface study across several universities generally echoed the same experience, as indicated above. This recurring Black experience at universities and other educational institutions focuses our attention on the ways in which Blackness is not just the antithesis of whiteness, but the antithesis of broader hegemonic Canadian constructions of Western Humanity (Walcott, 2014c, 2018; see also Dumas, 2018; Wynter, 2003). Where the dominant role of the university is the production of educated (i.e., rational), patriotic, respectable, bourgeois, Canadian citizens worthy of inheriting the neoliberal settler-colonial state (see hampton, 2020, p. 19), CH and other Black people exist as the negation of all these identities.

Against this background, the multiple experiences of being encountered as surprise shared by the Black people who participated in this study can be understood. If Blackness is in fact the antithesis of everything that the university is committed to producing, if that product can only be known in opposition to what Black people are, then Black people cannot properly be a part of the university community. By this logic, Blackness can only ever be surprising when encountered there. Recalling McKittrick, we see that surprise enables the fundamental rendering of the university as ontologically Blackless, regardless of how long Black people have been a part of the Canadian university, in order that it can go about the essential business of producing that which Blackness is not.

Of Rationality/Intelligence, Black Embodiment, and Blackface

The university's antiblackness is not simply directed at a nebulous concept of being Black. As the antithesis of the university's disembodied rational minds, Blackness, with the attendant associations with irrationality and lack of intelligence, is ontologically embodied. Black Canadian scholar George Dei (2017) has noted the associations of the body with irrationality and lack of intelligence in the context of the university:

Based on my skin color, I am often seen simply as an "emotional" being. I am constantly being urged to be a "rationale" [sic] thinker without questioning the basis of such Western logics of rationality. ... Our [i.e., Black scholars'] presence is under a constant gaze ... Our experiences can be invalidated, our knowledge-base questioned; and when we are critical, our scholarship is not only suspect and labeled as "anti-intellectual," we are often seen as angry intellectuals without a cause. (p. 11).

In the antiblack semiotic field, the Black body visually conjures these ideas of irrationality and unintelligence. Therefore, academic antiblackness is actively directed against the presentation of the Black body, as in Achille's, Zawadi's, and Franklin's experiences. Jalil Bishop Mustaffa (2017), drawing on Cornell West, alludes to this when he writes:

> White supremacy defines itself "by convincing [Black people] that their *bodies are ugly*, their *intellect is inherently underdeveloped*, their culture is less civilized, and their future warrants less concern than that of other peoples" ... The higher education system has helped operate and engineer all of these functions of white supremacy. (p. 713, emphasis added)

Lack of intelligence is therefore conceived of as housed in "ugly" Black bodies, and the university is implicated in the propagation of both concepts and the relationships between them.

Sylvia Wynter (1979) is helpful in further understanding how Blackness as the antithesis of rational Human Western subjectivities is signalled in the white Western imagination by the presentation of the Black body. Wynter writes:

> The Place of the NORM is constituted by and through the definition of certain desired attributes. The most desired attribute was the "intellectual faculty." The sign that pointed to one's possession of this attribute was whiteness of skin. The sign that pointed to its nonpossession was blackness of skin, which revealed non-human being. The black exists as the Symbolic Object constituting the Lack, the Void of these qualities that have been postulated as the absolute sign of the certainty of being human. That a man or almost a man can exist, lacking these things, sets into play the terror that these attributes can be lost. ... The Negro then becomes the SYMBOLIC OBECT OF THIS LACK WHICH IS DESIGNATED AS THE LACK OF THE HUMAN. (p. 152, emphatic caps in original)

Wynter here identifies the "intellectual faculty" as paramount for recognizing oneself as the Western Human subject. The Black body is set up within this construction of Humanness as the site at which the intellectual faculty cannot exist, while the white body is *supposed to* represent where the intellect faculty is expected. However, rationality and intelligence are by no means given just because one presents physically as a white person. White subjectivity, like all dominant subjectivities, is insecure, always at risk of falling into its constructed opposite – in this case the location of the constructed unintelligent Black subhuman (Wynter, 1979, p. 152).

The stakes around intelligence and Blackness are raised at the university in the context of (unevenly) broadening participation in higher education, and where, in its normative workings, intelligence is the main currency reckoned and accumulated as merit, or to one's "credit" (Harney & Moten, 2013) as belonging. They are particularly raised at the elite university, where being *"good enough* (ostensibly, smart enough) to get in" and "excelling" academically once "in" can potentially be mobilized to supersede social class, socio-economic, and ethnic identities that might otherwise suggest unbelonging (see Reay, Crozier, & Clayton, 2009). Academic excellence, or being "smart enough," insulates one from being "kicked out." The stakes are raised yet higher again by the increasingly neoliberal university with its increasingly unreasonable demands on students (and faculty), and where imposter syndrome reigns, but is misrecognized as a private psychological struggle rather than as a "public feeling" generated by neoliberal rationalities (Breeze, 2018; see also Gill, 2009; Reay, 2001). Under these conditions, the assurance of being "good enough" to belong is elusive and perilously fragile.

Wynter's (1979, p. 150) analysis of the relationship between Blackness and intelligence goes on to explain the role of the Sambo stereotype in reifying the association of Blackness with the absence of the intellectual faculty. Sambo is a site onto which one can project repressed fears of not personally measuring up to the "Norm of mastery," and at which those fears might be contained (p. 155). Of course, the Sambo stereotype is integral to blackface, having been deeply interwoven into it through minstrelsy (Lott, 1993, p. 7), making blackface the prototypical visual representation of Sambo.

It is with these conceptual tools that we might understand how it makes sense that blackface ritually occurs at sites of schooling – particularly at elite university sites where Black people are held at bay, and especially where Black people still dare to show up. Black people in the space of the university rupture the neat colour lines that are supposed to coincide with the university's boundaries, and that permit the construction of respectable, rational white Canadian subjectivities. As academic insecurities generated by the structures of schooling abound, Black people's presence potentially raises anxieties around falling out of respectability and into Blackness and what it ostensibly represents. This is managed in multiple ways institutionally, such as through well-worn discourses of merit and excellence. I suggest that blackface is another such strategy. The performance of Sambo, through grotesque blackface representations of the Black body, visually rehearses the antiblack geographies that attempt to fix both Blackness and intelligence in separate, non-coterminous locations. Blackface serves up conceptions of Blackness that potentially allay insecure white subjectivities and avert the fall into Blackness. Blackface is therefore experienced as soothing, as entertaining, as comic relief, not only by the performers of blackface but also by those who witness it and engage in discussions around it.

An online comment pushing back against challenges to a blackface incident at McGill University unwittingly demonstrates this racial dynamic:

> Blackface for Halloween. Seriously? Anything is an issue with these AA[2] students. As far as I'm concerned: a person can dress however they wish for Halloween. Isn't that the point? The personification of a fear. I see Black students pretending to be White every day. Chill down. (Heidelmann, 2012)

Here, Blackness in the university space is read as both fearful and as always already an attempt to be white – or as whiteface. Its logic creates a blackface double-bind. The Black person who is read as not openly contesting the white identity-formation functions of university is read as attempting to be white, but their existence as such serves as justification for blackface. On the other hand, the Black persons whose presence reads as more evidently insurgent, presumably like those to whom Heidelmann is responding, are apparently refusing to play the university game on the expected terms. They are a threat, but one that can be contained by wearing blackface to "personify the fear." In either case, Blackness is out of place and incites fear at the university, and blackface is apparently a reasonable response.

Overall, then, the university context is deeply conducive to blackface (explaining its prevalence there). Blackface is a product of the university space, not a haphazard intrusion upon it as university administrators are wont to claim. The philosophical and historical foundations of the university, and therefore its extant structures and social relations, produce blackface as a function of a constitutive antiblackness that is required to construct the university as a rational, egalitarian space that produces a particular kind of respectable Canadian subject. Donovan, a student nearing graduation at the time of his interview, shares a reflection that speaks to blackface as apt representation of the university and its structures:

> You already know my loving relationship with education. That's part of the reason why I said I wouldn't argue with someone who had blackface

---

2 "AA" presumably means "African American" here, a problematic misnomer for Black students in Canada consistent with the logics that cannot conceive of Black people with/in Canada. From the context, the comment is clearly aimed at Black people.

who walked by me. And I also wouldn't expect the university to respond to it when they don't have course offerings that reflect any type of anything that speaks to the [Black] population, the discourse, the research, anything like that. I didn't see myself reflected in the teaching staff. I don't see myself around campus. ... when I walk into the building and sit down in a class and I have [Black history] taught by – (*trails off, but names a course taught by a white professor that other focus group members are aware, and wary, of*). Anyways that's a whole 'nother thing! To me that's worse than blackface! ... When I agitate something very small and say, "Oh, well you know what? I want course offerings that speak to my history, my heritage," and I'm shut down by the dean ... I kind of feel like when I walk into campus environments after leaving a class, I would only *expect* to see people wearing blackface. It sounds crass, but I'm being serious! (U2FG2P1)

For Donovan, blackface visually captures the problematic ethos of the university that resists Black people, resists Black knowledge, and resists calls for change. Rather than find blackface surprising at the university, Donovan finds it more surprising that he does not see it all the time, everywhere.

Black Insurgency and Blackface

There is another dimension to be attended to. Both Donovan's reference to his attempts to agitate for change, however small, and Heidelmann's earlier comment that "anything is an issue" for Black students (which evidently produces a measure of fear to non-Black others) indicate that Blackness at the university is not solely some threat passively represented by the Black body. These comments gesture to an important way in which Black people live and take up space at the university despite its antiblackness. They gesture to the place of insurgent Black activist politics at the university.

With regard to blackface and Black insurgency historically, Douglas A. Jones (2013) has warned that we not ignore the "black social and political formations that also framed the production of minstrelsy" (p. 27). Jones, like other scholars, argues that blackface minstrelsy originated in the North and West of the United States where, as in Canada, slavery operated on a smaller scale than in the US South and where slavery ended more gradually (p. 26). In these kinds of circumstances where colour lines are not as clearly defined, racial thinking and racist representation, such as blackface, flourish (Pieterse, 1992, p. 62). Yet Jones (2013) insists that blackface not be understood to have arisen as solely an anxious white response to a *passive* Black presence – an approach that obscures and renders inconsequential what Black people were doing at the time. Instead, Jones argues that that blackface was also produced as a "buffer" against the increasingly assertive Black politics that characterized the North in the early 1800s, and which therefore also shaped the social-political context (p. 27). As a reaction to these conditions, blackface minstrelsy was an "aesthetic surrogate for the lack of slavery" under which terms it at least appeared to be clear who was free and who was not, who was respectable and who was not (p. 27).

Jones's warnings are in order for our consideration of contemporary blackface at the Canadian university, where dominant notions of both Canada and the university as egalitarian reign but also where Black activism has, at least since the 1960s Sir George Affair and Congress of Black Writers, long been a "gift that shapes reform" and reveals Canada and the university, despite their efforts to say otherwise, as deeply implicated in the relations of slavery and its afterlife (Walcott & Abdillahi, 2019). Here, the posture of Black life, its insurgent presence, its daring to show up, is what Jones (2013), drawing on Nahum Chandler, describes as "the menace of … black 'exorbitance' … the destabilization of normative understandings of sociality and historicity by means of a politicized, epistemic surplus" (p. 22). It reminds us of CH in hampton's study, who identifies her status as the university's antithesis as an identity she relishes. Black life lived on these terms at the university is not engaged in melancholic lament to somehow be made comfortable there, but as radical critique of the entire enterprise. Blackface at the university appears to also be mobilized as a response intended to push back against this critique.

That this active and activist Black presence at Canadian universities is salient to the ritual occurrence of blackface is evident not only from Donovan's and Heidelmann's comments, but in all the protracted debates after such incidents and the reactive white scholarship on the matter that take deep exception to Black indignation about blackface. These conversations attempt to resituate the university and Canada as bastions of fair-dealing rationality, often by asserting rights to (a paradoxically American understanding of) an unbridled freedom of expression. A recent example of this desperate effort appears in a book entitled *University Commons Divided: Exploring Debate and Dissent on Campus.* The author writes in reference to an incident including blackface and racist costuming at a university:

> If there was insensitivity to issues of race in the selection of costumes by party-goers at the three universities, there was also a lack of proportion in the responses to them. These were Halloween parties, not cultural mis-

appropriations, Nazi mimicry, or manifestations of disapproval of other peoples. So describing them risks diminishing real problems of intolerance, discrimination, and racism. It also risks backlash from a bewildered public observing these episodes. No country in the world has adapted to multiculturalism more successfully than has Canada; most Canadians know that and appreciate our diversity. (MacKinnon, 2018, p. 45)

The interdependence of hegemonic conceptions of the university, rationality, respectability, and Canadianness is rather evident here. They come together in defence of blackface, and to reassert the challenge that Black insurgency presents to these notions and their production at the university.

Conclusion

What, then, of the phenomenon with which we began: that of blackface as surprise at the university? As we saw in administrators' comments in an earlier section, making blackface surprise can serve as a pretext for not taking incidents of blackface seriously and for failing to take decisive action when they occur. However, this strategy accomplishes more than the immediate deflection of responsibility in the wake of a blackface incident. It accomplishes the more consequential outcome of denying that the university is a location that might produce blackface.

Once blackface is identified as surprise, the university aims its interventions at students ostensibly coming into the university as pollutants, and pursues these interventions in ways that never implicate the university itself. Donovan's insights again help us to understand how this might look on the ground when he says:

> Blackface is one of those things that if you are a white liberal, this is something you can take up as your fight. … They can be a good white person and let you know that, "You know, Johnny, you shouldn't do that because it's offensive to Black people!" And then they are praised for it. It's the same thing when you come to talk about the institution. I don't want to hear University 2 chastise some kid from China for putting on blackface, and then kick me out of class for telling them that their courses are garbage and they don't have anything for me. I'm not interested in that! And I don't want them to be championing it and putting it in the newspapers: "Great job! People in schools all over are doing blackface, but University 2 did a great job because they kicked out the Chinese kid." I don't want to hear it! (U2FG2P1)

According to Donovan, when the university considers blackface to come from ignorant people originating beyond its boundaries, rather than something fostered by the social relations of the university, it makes a show of being progressive and ahead of its peers while it fails to look inward and continues unchecked with the everyday antiblackness that Donovan experiences. This is an institutional version of the postracialist claims to Canadian progressiveness that we saw on the individual level in Chapter 3.

Yet I have argued that the discourse of surprise has a much broader reach in that it is applied to the presence of Black people at the university. Applying McKittrick's analysis of the politics of surprise, we can assert that presenting blackface as surprise is a necessary technique precisely because the university must deny that antiblackness is its bricks and mortar, and precisely because Black people are present at the university and use it as a site of Black insurgence. What is at stake for the university in doing this is its reputation as producer and home of rational, reasonable, liberal Canadian humanisms/humans: a position that claims to be at odds with colonialism, racism, and antiblackness but, as we have seen from Black participants' assessments as well as from the genealogy of the Canadian university presented above, is only possible *through* colonialism, racism, and antiblackness. Therefore the university cannot somehow simply divest of the logics that produce blackface while hanging onto its role as producer of Canadian rationality. Making blackface surprise becomes a way for the university to perform itself as being beyond its inglorious constitution, and indeed in the particular mythologies created by Canada and the Canadian university, as never having been antiblack while it remains an institutional instantiation of slavery's afterlife. The university is able to bridge its proclaimed values with the very different ones that keep it going.

Yet it also becomes evident that the more the university insists on its Canadian rationality and reasonableness, even in the name of responding to blackface but without owning up to its coloniality and antiblackness, the more it entrenches the very antiblack logics that both encourage blackface and produce that rationality in the first place. As such, far from contesting blackface, the university continually reproduces the motivations for blackface with its every expression that blackface is surprise, and drives antiblackness deeper with every insistence that the university is too rational, reasonable, and Canadian a place for blackface to be expected.

6 "Making Them Better Leaders": The Pedagogical Imperative, Institutional Priorities, and the Attenuation of Black Anger

This chapter considers some of the particular ways in which anti-blackness takes shape institutionally at universities. By examining institutional responses to blackface as expressed by university administrators in our interviews with them, we were able to identify the discourses that organize these responses and that, more broadly, perpetuate antiblack structures. Among these discourses, I am particularly interested in what I will call the pedagogical imperative, which administrators present as the rationale for the tenor of their responses. Though the pedagogical imperative is advanced and enacted by university administrators and offices that claim to value "equity, diversity and inclusion," and even by some offices that oversee university equity and diversity mandates, I argue that the pedagogical imperative is ultimately an outgrowth of what I contended in Chapter 5 is the university's role as an educational institution that produces whiteness through antiblackness and coloniality. The commitment of such institutions is to produce ostensibly progressive, postracialist, white Canadian leaders from its students. This mandate returns emphatically in the service of students who have become involved in what the administration largely sees as innocuous forms of antiblackness such as blackface that, because of Black people's protests, could derail their otherwise sure paths to leadership. These priorities necessarily involve constructing Black reactions to blackface as outrageous and requiring attenuation, resulting in the institutional disregard of Black members of the university and their interests in these circumstances. The chapter ends with a meditation on Black anger, and proceeds to imagine what institutional responses might look like if conceived through a commitment to take Black indignation seriously, and to eradicate Black suffering.

Presuming Ignorance

Chapter 5 argued that the Canadian university context fosters black-face, but that the university prefers to understand blackface incidents as coming from uncultivated new students who have not (yet) embraced the university's values. This preferred view seeks to make the university innocent by displacing antiblackness onto the bodies of incoming *individuals* with inexplicable values who are to be understood as unlike the enlightened people who more properly characterize the university.

Nevertheless, having thus absolved the university, the administrative response is wont to extend the story of innocence further by making blackface perpetrators ignorant. This presumption that perpetrators are simply oblivious was central to how every administrator we interviewed, without exception, explained their institution's response to blackface. For example, an administrator at University 2 says:

> In retrospect we probably should have come out a little more strongly at the beginning to denounce this. On the other hand, we just felt that it was kids being stupid, that there wasn't an underlying aspect of racism ... I do believe they just didn't think it was anything other than funny.

An administrator at University 4 makes the same presumption:

> Me, I think it's ignorance. That's for sure. I think there is a lack of sensitivity also. ... We are talking about young people who are eighteen, nineteen years old who on this point were particularly ignorant. So this was an opportunity to educate them.

What is striking here is the way in which both these administrators move seamlessly from what they would prefer to think about the black-face perpetrators towards asserting their certitude that what they wish to believe is, in fact, the case. This is an active task directing their psychic energies towards a particular reading. As the University 2 administrator continues to justify their university's response, we learn more about the process of this methodical psychic work. When asked about their first reactions after a blackface incident, they said:

> Well, first of all, I think you hope that when you have an incident like that it truly is based on ignorance – that the individuals involved really just didn't stop to think about the impact it would have. And you, and you truly hope that this was not in fact racism – that they knew it was

racism, that they wouldn't have known it was going to be distressing and in fact they didn't think about it. So – And it was Halloween, and a lot of people do stupid things at Halloween. And no doubt they'd been drinking and whatever. You try and look at it and say, "Please let this just be simply a lack of understanding and maturity, and not being used to living in a community that is incredibly diverse ... That was my reaction and was probably the reaction – it was the reaction of some of the other administrators.

The repetition of what they hope, indeed what they *truly* hope, what they make a deliberate effort to believe, the way it all eventually turns into a prayer, and the way this disposition is shared, together represent the layered process by which administrators doggedly will the perpetrators to be innocent. This process includes filling in details about the incident (for example, "no doubt they'd been drinking") to support their presumptions before ever speaking to those involved.

These presumptions are related to the logic and vigour (or lack thereof) of the universities' responses. As we see above, the University 2 administrator attributes an institutional response they admit was inadequate to the presumption of the perpetrators' innocence, while the University 4 administrator indicates that this presumption directed them towards an "educational" response.

It is important to clarify that my goal here is not somehow the inverse of the administrators' – that is, to insist on the perpetrators' *lack* of innocence. While it is unlikely that the perpetrators had no idea whatsoever that their blackface humour was risqué and would have caused offence, it is also beside the point. We have already seen that antiblackness is deeply embedded in Canadian national narratives and profoundly constitutive of white humour and pleasure (Chapter 2) and that the university itself is implicated in the production of blackface (Chapter 5). Therefore, to participate in the project of simply assigning individual blame would be to participate in, and settle for, the tactics typical of the university, which divert attention from institutional, societal, and systemic antiblackness and militate against change at those levels. Instead, my goal is to highlight the discourses and structural logics that produces universities' typical, unproductive, responses to blackface, and that renders more nuanced responses impossible. Where administrators so enthusiastically embrace the notion of idiosyncratic naivete located in random ignorant individuals, it is no surprise that the institutional response is driven by what I will call the pedagogical imperative.

The Pedagogical Imperative

The pedagogical imperative refers to the overdetermined ways in which the universities in this study, as educational institutions, claimed to be duty-bound in the wake of blackface incidents to respond with narrowly conceived educational efforts. This sense of obligation is clear from the words of a University 5 administrator:

> This is a university. This is a teaching institution. And one of the reasons that the students are here is that they don't know that [i.e., that blackface is provocative] already. They are here to learn, and we are here to provide an environment in which they can learn as safely as possible. (U5A1)

Similarly, a University 4 administrator explains: "For us, it was clear right off the bat: in the short term, it's crisis management, but in the direction of education, not in the direction of punishment. So, on that we were very firm" (U4A2). A University 3 administrator says: "I am really mindful of [University 3's] commitment to restorative justice and learning because I think when it becomes a penalistic, punitive, shaming then we further isolate and alienate our students who most need to learn" (U3A1).

These comments represent the administrators' tone across the multiple sites of this study. The logic is extremely seductive. How else ought a university respond, if not to educate? However, as I shall argue below, this educational response does not stand on its own but rather is informed by the ways in which universities are positioned within the Canadian settler-colonial nation state and its relationship to Blackness. This context produces the ways in which (1) the pedagogical intervention comes to be seen as one focused on a few misguided individuals; (2) the needs of these individuals, including their ostensible safety (but from what?), become top priority to the disregard of the needs of other students, particularly Black students; and (3) other possible responses that might involve greater accountability – particularly those that make the university accountable – are constructed as punitive, unsafe (for the perpetrators), antithetical to the pedagogical imperative, and therefore to be ruled out. On this, the University 2 administrator tells us more:

> There is a sense in which [we can say] that our society doesn't punish people immediately. Like we do give people a chance to say, "God, I made a terrible mistake. I will never make it again, and don't throw me out," kind of thing. And I think that is certainly the kind of approach we would want to take. But we come to universities to be educated. It's a part of what it's all about. (U2A1)

This excerpt can only be read as a fantastic, revisionist account of Canadian society and its schools, or at least as a perspective firmly situated in dominant racial and class experiences. It is glaringly disconnected from the experiences of Black people (as well as of Indigenous, racialized, poor, and migrant people in all their intersections) who are constantly under surveillance, punished, and incarcerated without even necessarily having made a "mistake." Therefore, in relief, it shows us the way in which an ethic of latitude and opportunity for reform comes to the fore when particular groups (by which I mean largely those who are white, middle class, and often, but not exclusively, male) offend, and particularly when those harmed by their offences are not bourgeois white people (by which I mean usually Black, Indigenous, and racialized people, but also often those who are women, sexual and gender minorities, and/or people with disabilities of all racial locations). The pedagogical imperative is thus laid bare as one constituted of this ethic. It seeks to give perpetrators an opportunity to "return" to innocence from racial offence. The University 3 administrator adds more about the urgency of this pedagogical imperative:

> When it becomes a penalistic, punitive, shaming then we further isolate and alienate our students who most need to learn. So by empowering them to say, "Yes, we didn't make a good choice, [it] wasn't our intention" – which often in my experience [it] has not been their intention to have the impact that it has had – and to work with them to make sure they are better educated and more aware so that they can be better leaders and role models and further educate the people that they are connected with in their networks to avoid similar mistakes. So that has been the approach. (U3A1)

The pedagogical imperative, then, becomes a way of producing the white innocence that has already been presumed. Notably, it is not a mechanism for assigning individualized innocence contingent upon an examination of the particulars of the situation. Rather, it is the mechanism by which to operationalize a broad presumption of racial innocence, independent of the details but based primarily on the (often male) perpetrators' whiteness.

Particularly troubling is the way in which, despite their behaviour – whether deliberate or naive – these white perpetrators are positioned as always already leaders whose paths to being recognized as such are at risk of being derailed by an ostensibly trivial incident. The pedagogical intervention, then, and its project of redeeming blackface perpetrators as innocent, responds to what is perceived as a pressing need to reconfirm white students in their presupposed status as leaders. The interests of perpetrators become quickly prioritized, making them those "who most need to learn." Then these interests are met through the pedagogical imperative, which students, after they have benefited from them, will be able to participate in by "further educating the people in their networks [i.e., other ontologically innocent white people] to avoid similar mistakes." The pedagogical imperative therefore offers a process whereby the perpetrators are able to reclaim their birthright to social power through claiming innocence.

A similar approach was taken in the case of a London, Ontario, police constable who was discovered to have dressed in blackface many years earlier. The London police chief, analogous to university administrators, appeared in media on the constable's behalf, announcing that she would be required to undergo "racial sensitivity training" but also reconfirming her leadership status and legitimacy as a police officer by stating that she had "in her nearly two years with the force ... shown herself to be an excellent police officer and highly engaged in the community" (CBC News, 2018). In a public apology letter, read by the police chief on her behalf, she pledges to take "training on cultural sensitivity, racism, bias stereotypes and the negative impacts of the same" but also to "look for opportunities to participate in internal training of London Police Service members so that other members of the London Police Service may recognize the importance of such a powerful subject" (CBC News, 2018). In this case, as at the universities, the process of confirming innocence and reinstating leadership through the pedagogical imperative is so complete when it is over that the perpetrators become *better* leaders who can now *also* claim credentials to teach others about the problems with blackface, "cultural sensitivity, racism," and so on. The pedagogical imperative allows perpetrators to smoothly transition from being uninformed to being enlightened, and their engagement with antiblackness becomes renarrated through the process as grounds for credible cosmopolitan leadership. Race offenders thereby become race experts in the postracialist state.

The pedagogical imperative, and how it is produced at the university, makes sense within the context of Canada, where national subjectivities take on a particular form. As Thobani (2007, p. 5) explains, in the national imagination the Canadian nation state is understood as possessing particular human qualities, which are then reflected back, in a process Thobani calls exaltation, onto the ideal national subject (always presumed white). Reciprocally, this white subject embodies these characteristics, which come of belonging to the nation. Thobani argues that these exalted human subjects are understood to be hard-working builders of the nation, who are also "law-abiding ... responsible ... compassionate, caring, and committed to the values of diversity and multiculturalism" (p. 4) but whose benevolence is at risk of being taken advantage of by Indigenous people and racialized migrants. Institutions within the nation are instrumental in this process of exaltation and the hailing of the national subject (p. 8).

Though Thobani's framework does not specifically account for the unique location of Black people in relation to Canada, it does make the university's pedagogical responses to blackface legible. As an institution of the nation state with an educational mandate, the university, I suggest, regards its students as national subjects in the making. The university's mandate, then, is to bring to full fruition the exalted qualities of these young diamonds in the rough, confirming them as the good, egalitarian subjects they must truly be, and who possess the innocence that comes with these claims. Further, within the context of racial capitalism in the settler state, the university also serves to produce and legitimize as leaders whose ostensible birthright it is to lead the nation, advance its interests, and to police the Indigenous, Black, and racialized others who might contest settler futurity and the racial, antiblack order.

These are the structures that bring the pedagogical imperative so forcefully into play in the wake of blackface incidents. The university sees blackface perpetrators as otherwise innocent (white) Canadian youth caught in a less-than-glamorous moment, and whose true character is threatened by Black people whose protests call into question their suitability as egalitarian, multiculturalist leaders. Yet since blackface is presumed to be nothing more than innocent, individualized youthful ignorance, this threat can easily be addressed through awareness-raising education, in a logic consistent with liberal individualist educational paradigms. Once awareness has been raised, the perpetrators will no longer be ignorant, will presumably not reoffend, and will now be back on track towards assuming their rightful places as products of the more enlightened university community and, more importantly, beyond that as leaders in/of the nation. One can therefore read the pedagogical imperative as a form of reparation and restoration for white perpetrators that propels them further into the privileges of leadership for which they are presumed to be ontologically poised. The pedagogical imperative is dedicated to making presumptive leaders into "better" leaders – "better" because they are assumed to now understand racism, but also have witnessed first-hand how to manage Black others. They are "better," perversely, in and through their participation in antiblackness.

The Pedagogical Imperative as Disregard of Black People

The pedagogical imperative is only part of the broader ways in which the universities' antiblack institutional structures serve the interests of whiteness, and therefore become preoccupied with the ostensible needs of white students after blackface incidents. At University 4, an administrator describes the climate at the university and in its student services office just after a blackface incident:

> And then there is a bunch of students in distress, meaning that they are scared; they don't understand anything anymore, and they don't know what to do. And we have the people who are in student services who are in distress. "What should I do? What should we do? How do we help them? Will we need to have psychologists in?" (U4A1)

In this statement, the students in distress are not, as one might otherwise imagine, Black students who have had to face the violence of blackface. Rather, the student affairs office is overwrought with the needs of the white perpetrators of blackface. The challenge that perpetrators felt to their sense of impunity and entitlement when their very public performance of blackface was identified as antiblackness – the very dissonance that might lead to meaningful learning about antiblackness – is narrated as distress. The perpetrators' distress then easily becomes the institution's distress as it rushes to ensure that these white students are supported in managing personal discomfort and the threat to their reputations. The sense of urgency and frenzy with which the university and its services respond in support of the blackface perpetrators is palpable in the excerpt above.

A University 1 administrator describes a similar instance in which student services rushes to support a blackface perpetrator facing accusations of racism:

> You know this person by this point was really upset and putting forward a lot of innocence about not knowing that this was inappropriate and that kind of thing. Because by that time the incident had taken off, and activists on campus had started huge social media campaigns against this person, and had outed them, and were running around campus with posters of them with their name on it. And so the respondent was terrified about what was taking place and felt that of course they were being hard done by – that kind of thing. Mind you, the way people found out about it was because [the perpetrator] had brazenly posted the picture on their own Facebook page. But it was getting out of hand from their perspective.

So ... we spoke to them about what blackface was and what it symbolized, and how it affected people. So that is typical for our office. It wasn't enough for example, for the activist community that was involved in dealing with it, and so they found their own means of dealing with it. But that's what we did in that particular case. (U1A3)

In this instance, the perpetrator repositioned themself as victim, and sought out the support of this student services office. The office obliged, directing its resources to serving and assuaging this person who had, in fact, perpetrated antiblackness. The evident corollary is that it did not meet the needs of Black students, who in this excerpt remain deeply unsatisfied with the university's response.

That this office took on the needs of white students while failing to respond to the needs of Black students becomes more poignant when we consider that this particular office at University 1 has an explicit equity mandate[1] and, like similar offices at many universities, nominally exists to address the needs of racialized and other students from marginalized groups. Yet, as part of the institutional structure of the university, it is unable to resist prioritizing white perpetrators' needs after a racist incident, when one would suppose that its services should rather support racialized students harmed by the incident. Nonetheless, as this administrator tells us, this kind of response is typical of their office.

To be fair, this redirecting of equity services does not go unchallenged even within these offices. In some instances, the staff within these offices included people from historically oppressed groups – including Black and racialized people – who in their conversations with us were cautiously critical of the way this institutional dynamic structured their work.[2] They recognized the ways in which these "restorative justice" measures were not at all that. Universities via their administrators generally claimed in our interviews to be supportive of Black students in the context of blackface. However, the ways in which they describe what actually happens on the ground suggest that whatever concern the university might claim to have about Black distress gets completely displaced by concerns about ostensible white distress. Ultimately, this

1 All the offices in which the administrators we spoke to worked declare commitments to equity and diversity. This office at University 1 is only different to the extent that its name and mandate claim to be explicitly committed to equity.
2 In at least one instance, Black and racialized people in these offices were actually prohibited by their white supervisors from speaking with us.

translates into a disregard for Black people's welfare, and a structurally produced indisposition to identify and respond to Black suffering. More importantly, it reveals the ways in which the liberal logics that undergird "equity" projects at universities default to antiblackness, and certainly do not envision Black freedom (Walcott & Abdillahi, 2019, p. 94). That Black people, given the university's abdication of responsibility, have to take things into their own hands if they want to see anything done is not understood as compounding Black suffering. And should Black students' interventions at this point take unfortunate directions (which the administrator implies may have happened at University 1, though I found no evidence of it in my research), this is often understood through the lenses of rule-breaking and aggression, rather than as a function of Black students' distress and the inadequate support available to them.

But of course Black people are distressed by blackface, and this distress is exacerbated by the universities' missing or inadequate responses. Jackie, a Black faculty member, describes what this looked like at University 2 after a blackface incident:

> The Black students on campus ... were fairly disturbed about it ... The university administration was asked to respond. It was brought to their attention. I don't believe any response was forthcoming ... my memory is that the University itself never came out with a very clear and strong categorical statement rejecting blackface, talking about the need for inclusion, et cetera, et cetera ... You really could have gotten a sense of the real despair and anger on the part of Black students and their allies ... I don't think the university spoke out or took the lead on this as you would imagine they should if they are advocating on behalf of students, faculty, and staff who have experienced or been injured by incidents of racism. (U2F1)

When we cross-referenced these remarks, we discovered that, indeed, the university never made a public statement condemning the blackface incident, nor did it express any commitment to foster an equitable climate for Black students. But this kind of statement appears to be what Black students across the sites in this study expected from their institutions. Miremba at University 1 has this expectation, and expresses disappointment in her university administration's failure to come forward:

> There's not that environment where someone would go to the administration and say, okay, this and this happened. I feel like that space hasn't been created by the administration. And even when [a racist incident] happens, I feel like there's this idea that because we're a minority it doesn't warrant

administrative action. Like, if something like this was to happen [again] I know for a fact that the president wouldn't come out and give a comment on it or something like that … no one feels they need to say something about it. (U1BSOFGP2)

Miremba feels her university makes no effort to be attentive to the concerns of Black students. For her, the university's disregard of Black people is reflected in its refusal to make even nominal statements that express disapproval of blackface.

The reluctance to categorically and publicly denounce blackface in partial response to the demands of Black students is directly related to the duty the university feels to white perpetrators and the resulting pedagogical imperative. So, for example, when we asked one administrator to comment on their refusal to issue a statement, they told us:

This is a really awkward position for me to be in because I would like to have the message that these types of events do not line up with the values at our university. And we are really pleased to be working with the students engaged in learning to mitigate this happening in the future. But I don't want to go on record to say all the reasons why these students screwed up, because I need them to work with me to make it better and I'm going to have more success at that if they don't feel like I'm throwing them under the bus in public. (university number withheld to maintain confidentiality)

This administrator displays that they are most invested in, and most proud of, the pedagogical imperative – the fact that they are "working with the students engaged in learning" – and therefore that, for them, making a statement that condemns the incident (which of course need not mean condemning the perpetrators) cannot happen because it would ostensibly interfere with the pedagogical imperative. In the end, this university also never made a statement, though in the events surrounding this incident the perpetrators repeatedly pushed back in public to insist that what they had done was reasonable and should have been allowed to continue – a context of which the administrator was fully aware. With the reputation of the university at stake because of the complaints of vocal alumni, this administrator did, however, follow through with sanctions aimed at the offending students.

At University 2, an administrator similarly resists a public statement, saying:

So yes, we [administrators] agreed [in private meetings with Black people on campus] it was racist. So then the question is, "Okay, what do you do by coming out and saying, 'Well that was racist' and whatever?" The kids knew when they were told about it; they apologized profusely. They realized they really screwed up here and that indeed what they had done was racist. They got it. They understood that. So do you make it more than that, when the students themselves truly understood after they had been given quite a lot of talking to about why this was so inappropriate?

Here again, with a focus so squarely and exclusively upon what individual perpetrators are learning, the university disregards Black people's calls for it to affirm its nominal commitment to fostering a campus climate that is equitable. For them, all the necessary work is done if the perpetrators (and apparently only the perpetrators) "get it." To go further to make a public statement that would reach a broader audience and announce the disapproval of blackface would, that university claims in private, be overkill. Furthermore, in this instance, the apologies that the perpetrators are said to have made were apparently made to the administration behind closed doors, if at all. The university never required the perpetrators to apologize to Black people on campus, either in person or in writing, publicly or in private.

Most would agree that blackface is towards the lower end of the scale of the always egregious kinds of antiblack violence that Black people routinely experience at the university. As Donovan suggested to us in the previous chapter, it is a topic on which individual white persons can, at little cost to themselves or the status quo, make a good show of being anti-racist. I am therefore not positing these kinds of statements, despite students' desires for them, as an adequate or sufficient response to blackface and antiblackness. Nevertheless, that it is as difficult as it is to get universities to make categorical statements denouncing blackface seems to gesture towards the fundamental ways that Canadian universities exclude Black people by default. It is a manifestation of the foundational contradiction for Canadian universities as educational institutions within an antiblack, settler-colonial nation state. How will they denounce antiblackness while they are charged with teaching white students to know Canada as innocent, and to know themselves as exalted, rational, egalitarian Canadian leaders in relief against Black, Indigenous, and other racialized persons?

Attenuating Black Anger

The university administration's approach to Black people after blackface incidents is not limited to disregard. Indeed, above where administrators at Universities 1, 3, and 5 speak about frightened perpetrators and providing "safe places to learn," they take up the discourse of safety in its usual antiblack expressions, requiring that we attend to whose safety is being considered and at whose expense. In this instance, it is clear that Black people subjected to blackface are illegible to the university's systems as those who might be in distress, and are not understood as those whose safety the university should guarantee. Rather, Black people are understood as potentially violent aggressors who *cause* distress and unsafety for innocent white perpetrators.

Ultimately, then, Black people or the presence of Black people, rather than antiblackness, becomes the problem that must be solved. This logic is evident in administrators' understandings of where the problem with blackface starts. A University 2 administrator tells us:

> When I was growing up, a long, long time ago, we had minstrel shows on TV. Like it was – and people loved it – on public television! You watched blackface singing and dancing. So if kids grow up in parts of this province where their families may also have lived through experiences like that without ever, ever understanding that that actually is racist ... We're pretty sophisticated communities in universities, and we're also in incredibly diverse areas. And it does lead to you having a deeper understanding of the impact of something on others, which doesn't occur if you go to other parts of Canada. You do not see racialized groups walking on the sidewalks [there]. ... So if you have grown up where there may have been very, very few racialized students in your class ... it's not surprising to me that indeed kids have never been exposed to the impact of their behaviour before. I'm sure in some communities in Canada if somebody dressed in blackface nobody would care, right? ... Here it matters, and part of our job is to explain why it matters.

Though this administrator now claims to understand that blackface is a problem, and that it should be discouraged in a "diverse area" like their university, their identification with a moment and a space where blackface was accepted as just harmless fun, juxtaposed with their understanding of where blackface "matters," displays an underlying logic that makes the presence of Black and other racialized people the source of the problem. Since there are (presumably white) communities past and present where no one would find anything wrong with blackface, embedded antiblackness becomes innocent ignorance. The problem is not understood to be Canada's default antiblackness across its expanse, nor is it understood to be that in the absence of Black people this antiblackness goes unchallenged. Blackface (only) becomes a problem "here" in a "diverse area" because Black people are "here." If we weren't, apparently there would be no need for intervention. Therefore Black presence and Black responses to antiblackness are what produce racial conflict.

The onus is then apparently on Black people at the university to commiserate with blackface perpetrators who are presumed to be hailing from these white areas where antiblackness is normative, while other people learn at their expense. Apparently Black people should likewise be patient with the universities' deficient responses that flow from rushing to protect, create safety for, and recuperate whiteness. Problems only arise where Black people are not willing to be "understanding" in this way. The University 2 administrator demonstrates this disposition where they say:

> Our [Black] community, though, were not thrilled. They felt that we did not respond as promptly or as vigorously as we should have done and so we did get a fair number of complaints … And so as [an administrator], I had to endure – and I think that is probably the right word – a number of quite heated and difficult discussions with individuals who came to see us and discuss their deep concern…. In retrospect … we probably should have come out a little more strongly at the beginning to denounce this. On the other hand we just felt that it was kids being stupid, that there wasn't an underlying aspect of racism.

This administrator communicates that they consider Black people themselves to be unreasonable by stressing that dealing with Black concerns was a burden to be "endured" (a choice of term they emphasized) rather than, say, a moral obligation flowing from an institutional commitment to equity. Black people are constructed as heated or angry – even violent. They cause fear, and therefore this anger must be attenuated – either by the Black people themselves, or by the administration.

An administrator at University 5 also represents this demand on Black people to tolerate antiblackness and attenuate their anger, as they reflect on the conversations on their campus after a blackface incident:

> So I can be angry and outraged about someone's behaviour or their actions or their discourse but if I approach them with that anger forward then I am encouraging them to harden their position. If I hold that anger and I assume that until I have evidence of the contrary that they are not malicious in what they are doing and I ask them, "Why are you doing that?" or "Here is my position on this. What is your position?" If I tell them there is a problem here and here is why I think it's a problem and here is how I think you can be part of the solution, in the vast majority of cases I find,

and I think you will find, that people are on board with being part of the solution. ... So yes, that outrage ... motivates my approach to them but it can't define my approach to them.

As this administrator presumes to place themself in Black people's shoes, their message can be read as a call for a particular kind of civility – where being "civil" places deeply antiblack demands on the Black person to ignore the socially embedded antiblack foundations that make a blackface act possible in the first place, and therefore to withhold outrage in the interest of the pedagogical imperative. It also suggests that if change does not occur, it is because Black people have taken the wrong approach. The institution's duty to change (if it is to claim to be equitable) is displaced onto Black people.

A version of this call for Black people to attenuate their anger that superficially appears more benevolent, but is equally pernicious, is evident where a University 1 administrator says:

I also support, and try to support, students to have the right to the feelings that they should have around this, and help them sort out how to manage those feelings in a productive way ... who can they talk to to vent about this, as opposed to what often happens, which is what we're dealing with right now: I may just go on Facebook and talk about this, how awful it was, and how racist this person was. Then it becomes this huge, polarizing, very hurtful explosive thing on Facebook. Which they have a right to do that, but as adults here and trying to help them figure out ... how do you manage that impact in your feelings in a way that doesn't make you even more unsafe with the choices that you make in terms of dealing with this. And there's often times this feeling that the university needs to expel them from the university. We can't expel someone for – You know, and it's trying to manage messaging without sounding – we're not minimizing this, but we also have to go through a process where we are giving people the opportunity to learn something from this in a meaningful way. (U1A5)

This administrator claims this response to be one that is protective of Black people. However, it is no less a call for Black people to attenuate their anger in the interest of white perpetrators' education, and still understands Black people as calling for punitive action rather than for a response that considers their security – indeed their humanity – first, and that then, secondarily, might also be potentially pedagogical.

While as I will argue later, Black anger is in no need of justification under these circumstances, it is worth pointing out the simple fact that in no instance covered by this research were Black people calling for punitive measures. Rather, in addition to calls they made for public statements from the university, concerning measures that might be focused on individuals, some Black students would have liked to see perpetrators made accountable for their behaviour and for learning in some way. This might be by making a public apology and/or speaking publicly about what they have learned since the incident (such as in a class, a public performance, or a student newspaper). However, most felt responses focused on a few individuals considered exceptional rather than on the university community as a whole were futile. Instead, they called for measures that, in fact, do not or only peripherally involve the perpetrators. Understanding that antiblackness is embedded in the institution and that blackface is in many ways produced by the institution, they called for educational opportunities for the entire university community, and/or they called for institutional change to address the more persistent and less episodic conditions of antiblackness in the university (such as addressing the under-representation of Black faculty, staff, and students and the marginalization of Black knowledge at the university). Together, these broader asks attempt to establish a community norm against blackface, to rupture the denial of antiblackness and systemic racism, and to hold the university accountable for its own antiblackness.

These measures that Black people in the study are calling for can be distinguished from initiatives, which have become more popular in the years since I started investigating blackface, that implement antiblackface training in first-year orientation activities, in residence halls, or before Halloween. Much like the pedagogical interventions with perpetrators after an incident, these latter initiatives are still based on the construct of the ignorant incoming student who needs to be initiated into the otherwise egalitarian university, and they address blackface as though it can be considered apart from the university's constitutive antiblackness.

The call to attenuate Black anger and the general disregard of Black people's reactions to blackface are informed by the illegibility of Black concerns in the national context. This reaction to Black anger is consistent with the terms of the settler-colonial nation state and how Black people are presumed to be located within it. In the settler terms of the Canadian nation state and its exalted subjects, it is white people of British and French ancestry who are industrious, deserving, and benevolent. Under these terms Indigenous people are undeserving because they presumably did and do not know how to make the land productive, and so had nothing to do with making the bustling nation state what it is. Simultaneously, through the active erasure of the long Black presence in Canada, Black people are always framed solely as recent immigrants (Walcott, 2003b, p. 43) who benefit from the largesse of the nation state and its people, and who are therefore takers and not contributors. If "the only good immigrant [is a] supplicant to the nation" (Thobani, 2007, p. 252), Black critiques of the nation state and its "true citizens" – particularly with respect to antiblackness – are understood as ungrateful, unreasonable, and always asking for more. Under these conditions, what is valued by the state, its institutions, and in dominant discourse is the attenuation of Black anger or indignation, if there is any room for it to exist in the first place. We see an example in the case of former Montreal Canadiens hockey player P.K. Subban. Subban has frequently been the subject of blackface incidents (CBC News, 2015; Petchesky, 2010; QMI Agency, 2014) as well as other expressions of racism. In an instance in which (American) hockey fans tweeted offensive comments containing racist epithets about Subban, a Canadian news reporter, speaking in concert with Subban's teammates, writes:

> "He handles it really well. He's a professional. He understands that the best way to handle it is to ignore it and to understand that their opinions don't really mean anything." … Subban's self-composure, at least in this context, shows the measure of the man. … "It says a lot about him as a person … The fact he's able to just shake it off and go along with his life. It doesn't really affect him too much, and it shouldn't." (DiManno, 2014)

The reporter admits that Subban had "every right to be angry" (and perhaps the forthrightness of this claim is not unrelated to the fact that the perpetrators in this case were Americans and not Canadians), but also that Subban himself was mostly silent on the matter, saying only, "I don't know. It doesn't even matter." Whatever his motives in not speaking out – motives that it is reasonable to presume are self-protective – Subban's attenuation of his anger is highly praised as *the* fitting response to antiblackness. The reporter concludes that "in Subban's silence Friday there was a certain eloquence. Yet also, I think, an unspoken sorrow. What can he say?" Indeed, what can Subban say within these constraints that can be heard without risking his reputation as a model Canadian of Black migrant origins? He is lauded for choosing to suffer silently and to attenuate his anger.

The call for the attenuation of Black anger at blackface is not unusual in the context of unequal social relations or in education. Sara Ahmed (2012) reminds us that positioning Black and racialized people as angry in the context of the university serves as a defensive strategy against the accusation of racism by suggesting that we "talk about racism because we are angry, rather than being angry because of racism" (p. 159). Additionally, in an article exploring the role of emotions in education, Michalinos Zembylas (2007) observes that despite the variety of historical approaches to anger in the West, they all view anger as fundamentally irrational, as dysfunctional, as uncivil, as always needing to be managed, even where anger might be considered justified (pp. 16–17). Drawing on a number of contemporary anger theorists, Zembylas reminds us that anger cannot be understood apart from the nexus of power relations in which it occurs. Zembylas identifies educational initiatives dependent upon calls to manage anger or express it "appropriately" as dominant moves to silence the oppressed in the face of their oppression (pp. 19–20). Thus, whether these calls are unapologetically racist (as with the administrator at University 2) or presumed benevolent (as with one of the administrators at University 1), framing Black anger as a problem needing to be managed is exposed as a pure expression of dominant power in the service of the status quo. The demands made upon Black people to attenuate their anger in the face of injustice are shot through with the politics of antiblackness that make Blackness always the foil against which civility and rationality are defined. This is entirely consistent with the educational mission of the settler-colonial university as discussed in Chapter 5.

Black Anger and Pedagogy

As we have seen from administrator responses above, the anger of those Black members of the university community who object to blackface is read as aggression – distress-causing, fearful, punitive, and as forestalling a particular pedagogy. Black people note the double bind this places them in, as in an instance (not directly related to blackface) in which students had met with administrators at the University of Toronto to demand it collect race-based data about its community. Drawing on one students' reflections, a *Toronto Star* article reports:

> Barriers remain, including tension between student groups and administrators. "We felt as if they were scared of us. That was the aura in the room," said Khogali. "That's problematic if we want to work to implement policies of equity that improve the entire quality of life for everyone in the institution." (Reynolds, 2016)

Even in this instance where the administration agreed that the labour that Black students were engaging in was an integral intervention for the sake of equity across the board at the university, the students left the table feeling as though they were seen as little more than aggressors.

But make no mistake: the Black people in this study were definitely angry about blackface, and the broader forms of antiblackness they face in their universities. I make no attempt to claim otherwise. Thus, my concern is with the ways in which university administrators, in their institutional roles, consider Black anger instead of white antiblackness to be the problem to be managed – a corollary to the ways in which they prioritize white innocence over Black distress when offering support. My objective in this final section of the chapter is to consider Black anger on Black terms, and beyond the routine antiblack terms with which it is regarded in the situations I have been describing. I take up the ways in which this Black anger is a pedagogy of its own, and a way to make Black life at university. However, unlike the pedagogical imperative, it does not seek to recuperate whiteness and reify a colonial order. Rather, it is a pedagogy that calls for radical transformation. I conclude by imagining, in the context of blackface, what might happen if universities' institutional processes could give way to Black anger with a view towards a broader pedagogical project of justice and the eradication of Black suffering.

I open this consideration through Audre Lorde's meditation on anger. Lorde speaks from her location as a Black lesbian, and so her insight into anger emerges out of a particular set of interlocking experiences with dehumanizing racialized, gendered, and sexualized power structures. Without losing sight of that specificity, we can also apply the principles more broadly to Black identities to the extent that Blackness as a whole is dehumanized and subject to wanton suffering.

In her 1993 chapter "The Uses of Anger" Lorde identifies, without romanticizing, the ways in which her anger as a Black woman has been a way of knowing: of knowing that which is deadly and threatens Black survival (p. 131), of knowing circumstances that would relegate us to the realms of the unhuman (p. 129), and, where necessary, of knowing who her potential allies might be (p. 127). Ultimately, Lorde understands Black anger that moves in this way as love for self and community (see also Zembylas, 2007, p. 23), as survival, and as a way to keep in view the concrete goal of ending Black suffering (p. 132; see also Dumas, 2018). Lorde's clear point is that Black anger is part of sustaining Black life; it is abandoned at our own peril. This Black anger is politically salient for signalling and contesting injustice, where silence in the face of injustice should be what is considered pathological (p. 129; Zembylas, 2007, p. 25). Lorde asserts, "My anger has meant pain to me but it has also meant survival, and before I give it up I'm going to be sure that there is something at least as powerful to replace it on the road to clarity" (p. 132). Lorde thus identifies Black anger as pedagogical, and as a way of knowing. Black anger, with its associated pedagogy, is a vital component in a project of Black survival, where survival is not just about existing. Black anger envisions Black freedom.

When considered from this vantage point, the institutional negation of Black anger through the call for its attenuation is an injunction against Black freedom, a demand that we not transform the terms of our existence, and a reification of the terms of our unfreedom. These effects are intensified where the demand to attenuate Black anger occurs alongside a demand to prioritize a kind of white learning that reifies postracialist white innocence. Lorde (1993) refuses the ways in which Black anger is legitimized only if it can be considered to be "in the service of other people's salvation or learning" (p. 132). This, of course, amounts to the kind of instrumentalization of Black being as resource to meet white needs that constitute slavery's afterlife. In sum, the call to attenuate Black anger and the accompanying pedagogical imperative are antiblack violence!

In the face of such violence we are brought back to Fanon (1961) and the violence that decolonization requires as a response. To understand the kind of Black anger that shows up in the wake of blackface as gesturing towards Black freedom is to identify it as disruptive, though Lorde (1993) distinguishes the disruptiveness of Black anger from the destructive wrath that emanates from hatred (p. 130) and from institutional/colonial power that seeks to annihilate (p. 131). Indeed, such anger is ontologically disruptive of these antiblack colonial structures. Black anger is constitutive of, and constituted by, the disruption of antiblack violence, and it refuses the dehumanization of Black people. Ultimately, then, the kind of Black anger that we see in contexts of blackface *is* violent on Fanonian terms whereby this violence is that which is necessary to interrupt conditions of colonial domination. And unsurprisingly, this is seen as threatening and unsafe by those who support and are otherwise invested in colonial conditions. Applying Fanon to notions of education and pedagogy, Leonardo and Porter (2010) posit that in contemporary postracialist conditions, the white fear response to Black anger arises not from a fear of physical violence as much as from a fear that attending to Black anger will expose white supremacy as ongoing, embedded into the rhythms of the "normal" life that whites want to understand as egalitarian, and will cause them to discover their deep personal investments in it (p. 150). While I would not so quickly dismiss a white fantasy of physical Black violence, I agree where Leonardo and Porter define the transformative potential of the knowledge produced by Black anger as "a humanizing form of violence ... a pedagogy and politics of disruption that shifts the regime of knowledge about what is ultimately possible as well as desirable" (p. 140).

Where Black anger is accepted on its own terms, where it is not coerced into the service of whiteness but where the pursuit of Black freedom is sufficient, it is also the case that its pedagogical salience reaches beyond what Black people can come to know from it. In other words, there is opportunity for white perpetrators and the university (as community and institution) to learn – paradoxically, where white learning is *not* the goal. So what might it look like if a university were to be able to sit with the reality of Black anger and engage its pedagogy in the context of blackface?

Such an approach would reject the attenuation of Black anger. Understanding the call for attenuation as a manifestation of the university's antiblack commitments, it would reject the accustomed appeals to innocence and for safe white learning. It would examine the affective economy under which Black anger with its liberatory potential becomes aggression while the pornotropic antiblack violence of blackface becomes innocent humour. Instead, an approach that takes Black anger seriously might permit perpetrators to face that anger, rather than shielding them from it. Attending to Black anger would allow perpetrators to come to realize their existence as racial beings as they discover that the very foundation of their humour and pleasure is antiblack. This learning might also be made available to the entire campus by way of categorical statements by the university denouncing blackface's antiblackness in response to the conditions that Black anger makes evident. Instead of addressing blackface in ways that participate in exalting the Canadian national subject (Thobani, 2007), blackface could be read as a site where the claim of this exaltation unravels, and therefore as one site from which to begin the dismantling of accustomed paths in favour of new ones.

And to be clear, such an exchange would not be a problematic airing of black pain for cannibalistic white learning – a dynamic that I have challenged elsewhere (Howard, 2006). Rather, it would be an opportunity to consider a counter-storying of blackface, different from dominant societal interpretations. In my research, I have found that in the absence of a university response in the aftermath of blackface, these kinds of learning settings and teach-ins (with Black people as their primary audience) are normally organized by Black university communities rather than by university administration, and that they produce the most meaningful outcomes for all parties, including perpetrators (see, e.g., Kyei et al., 2009; Powell, 2009).

Zembylas (2007) proposes the value of embracing subaltern anger in producing a form of what he calls "witnessing" – "a collectivised engagement in learning to see differently" and then "a call to action ... as a result of learning to see differently" (p. 26). Seeing differently would mean unsettling the seductive normalized discourses of educational mission, conciliation, and pacification as well as the antiblack foundations upon which they stand, redirecting towards what the university's pedagogical imperative ought really to be. Where Black anger is not considered something to endure and dismiss, Black anger considered in the context of institutional responses to blackface might be an opportunity for the university to understand its own foundational commitments to antiblackness, and how these are instantiated even through its structures that claim such names as "student services," "equity," and "human rights" by way of how it mobilizes its pedagogical mission. It should provoke contemplation of what might really be required to achieve Black freedom in the university, if that is indeed the goal. It should provoke an understanding of serving students that does not always already exclude Black people and make us who these "services" are protecting against. Engaging Black anger will make clear that change is much bigger than just stopping or covering up blackface, but extends to the ways that the university conceives and operationalizes its mission.

Ultimately, taking Black anger seriously puts the university in a place where it has a choice between maintaining its colonial character or engaging an educational agenda that seeks justice, decolonization, and Black freedom. Indeed, such a mode of engagement takes up Walcott and Abdillahi's (2019, p. 91) provocation of a Black Test: one that evaluates university actions based on whether they make the conditions of Black life better. This, of course, constitutes a thorough upheaval of everything that the university is and has been to date, such that quite simply the university would become unrecognizable in beautiful new ways. Therefore proposing it here joins with other scholars' call to a radical imagining of a Black future at the university (Dumas, 2018, p. 43). That the university as institution is not currently up to that task is entirely clear (Kelley, 2016b). Whether some university administrators, and indeed other members of the university community, might decide in favour of becoming co-conspirators with Black people and take up this charge to work within and against the university remains to be seen.

7 Learning to Get Along at School, or Antiblack Postracialism through Multicultural Education

This chapter shifts attention away from the university site to consider antiblackness in pedagogies used in state education in the years before university. It is based on the conversations we had with students during interviews and focus groups about whether and how pre-university schooling and/or the absence of particular pedagogies might be implicated in the occurrence of blackface and other forms of antiblackness at university. The experiences participants share suggest that antiblackness is instantiated in pre-university public schooling through the absence of critical forms of education, but also through specific pedagogies I will refer to here broadly as post-racism,[1] multicultural education – a particular way of approaching issues of Blackness and racial diversity in Canadian schools.

I discuss these forms of education, and participants' experiences with them, alongside the longer histories of multicultural education and Black education in Canada to argue that these pedagogies serve as a seduction into post-racism thinking, are informed by the hegemonic context of Canadian multiculturalism and its antecedents, and are the legacy of the characteristic antiblackness of education in Canada. I conclude that these pedagogies foster rather than prevent appropriative behaviour, including blackface, and that they attempt to render Black students apathetic to antiblackness by undermining their embodied and community knowledges. I also argue that the continued existence

---

1 In this chapter, I distinguish between *post-racism* – a spurious claim, made particularly in Canada, to have transcended racism – and the closely related but different notion *postracialism*, which refers to the mechanisms that perpetuate racism precisely through the claim to be beyond race and racism, that is, through claims to post-racism (Goldberg, 2015).

of these pedagogies in the 2010s and beyond is consistent with a pattern whereby Canadian education systems resist and forestall radical Black educational thought and initiatives. The chapter concludes with a call for safeguarding spaces of Black counter-knowledges and educational activism.

Teaching Post-Racism: Omission, Commission, and Multicultural Education

In the 1980s and 1990s, in the wake of the 1982 Canadian Charter of Rights and Freedoms, there was a brief time during which ministries of education across Canada were at least naming racism, and "developing policies and processes to 'review curriculum and learning to ensure that they are free of racial, ethnic, cultural, gender, and socio-economic bias'" (Joshee, 2004, p. 145). Though we know that policy-writing on its own is non-perfomative (Ahmed, 2006), this moment seemed promising in that it was naming racism and promising to implement anti-racism. In Ontario specifically, a thrust towards anti-racism education was institutionalized by the Ontario New Democratic Party (NDP) government in the 1990s, and regulated by the Ministry of Education's Policy Program Memorandum (PPM) 119 (1993), *Development and Implementation of School Board Policies on Antiracism and Ethnocultural Equity*. When the government changed hands in 1995 to the Progressive Conservative Party of Ontario, it scrapped both the Anti-Racism Secretariat and the Ministry of Education's Anti-Racism, Access and Equity Division established by the NDP (Dei, 2003, p. 3). The dismantling of efforts to address racism in/through education in Ontario mirrored similar moves across the country as Canadian education became increasingly impacted by the logics of neoliberalism. However, PPM 119 remained on the books in Ontario, though in many school jurisdictions it was unenforced and therefore became dormant. This remained the status quo, even after the government changed hands again to the Ontario Liberal Party in 2003.

In 2009, largely as a result of lobbying by the Equity Summit Group, a collective of school board equity consultants, PPM 119 was revised and renamed *Equity and Inclusive Education in Ontario Schools*. This equity strategy was ostensibly intended to revive the lagging focus on social justice in education in Ontario, while broadening the scope of PPM 119 to address other forms of structural inequity in addition to racism that had not been explicitly addressed in the original document.

Knowing this history (and similar histories in other provinces), and given that several of our respondents (from both Ontario and Quebec universities) attended school in Ontario within this era, we asked students who went to school in Canada whether they recall having received any kind of anti-racist education in their years before university, and / or any education that they felt might inform, even prevent, whether and how blackface occurs at university. The participants' answers starkly indicated that, for the most part, they had had nothing that would qualify as such. For example, among the Black respondents, Patrick at University 7 told us:

> I can't think of anything specifically that I've had in terms of anti-racist education K to 12. Maybe the closest thing, and again I can't really remember, would be some things in religion courses or world religion, where you talk about different religions around the world and respecting them differently and learning about them. But anything particularly anti-racist from K to 12 would have been non-existent. (U7S1)

More whimsically, a focus group of Black students at University 2 used humour to point to the dearth of this kind of education in their years before university. When asked about it, they responded with giggles and peals of laughter throughout the entire exchange:

> LANCE: Pardon? (*Interviewer begins to repeat, but is cut off*) No, that's the answer!
> INTERVIEWER: Oh! We were getting ready to elaborate.
> LANCE: That's the answer!
> SONJI: (*whispering*) It doesn't exist! (*at regular volume*) It'd be, like, "What? Anti-racism? Anti-what? What's this foreign – ?"
> LANCE: – foreign language? ... That word "equity" didn't exist in my high school. We didn't have any anti-racism or equity. (U2BSOFG)

Valerie in the same focus group adds, "I didn't get any education on anti-racism in high school. Not that I remember! ... We didn't have anything about equity-based or anti-racism stuff in my school before coming here, no." (U2BSOFGP2)

Non-Black students who participated in focus groups had much the same recollections. For example, white students said:

> We were never exposed to that. It was very Eurocentric. We were never exposed to that kind of learning. (U2FG1P7)

That's what I was going to say. In high school we don't really learn about this kind of stuff at all. (U2FG1P9)

Racial and ethnic education in high school ... even history and civics there wasn't a lot of discussion of race relations, and Canadian history was all about what those old white dudes did in [City 1], you know. (U1FG1P2)

These responses suggest that it was very rare for participants to have received any serious critical attention to matters of race, never mind Blackness, in their schooling and, in the context of this research, certainly nothing that might have mitigated participation in blackface.

However, to say that they received no critical education around race and Blackness in school is not the same as saying that they were not, in fact, schooled into a particular way of thinking about race, racism, and Blackness. For within this broader general climate of omission, and alongside a few accounts of educators teaching blatantly antiblack knowledge, the students did identify what amounted to a pedagogy in these matters that took a very particular form. Valerie at University 2 tells us:

I was multicultural chair at my student [council], and we had one multicultural day of the year. And all we really did, though, was we brought food and stuff from different cultures, and we had the different countries and their flags and stuff. And then we would have performances. But that's it. That's about it. (U2FGBSOP2)

What Valerie describes is a very common pedagogy in Canada, rooted in multiculturalism, that understands its educational objective to be that of fostering "cultural harmony" and that ignores racism and racialization. It characteristically understands those who are racialized as always already originating beyond Canada's borders (thus the focus on flags), and it views opportunities to share cultural practices, often pertaining to "food and festival," as the solution to cultural misunderstanding.

Ava at University 3 shares about her student club, which was similar:

I don't think I got any of that [kind of education] in my high school or my elementary school. I mean, we had like the STOP campaign when I was in elementary school – like Students Together Opposing Prejudice – but how do you really explain prejudice to ten-year-olds in a kind of way that they actually understand and take in? (U3FGP3)

In Ava's opinion, the club had minimal impact, which she attributed to a faulty premise that younger children cannot understand systemic inequity. However, what appears more important is that the club stopped at notions of individual prejudice – similar to the focus on cultural harmony – and Ava indicates that she learned little about Blackness, antiblackness, racism, or structural oppression. Further, Ava did not speak of having experienced these more critical forms of education in later years when, presumably, students would have been more mature and the conversation might have been more sophisticated.

When asked about specific initiatives in her schooling, Sonji at University 2 tells us about assemblies, which she, like Ava, viewed as having minimal impact:

> It's the most ineffective education ever. … this is what they will do. Basically – I am trying to remember; I was there last year, it shouldn't be this hard – but maybe they will have one assembly that they will devote to every single diversity issue, and they will do it like once every two years or whatever. And so they will have the one assembly with teachers just standing there. … I went to a uniform school or whatever, so they will be like, "Come to school on time. Don't fight each other. Now wait, don't be a racist!" [Anti-racism education] doesn't really exist. And then that coupled with the fact that all we learn about is white people. It's kind of like a double negative. (U2FGBSOP3)

Sonji's account of these forgettable assemblies and the casual injunctions against racist behaviour indicates the marginal place that even these inadequate approaches to racism take within the school culture.

These excerpts suggest a number of things that were borne out across the interviews with students who had been educated in Canada (often Ontario) before coming to university. First, we see that these programs are superficial and mainly extracurricular and episodic rather than critical, within the curriculum, and sustained. They treat racism and antiblackness as being unworthy of substantive attention because they are presumed of little relevance in Canada, as we shall see. In other words, they largely take a post-racism approach. Second, they are largely student led, with teachers minimally involved. Sonji's observation that the teachers are "just standing there" at equity assemblies while students presented captures this uninterested, hands-off approach quite well. Third, it was evident that Black and other racialized students seemed to end up being primarily the ones to become involved in leading these kinds of initiatives. It appears that Black and racialized students seek out forms of learning at school about the racial terms of their lives, identities, and experiences, and/or that these students are guided towards these initiatives by schools. The programs available at school to respond to this kind of student need at best take an approach that translates antiblackness and racism into prejudice and bullying, and at worst exist to placate the students, as we shall see. That these initiatives are occasional, extracurricular, and student led (with a possible staff advisor) sends implicit messages to the students about their relative unimportance – a message students are able to recognize as such in retrospect, if not as they occur. The casual, superficial, extracurricular approach, and the ways that behavioural norms are enforced (as in: "Don't be racist!" is made to be of the same order as "Don't be late!" at Sonji's school), guide students towards dismissive, post-racism attitudes and away from substantive engagement with matters impacting the lives of Black students, as Sonji goes on to explain:

> I think, number one, people are like, "Yeah, yeah, don't be a racist? Everyone knows that, silly! Come on, now. I love all people!" But it's like we don't speak about what ingrained societal racism exists, and we don't speak about things like blackface and issues that are still there and derive from issues that happened long ago. (U2FGBSOP3)

That these kinds of approaches are inadequate ways of educating about and addressing racism and antiblackness is not new information. This has long been signalled by scholars in Canada in relation to similar pedagogies that have preceded it (e.g., Dei, 1996; James, 1995; Lee et al., 1998; Thomas, 1987). Rather, with reference to this book's engagement with blackface, what I am interested in here is how these students understand these pedagogies in relationship to blackface and other antiblack experiences in university. I reflect on what it might mean that these pedagogies persist in this post-racism form up to the contemporary moment, their impacts on Black students, and the importance of Black community-based initiatives in countering them.

Canadian Post-Racism Multicultural Education in Context: Historical Antecedents

The approaches to education that students describe cannot be fully understood without examining the contexts of their production. Though some bear the label "multicultural," they do not abruptly appear after multiculturalism became a dominant discourse in Canada. Rather, they are the legacy of a long educational trajectory developed in response to the cultural and linguistic diversity, and within the racist structures, that have always been endemic in Canada. Joshee (2004) locates the beginning of this kind of education prior to Canadian federation in an overtly assimilationist agenda initially to turn immigrants into "good" British citizens in North America, and later, after federation, into patri-. otic Canadians, while coaxing white Canadians to mingle with new immigrants to expedite the assimilation process (p. 135). This citizenship education was also developed to quell the radical influences of burgeoning labour and white feminist movements in the 1920s and 1930s, and to bolster support for Canadian war efforts among a diverse populace during the World War II years (p. 137).

The next iteration of this educational trend, now calling itself multicultural education, was an outcome of the 1963 Royal Commission on Bilingualism and Biculturalism (B&B Commission), which was struck partially to stabilize the nation state in response to rising Quebec nationalism by equalizing the places of English and French as "founding races" of Canada (Haque, 2012; Thobani, 2007; Walcott, 2014b). However, the B&B Commission's consultations brought to the fore the concerns of racialized and linguistic groups who were neither linguistically nor culturally French or English (even if they spoke French and/ or English), and who contested the fact that the bilingual/bicultural framework erased them. The federal government's subsequent 1971 Multiculturalism Policy was an effort to manage the demands of these groups. However, it did not undo the racializing effects of the bilingual/bicultural framework, but rather mystified the racial-colonial logics that undergird Canadian bilingualism and biculturalism that frame French and British whiteness as language, reframe colonization as "founding," and reconceptualize non-British, non-French "others" as belonging to the realm of culture – that is, intrinsic, immutable, cultural Otherness (Haque, 2012; Walcott, 2014b). Thus, multiculturalism and the multiculturalism education associated with it[2] came to have an emphasis on sharing culture but no substantive attention to Canada's histories of colonialism, antiblackness, and racism.

From this history, it becomes clear that the contemporary postracism, multicultural forms of education that students report experiencing in 2013–14 are rooted historically in conservative and

---

2 While education in Canada is governed at the provincial level, federal influence on this provincial jurisdiction was particularly deliberate in the areas of citizenship and multicultural education at this time (Joshee, 2004, p. 128), and thus multiculturalism education gained traction across Canada.

nationalistic efforts to manage racialized people and radicalism in Canada. Given these roots, they remain *counter to* goals of social and racial justice.

Multiculturalism: Harmony, Exchange, and Blackface

The students we spoke to were well aware of the ways in which the peculiar post-racism education they experienced is couched within dominant Canadian national narratives of post-racism multicultural-ism. A white student told us:

> I think there is a lot to be said about our public education system and the investment the government has in teaching all students that, like, Canada's so multicultural and, like, we don't have racism here. That's the image that we're supposed to consume. (U1FG1P3)

This student connects the post-race approach to racism (as that which everyone already understands, and that which is already past) to the national post-racism mythology of a peace-loving, egalitarian nation that Canada is invested in propagating. Sonji speaks of the same dis-course about Canada in specific reference to the ways it views Black people's relationship to the nation state:

> A lot of Black issues are kind of ignored especially in Canada, because in Canada since we didn't enslave people as long as our US counterparts and since there are less Black people and not really a climate for [plantation slavery] in Canada, racism is somehow less of an issue, a lower issue, for a lot of schools. So it is not taught, or it is not even aware [*sic*]. A lot of people are taught since we're multicultural, to ignore issues. (U2FGBSOP3)

Sonji too connects Canadian national identity – in this case, that it denies Canadian antiblackness or suggests that it is kinder and gentler – to the ways in which schools dismiss serious consideration of what Sonji calls Black issues.

In Chapter 3 we saw how Canada's national sense of post-racism egalitarianism flows from the dominant discourse of multiculturalism, as well as a mythical rendition of its relationship to Blackness. Here I look more closely at the Multiculturalism Act, the discourse it pro-motes, how these have shaped educational initiatives in Canada, and what this might have to do with blackface. Through the act, race is reframed as culture and culture as fungible. There are two mentions of race in the act, though notably none of racism. The first is in section 3(1) (a), which declares it the policy of the Government of Canada to "recognize and promote the understanding that multiculturalism reflects the cultural and racial diversity of Canadian society and acknowledges the freedom of all members of Canadian society to preserve, enhance and share their cultural heritage." In this clause, (an essentialist notion of) race – disconnected from social structures – is made analogous to (simplistic understandings of) culture, and both are subsumed under multiculturalism, much as we saw in some of the educational initiatives participants describe above.

The second mention is in section 5(1)(g), where the minister responsible for multiculturalism may "assist ethno-cultural minority communities to conduct activities with a view to overcoming any discriminatory barrier and, in particular, discrimination based on race or national or ethnic origin." Here, in addition to the conflation of race with ethnoculture, there is a clear absence of a reference to structural racism in favour of "discrimination based on race," with an implicit focus on individual interactions. The way in which this kind of discrimination is to be addressed is apparently through activities put on *by* "ethno-cultural minority communities" to address discrimination against themselves – activities that the minister assists but does not take responsibility for.

There is, of course, no specific attention to Blackness, and no mention of Canada's history of slavery or how its afterlife might produce unique "discriminatory barriers" for Black people in Canada. Instead, Blackness is subsumed under race, race is understood as culture, culture is understood as static (with a one-to-one relationship between "ethno-cultural" groups and "their" cultural heritage), and the act makes culture fungible – that is, a commodity to be shared and exchanged in the interest of social harmony. This is evident in several clauses of the Multiculturalism Act:

Section 3. (1) It is hereby declared to be the policy of the Government of Canada to:

- (*a*) recognize and promote the understanding that multiculturalism reflects the cultural and racial diversity of Canadian society and acknowledges the freedom of all members of Canadian society to preserve, enhance and *share* their cultural heritage;
- (*b*) recognize and promote the understanding that multiculturalism is a fundamental characteristic of the Canadian heritage and identity and that it provides an *invaluable resource* in the shaping of Canada's future;
- (*g*) promote the *understanding and creativity* that arise from the *interaction* between individuals and communities of different origins

Section 5. (1) The Minister ... may:

- (*c*) encourage and promote *exchanges* and *cooperation* among the diverse communities of Canada;
- (*e*) encourage the preservation, enhancement, *sharing* and evolving expression of the multicultural heritage of Canada (Government of Canada, 1985, all emphases added)

This logic – race as culture, culture as fungible – seems to be what informs the post-racism multicultural educational experiences that our participants describe having in their pre-university schooling. This was evident in Valerie's multicultural club with its food and flags, as it is where a white student at University 3 recounts:

> In my high school and my elementary school, frankly we did have a lot of integrative – not multicultural events; I wouldn't call them multicultural because "multicultural" has many implications – but where everyone brought in, from their own home, cultural things. And it wasn't whored-out culture. It was very authentic. They were saying, "This is what my family brought from this region or this place; this is what it means to me, to my family." (U3FGP5)

Interestingly, this participant tries to distance his experience from the label "multicultural" in a focus group conversation during which other participants were somewhat less sanguine about initiatives bearing that label. Nevertheless, what he describes participates clearly in a multicultural project of "sharing and exchange," as well as the logics that produce anyone who is not white of British or French heritage as always already a visitor, hailing from a home that is elsewhere.

Other participants in the study, however, argued that this multicultural tourism approach might not just be crudely reductionist but also actively produce hegemonic ways of thinking that have racist consequences. In a University 2 focus group, a student who identifies as Latinx observes:

> I feel like education is huge, especially when we're talking about like just the way – When I reflect on high school, elementary school – it was the best building ground for these kinds of racial tropes to come up. It was the oversimplified historical tropes. (U2FG1P2)

This student felt that their pre-university educational experiences in schools prior to university failed to support them as a Latinx student, and that these experiences inducted them into a post-racism thinking that might produce blackface. They build on this idea later with another participant:

> PARTICIPANT 8: I feel like that kind of basic "Oh, we are a mosaic, and Canada – " kind of multicultural education has no impact on [preventing racist behaviour] because you don't go into the history ... And it kind of just creates this image of, "we are all equal now, and we are all happy. So it doesn't matter if you appropriate other people's culture because we are all part of the same culture now and we belong to the same mosaic. And if you need to take pieces from somewhere else for a little while, well that's okay."
>
> PARTICIPANT 2: I really like that point. The multicultural stuff is like the perfect breeding ground, because you have a whole bunch of cultures in one room showing their costumes [sic], their food, without any political education, or knowledge, or the consciousness to respect one another.
>
> PARTICIPANT 8: Yeah, it's like if you wear your costume [sic], maybe I can wear your costume [sic] for a day too. (U2FG1)

These non-Black participants are speaking from experience. Both remember and regret having been involved in appropriative behaviour. Participant 8, who is white, admits to willingly being dressed up by her parents "as a Mexican convict" at age eight. Participant 2, Latinx, remembers dressing in a Halloween outfit with a "Rastafarian hat and fake dreads" while in high school. Similarly, a white participant at University 3 says: "I would wear a lot of costumes of traditional outfits of different cultures because I was very much interested in other cultures. But upon realizing how offensive [it was], I stopped that immediately" (U3FGP1). These three students suggest that the logics and licence that produce cultural appropriation are cultivated by the fungibility inherent in post-racism multicultural education, and we have already seen how cultural appropriation becomes appropriation of the body when Black people are the subject of portrayal, since the logics of the afterlife of slavery render not only Black cultural production, but also the Black body itself, available, tradeable, and fungible.

With respect to blackface, then, the influence of post-racism, multicultural education partially explains how these appropriative moments might be produced. If being a good multicultural Canadian means sharing and exchanging (ostensibly static) cultures, then perpetrators might view acts of mimicry as goodwill rather than appropriation. That this might be the case does not, of course, detract from the offence, from individual accountability in the matter, or from the fact that others might engage in appropriation, particularly blackface, for more nefarious reasons. Rather, the point is that the education the perpetrators have received, and the broader national narratives and policy context within which they are embedded, foster logics that produce and normalize these kinds of acts and render them unproblematic.

Surely there are classrooms where appropriate forms of critical education around racism and even antiblackness are offered in Canadian elementary and secondary schools (often by Black and racialized teachers), though none of the fifty-four student participants who did their pre-university education in Canada could recall having experienced anything like it. And clearly not all students exposed to postracism, multiculturalist pedagogies engage in blackface and cultural appropriation. Nevertheless, on the basis of what our respondents told us, the reasons they do not participate in blackface are not attributable to anything they learned in their pre-university schooling, while the reasons they do sometimes are. Contrary to any idea that K–12 education in schools might mitigate the occurrence of blackface, then, it appears that in the opinion of both Black and non-Black participants their K–12 education, like the university climate, is implicated in the production of blackface and broader forms of antiblackness. Moreover, antiblack appropriative behaviour is produced precisely through the post-racism, multiculturalist pedagogies that schools might understand as promoting egalitarianism. It is therefore clearly not the case that university students who engage in blackface have somehow failed to embrace what their pre-university Canadian schooling has tried to instill. Rather, as products of that schooling and the particular post-racism, multiculturalist understandings it promotes – indeed, as university students who are ostensibly among the best and brightest graduates of K–12 education – these students are set up to behave in exactly these problematic ways.

Multiculturalism and MLK: Postracialist Silencing and Stifling Black Embodied Knowledge

Post-racism, multiculturalist pedagogy not only informs non-Black students' behaviour at university, but also crucially impacts Black students in negative ways. The members of the Black student organization at University 2 had an extended focus group discussion about how this pedagogy attempted to override both their embodied responses to antiblackness and the knowledge that their families and communities had instilled in them thus becoming postracialist. Instead, it set norms for the post-racism way in which they were expected to engage (or more precisely, disengage) with thinking and initiatives that seek Black liberation. In this conversation, Martin Luther King Jr. featured prominently as a figure around whom schools created a particular kind of discourse to achieve these ends. Lance tells us:

> We didn't have any anti-racism or equity, or what could pass for it. Well, I guess our Black History assembly. That was terrible! It was always focused on Martin Luther King, but they always just showed him – They created him as a pacifist, he was very passive. That's it! that's the only side they would show. And they wouldn't at least contrast that with Malcolm X. They didn't do anything like that. It was like, "Martin Luther King! Smile, everyone!" Honestly that was it. (U2FGBSOP1)

In addition to the problematic manner that histories of Black struggle are located beyond Canada in this school's Black History assembly, Lance's account of the assembly's postracialist pedagogy that made Martin Luther King Jr.'s philosophy of non-violence first pacifist then passive is instructive. Whether deliberate or not on his part, this slippage parallels Lance's opinion about the way that the revolutionary politics and practice of King are re-storied in schools. For Lance, the way they are taught about Martin Luther King Jr.'s life and work is not intended to inspire students, and particularly Black students, to engage in resistance and pursue Black freedom. Rather, he experienced this pedagogy as a call to be docile. Lance tells us it fails even to employ the very hackneyed, binary ways in which MLK Jr. is set up against Malcolm X (though when this binary is employed, it is usually also with a view towards creating docile Black students by repudiating Black resistance rather than to offer several alternative forms of Black struggle). Students are left without a diverse range of Black historical figures with whom they might identify. Rather, they are presented with a distorted, hegemonic view of a single one.

This sanitized version of MLK Jr.'s work through educational initiatives at school is a phenomenon that all three participants in this focus group understand well, though they attended different schools in different years. Sonji tells us more about how this pedagogy sets the terms for how Black students should behave:

> We are at a point in society where everyone is like, "Equality means that everyone sits down and shuts up. Equality means you don't get mad about issues and we're all Kumbaya." But when it comes down to it, there's still all these issues, but we don't say shit. Sorry. Like we're at a point where our way of talking, our education in high schools, in elementary schools is: "just put a smile on your face no matter what," is the type of education we get. We get the very centralized "Martin Luther King

says all Black people and white people should hold hands" but we're not going to ever talk about other things. It's a very one-sided, conditioning way of teaching. ... And it's not even a full explanation of Martin Luther King, because they don't talk about his radical days. They kind of talk about it in this very, like, "Martin Luther King taught us that everyone was supposed to hold hands and there was supposed to be no violence and no voice. Like this is the way that they teach Martin Luther King." (U2FGBSOP3)

In this rich excerpt, Sonji argues that Canadian post-racism both produces and is reified by the postracialist pedagogical discourse about Martin Luther King Jr. whereby King is transformed into a smiling, hand-holding figure. Students are initiated into a post-racism view that understands antiblackness as always already a thing of the past, at least in Canada, and therefore that Black people in particular should now also just smile. The effect is that it silences Black students, actively undermines Black dissent, and forecloses on critical discussions about Canada from the perspective of Black people. MLK Jr's non-violent strategy for contesting antiblackness becomes a demand for a kind of civility that ultimately means "no voice."

Complementing this dynamic is the way that many of the adults in schools approach racist incidents. Lance shared an occurrence where an altercation between students became physical when a Black student was insulted with an antiblack slur. The outcome was that the Black student who was the target of the slur was the only one penalized – made to "look like a demon for punching [the aggressor] in the face – like she was a monster!" (U2FGBSOP1). This approach, which fails to account for the historical weight of racist name-calling and punishes Black students who are the target of antiblack abuse, is all too common in anecdotal reports from Black students and families in Canada. It, along with the post-racism, multiculturalist pedagogy instantiated in this MLK discourse, sends clear messages about how Black students are expected to respond (or more accurately, to not respond) to antiblackness directed towards them, and about how much schools care about these racial justice issues.

Impacts of MLK Pedagogy on White and Other Non-Black Students

The consequences of this MLK pedagogy for Black students extend to their experiences at university. First, Black participants reported that many of their non-Black peers carry the hegemonic expectations of Black people inculcated by this discourse. Sonji tells of encountering this very logic when she tries to contribute to discussion in classes at her university.

> I have been conditioned with Martin Luther King at this university a bunch of times. And I think that it's kind of because when we learn about Black people in Canada [in K–12], where and what we learn about racism in itself is very – ... We had a discussion-based class where I see these people three times a week. So I have said some things throughout the year that may have rubbed people the wrong way, because I am not going to give you a filtered view on an experience. ... but a lot of people have said, "You have such a negative view" – quote-unquote negative because I guess the Martin Luther King explanation is very positive ... I got scolded and basically the whole classroom was against my points and I got called a racist ... I got conditioned with Martin Luther King ... It's very conditioned: "Martin Luther King and Gandhi said, 'Don't say anything, and smile, and that's how you're going to make change.'" ... and they'll try to [say that] I'm being violent ... "If you want things to change for you, you're going to have to be more like Martin Luther King." This is the type of stuff that they say to me ... And I think that it's weird because it's not even Martin Luther King. "You all didn't even read Martin Luther King! You are getting the grade seven assembly Martin Luther King." (U2FGBSOP3)

Through this account of a communication dynamic experienced at university, which Sonji traces back to the MLK pedagogy of the "grade seven assembly," we are able to learn about the very real consequences for Black people of post-racism, multiculturalist pedagogy beyond their years in K–12. Sonji repeatedly uses the metaphor of being "conditioned" to mean variously how her non-Black peers at university have been inducted through MLK discourse into a set of expectations of Black people, and the ways she is disciplined and muzzled by those expectations. When Sonji speaks from her experience as a Black woman, she is considered to be violent, and to be violating the rules about how she is supposed to feel (Wingfield, 2010) that she is expected to learn from Martin Luther King's life. In other words, as we saw in the previous chapter, she is upsetting the classroom conditions of "safety" demanded by white people (but also other non-Black people, according to Sonji) that protect them from confronting the whiteness of their Canadian subjectivities (Leonardo & Porter, 2010), and therefore from addressing their complicity in Canadian antiblackness. These kinds of expectations constitute profoundly post*racialist* conditions at university. Racist conditions, and specifically antiblack conditions, are advanced under the claim that racism is past, reproducing the terms of Black unfreedom.

Black Students Navigating Postracialist MLK Pedagogy

Though Sonji speaks of the significant distress that constantly having to face this postracialist muzzling causes her, she also says she is able to overcome the conditioning. However, not all Black students as easily resist succumbing to the pressure of post-racism conditioning, which accounts in some ways for the attenuated reactions to blackface that some Black students have. Both Lance and Valerie in this focus group admit to "brushing off" their experiences of blackface, even though they both sensed that something was wrong. Lance speaks about his reaction to seeing pictures of a blackface incident at his university on social media:

> I literally was scrolling. I remember I just saw sadnesses about it ... so I was looking at it and I was saying, "Okay. I get why people are mad, but everyone, like, relax!" It annoyed me but it didn't enrage me like I saw a lot of people were ... I kind of brushed it off as, like, nothing, which is embarrassing to say. I was annoyed that people thought that it was funny. I didn't find it funny at all. ... I thought it was stupid ... They are just taking it as if it's, uh, whatever, and they can wear stuff that's a part of me and they can just take it and make it a joke almost. It was a joke to them, and that annoyed me so much, but then I was just like, "Okay. Whatever!" (U2FGBSOP1)

Valerie shares her response to the same incident:

> Well, as I said, some of those people, I was acquainted with them. And I was new at the school, and I didn't want to lose friends or anybody. So I kind of just brushed it under the rug. I didn't really think anything of it, to tell you the truth. Like when I saw it I was like, "Oh, okay. Well, that sucks, but whatever. I have friends," like, you know? ... And I only heard it from one side too, like the [white people in my dorm]. I didn't hear from the BSO [Black student organization] or any of the articles or anything. ... It kind of sucks because they painted their face black, and like I'm Black. ... Like, you know that it's bad, but what can you really do about it? ... I feel like they're taking a part of me and making it into a costume ... but I didn't do anything about it. (U2FGBSOP2)

Both Lance and Valerie admit to not knowing much "about blackface or my Blackness" at the time of the incident. That is, they did not know the history of blackface, but more importantly, partly due to their school "conditioning" up until that point, they did not have a well-developed understanding of what it means to be structurally located as Black, and were not consciously politically involved in contesting antiblackness. Nevertheless, they both had negative reactions to the blackface incident – feelings of sadness, annoyance, "it sucks." Despite their cultivated, post-racism consciousness, they both had an embodied understanding of blackface as a performance of Black enfleshment – the appropriation of their bodies and subjectivities. Unfortunately, they had also learned to dismiss this embodied knowledge. They had come to think that there was little they could do to address antiblackness, or even that it is not worth addressing. They therefore resigned themselves to live with the kind of violence it represents.

In the same way that they learned to dismiss their own embodied reactions, they also learned to dismiss Black knowledge passed on to them through their communities and families. While Valerie says that her parents never spoke to her about being Black, she tells of an older brother who did, and who warned her of antiblackness she might encounter in interactions with white people at school. She remembers that she would dismiss him: "I would always be like, 'Why are you saying this? I have so many white friends,' and blah blah blah." In Lance's case, his parents and community *had* educated him about what it meant to be Black and had taught him to be prepared for encounters with antiblackness. Our focus group caused him to reflect on how he had come to discount this education:

It's weird because my parents did ingrain it in me … my parents definitely educated me on stuff like that. So looking back I don't get how I wasn't – It's not making sense to me right now that it wasn't a big deal, because it's not like I was ignorant of everything, and oblivious, and walking around all sunshine and rainbows and stuff like that. I actually knew! So it is weird to me that it wasn't a big deal. But definitely my parents and my parents' friends let us know what was happening, but I guess – [*trails off*]. You talk, because I am trying to think a little. (U2FGBSOP1)

After thinking about it for a while, Lance ultimately pins the disconnect on how he was taught at school, and the kinds of post-racism relationships he had in which contemporary antiblackness was not understood as a cause for concern:

I guess that is how I grew up. Like, I knew about things because of my parents, but I guess in school they weren't highlighted. I wasn't surrounded by people who cared, so why would I care? My friends at the time – and they still are my friends now – they didn't care. Why would I care? If it's not a big deal to them, why should it be a big deal to me? But it should. I am not white; I am Black. That's the first thing that should be a big deal because everyone around me who is white would say, "Hey it's not a big deal. You shouldn't worry," [and I would be like,] "Well okay. I guess I shouldn't worry. They are not worrying." But I don't look like them ... It's definitely because the people around me weren't making it a big deal, I guess. (U2FGBSOP1)

So the attenuated response to blackface and to antiblackness is, for some Black students, related to the post-racism education they had experienced and that structures their relationships with non-Black people. Both dismiss antiblackness and place the onus on Black people to prioritize a superficial interpersonal harmony. Indeed, Valerie's excerpt suggests that her relationships with white people played into the decisions she made to dismiss her embodied reactions; she did not want to lose friends. Lance felt similarly. He told us that because of his relationships with white colleagues, "At the time I was just kind of like, 'Oh well, I am not getting involved. I don't want people to see me doing this and this and this and that.'" They both felt that keeping their relationships with white people was contingent upon ignoring antiblackness – a reasonable conclusion for them based on their post-racism education. The demand through post-racism MLK Jr. discourse to have and maintain "smiling, hand-holding" relationships with white people comes at the expense of any critical discourse about antiblackness, undermines their embodied and community-based Black knowledges, and constrained their responses to blackface.

It is also clear that not every Black student is affected in this way. For example, Sonji says that this was not her experience. She says that she has "always understood" what was politically at stake in her responses to "Black issues," and always been clear about the limit on how far she would be willing to go to maintain relationships with non-Black persons. She recalls:

I've always been very aware ... I do attribute a lot of it to my mom and my parents because the way of society was very ingrained in me when I was little. A lot of pride was ingrained in me in being different. I might even attribute that to being part of a very proud diasporic community. But even then my mom was very apparent [sic] about the way the society works ... I remember being young, young; my mom would be washing my hair in the bathtub, my mom would be telling me, preaching to me. And I am too young to understand this. But when you grow up learning this and then you start to pick up what's going on, and then reading history and things like that, it kind of made me into the person that I am to where I can go into these university experiences and have this experience being very aware from the start. But my mother would preach. She would be like, "Listen … You're a woman and you're Black. This is how life is … You have to be aware of it, and you have to be able to work around it." So she conditioned me to look for these experiences, but she also conditioned me to speak up in these experiences. So I knew what right and wrong was. (U2FGBSOP3)

The education that Sonji's mother provided was deliberate and persistent, and thereby achieved its intended effect. Sonji attributes to this education her ability to expect, understand, and identify antiblackness directed at her as a Black woman, and to not shy away from participating in contesting these conditions.

Canadian Post-Racism Education in Context: Keeping Black People and Black Ideas Out

It is important to contextualize the specific effects of post-racism, multiculturalist pedagogies on Black students within the histories of Black education in Canada in order to make sense of why and how these persist. From the outset, schooling for Black people in what is now Canada was never guaranteed, and had to be struggled for within a context of white supremacy and Black exclusion. Specifically, the earliest forms of education for Black people in what is now Canada were offered, if at all, with/in contexts of enslavement (hampton, 2020, p. 15; Winks, 1997, p. 55), certainly not envisioning Black freedom.

In post-slavery Canada, despite the assimilationist approaches to education that dominated the late nineteenth and early twentieth centuries, Black people (and people from the Asian continent) were considered unassimilable (Joshee, 2004, p. 131). Therefore, as the Black population grew through the migration of Black Loyalists and fugitives from slavery in the United States, Black schooling took various segregated forms because of the ostensible negative influence that white communities felt Black children would have on their own offspring (Bramble, 2000, p. 99; McLaren, 2004, p. 33). Segregated schooling often existed in practice, even where it was prohibited by law, as authorities generally refused to enforce the law against the will of white parents; and it existed more formally by law where there were larger numbers of Black people, and where Black people did not already live apart from white communities because of de facto segregated neighbourhoods (Bramble, 2000, p. 101; McLaren, 2004, pp. 34–5; Williams, 1997, p. 61; Winks, 1997, p. 363).

Most, though not all, Canadian schools had become integrated by the beginning of the twentieth century, and the antiblackness that had previously worked to exclude Black people from schools altogether now informed their experiences within integrated schools (Bramble, 2000, p. 104). Thus, in integrated schools Black students were still sometimes physically separated from white students and regularly faced overt racism, low expectations, and disingenuous counselling that often caused them to leave school of their own accord – either convinced by what their teachers were telling them or, more often, to escape the stifling racist conditions (Bramble, 2000, pp. 103–4; Dei et al., 1997; McLaren, 2004, p. 34; Williams, 1997, pp. 61, 123; Winks, 1997, p. 388).

As indicated above, the brief turn in the early 1990s towards somewhat more promising paradigms of education, designated as anti-racism education, seemed to occur only at the policy level and was quickly swept away by neoliberalism – or more specifically, racial neoliberalism – which deems these forms of education expensive and superfluous and requires a docile labour force that continues to be stratified by race and gender.

Nevertheless, Black people have always actively resisted the antiblack conditions of education and held out radical visions of schooling not predicated on Black exclusion. During the era of segregated schooling Black communities contested educational antiblackness by petitioning educational and legal authorities, and where Black people – usually Black women – set up schools and other educational initiatives to meet Black students' needs (Bramble, 2000, p. 103; hampton, 2020, p. 17; hampton & Rochat, 2019, p. 152; McLaren, 2004, p. 36; Williams, 1997, p. 62). Though primarily created to address the educational exclusion of Black children, these initiatives were usually open to all, including Indigenous students, and sometimes had flexible fee structures that eased financial barriers (McLaren, 2004, p. 38).

Other iterations of a radical Black vision of education were in poignant evidence at the university level in 1960s Quebec. By this time, post–World War II, it had become federal policy for Canada to financially support international students, including those from Africa and the Caribbean, to study in Canada. The policy was part of a broader colonial approach to development primarily intent on fostering "political goodwill [abroad towards Canada], especially anti-communist attitudes" in the Cold War era (McCartney, 2016, p. 5). Consistent with "keep Canada white" immigration policies, this education policy rested on the expectation that international students would not remain in Canada (McCartney, 2016, p. 5). Notably, this immigration and education policy existed alongside the de facto educational exclusion of Black

Canadians, particularly at the university level where long-standing Black communities in Canada were severely under-represented (Williams, 1997, p. 123; Winks, 1997, p. 387).

It was during this time that Black university students in Montreal from the Caribbean and Africa, in concert with global decolonial movements and the general thrusts for civil rights of the era, organized educational forums for sharing and producing radical, anti-colonial Black and Caribbean thought through several clubs and conferences, including the 1968 Congress of Black Writers at McGill University, each of which brought Black thinkers, writers, and activists to the universities from across the Black diaspora (Austin, 2013).

The 1969 Sir George Williams Affair at what is now Concordia University also took place in this era. Beginning, as it did, with a request by four Caribbean students that the university intervene against what they experienced as a white professor's racist grading practices, it too represented a vision of Black freedom in education. When the university failed to respond appropriately, the complaint developed into a peaceful takeover by Black students and their allies of the university's computer lab (Austin, 2013). The affair ended with a violent police invasion of the computer lab, during which several students were injured and ninety-seven students were arrested – among whom forty-two were Black, some of whom were eventually deported (Austin, 2013, p. 135).

Immediately after the Sir George Affair, several federal MPs sought to have the government halt aid to international students, as part of a broader pushback against the sitting government's less racially restrictive immigration policies meant to meet Canada's increasing labour needs (McCartney, 2016, p. 11). While student protest at Canadian universities by Canadian students (of all backgrounds) had been on the rise since at least the 1930s (Lexier, 2007), international students, a significant proportion of whom were Black, and who would largely be the international students MPs had in mind in relation to the Sir George Affair, were now seen as a "threat to otherwise orderly higher education institutions" that needed to be kept out (McCartney, 2016, p. 12). What I highlight here is the way that the congresses and the Sir George Affair represent radical visions of a different kind of education that embraces Black people and Black thought, as well as the state's active rejection of these Black visions of education in Canada.

Since Canada's labour needs persisted while immigration flows from traditional European sources were drying up, the Black population in Canada grew as Black people grasped these employment and immigration opportunities. The number of Black students in Canadian schools also grew, but Black students have continued to face the antiblackness that is endemic to Canadian schooling.

Black educators and Black communities have continued to be vocal and active on various levels, to challenge the inequitable conditions of education for Black students and to bring transformative change to Canadian education systems. Black educators, again often Black women, have worked subversively within the limits of their positions of employment to combat the erasure of Black people in curricula and to challenge antiblack streaming and disciplinary practices (Aladejebi, 2015a; Howard, 2014b). Black families and parents, often mothers, have intervened incessantly for the equitable treatment of their children in schools (Adjei, 2018; Dei & Kempf, 2013, p. 66; Lawson, 2019). Numerous historical and current Black-community-based initiatives have been established over the years to advocate for equitable Black education and to offer supplementary forms of education to address the shortcomings of state schooling. These various actors have signalled the urgent need for K–12 educational change, which would include introducing Black histories and Black Studies into curriculum and establishing alternative schooling options, including Afro/Africentric- and Black-focused schooling.

To return to Black students' experiences, then, it is clear that the small number of students quoted in this chapter are only a very minute sample of Canadian students. They are not intended to be representative in any statistical sense. Nevertheless, that Black students should tell us of these experiences in 2013–14 seems significant against the history of antiblack education and Black educational activism in Canada. The outcomes of these contemporary post-racism, multiculturalist pedagogies are deeply antiblack, and are structured by the contexts that have produced them. Antiblackness has always been a feature of education in Canada, attempting to exclude and marginalize Black people. Contemporary forms of education continue this tradition, seeking to silence Black students, mystify the racist terms of their existence in school and in Canada, and pre-empt their involvement in contesting antiblackness. As such, I claim that post-racism, multiculturalist forms of education and their deeply antiblack outcomes cannot be seen simply as a matter of well-intentioned but inadequate pedagogy, or as a benign failure to create a more critical curriculum. They are, instead, consistent with a long tradition of upholding antiblack structures in education, and determined resistance to radical and inclusive visions of education that Black people have continually offered and pursued. As such, they are a response to the material and political facts of Blackness and Black resistance. They are consistent with Sojoyner's (2013) observation that education policy and practice "are best understood as attempts to make Black liberation irrational and Black subjugation, its logical converse, commonsensical ... the structure of public education is ... culpable in the enclosure of Black freedom" (p. 242).

Conclusion

This chapter has looked at post-racism forms of education in contemporary Canada in the pre-university years. It has argued that education is informed by the broader discourse of multiculturalism as expressed in Canada's Multiculturalism Act, as well as by the long history of antiblackness in education in Canada. This education contributes to producing Canadian subjectivities that will understand Canada as having transcended antiblackness. It does violence to Black students in a form of gaslighting, and also by teaching non-Black people how to participate in this postracialist gaslighting. White and other non-Black students who uncritically absorb the messages of this education come to understand antiblackness as no longer an issue in Canada, and therefore to understand efforts to challenge antiblackness as superfluous. Some come to understand blackface and other appropriative acts simply as following the expectation that Canadians "share their cultures" in the interest of social harmony. Others learn to hostilely reject those who speak out unequivocally against antiblackness – in this case, the antiblackness of the university. These are the kinds of non-Black subjectivities discussed in Chapter 3, and the current chapter elucidates how these subjectivities might be produced and/or reified in schools.

At the same time, pedagogies in schools attempt to seduce Black students into post-racism and lull Black students into ignorance and apathy towards the necessary, ongoing struggle for Black freedom in Canada. Black students are disciplined through a postracialist pedagogy that makes antiblackness unspeakable, and they are encouraged to accept relationships with non-Black people on terms that require that they themselves not become politically engaged. Black students subjected to post-racism pedagogies are further taught to negate the embodied and community knowledges that would provide a measure of psychic protection from antiblack hostility, and offer strategies of resistance.

This chapter has also attended to the power of a radical black education outside of school, such as that which Sonji's mother provided. Only a very intentional and determined pro-Black pedagogy that is rehearsed often at home or in community is able to resist schools' negation of Blackness and Black struggle. "The talk" that Black families often have with their children to warn them about interactions with the police and injustice in the criminal justice system more broadly has recently become topical in mainstream media. Here, as I and other Black educators have long done (e.g., Howard, 2014b; Lawson, 2019), I redouble a call for Black parents and communities to resist postracialist seductions and engage in similar "talk" with their children about what they can expect in their interactions with educators and educational systems, which often begin at a much younger age. This talk would not only address the criminalization of Black children, youth, and their families by schools, but must also address curriculum, pedagogy, and particularly the epistemic violence that takes place under such egalitarian-sounding banners as multiculturalism.

Of course, as we have seen, this is a kind of work that Black families and community organizations have done since the earliest days of free Black presence in Canada. There have been community-based initiatives such as the Black Action Party, Quebec Board of Black Educators, La Maison d'Haiti, and Nous Gen Peyi Tou (Montreal), the Black Education Project, Organization of Parents of Black Children (Toronto), Black Learners Advisory Committee, and the Delmore "Buddy" Daye Afrocentric Learning Institute (Halifax), to name only a very few. There have been some very notable public successes of this work, such as the creation of an African Canadian Services Branch located within the Nova Scotia Department of Education and Early Childhood Development, and some Africentric programs and an Africentric school in Toronto (though to widespread public dissent, including from the then premier of Ontario; Howard, 2013). At the same time, we must not ignore the less visible but no less crucial effects of this educational activism in sustaining individual Black students like Sonji, and in providing grounds for self-recovery for students like Valerie and Lance. In other words, its salience must not be neglected in the day to day of making Black life possible in schools.

This important work in Black families and communities, and by Black educators in education systems – much of it the work of Black women – must continue both to offer critical, pro-Black spaces of education apart from schools and to advocate for the creation and maintenance of such spaces within state systems of education. Much of our hope lies in maintaining these spaces, and protecting them from infiltration and take-over by hegemonic logics that will again pathologize and do violence to Black students and Black families.

It is heartening that each of the Black participants in the study who admits to having been influenced by post-racism education has now come to more critical understandings. Chapter 9 will address some of the ways that this awakening might happen at university.

8 The Costs of Belonging for International Students

Of course, Canadian pre-university schooling systems are not the only path that students might take to get to Canadian universities. Some students come to Canadian universities from other countries without having attended school in Canada. If antiblack pedagogies, and invitations to "belong" in postracialist ways, are written into state education as we saw in the previous chapter, they are also written into the ways that Black migrant students are invited to "belong." This chapter is, in some ways, an attempt to understand the perspectives of the few Black participants whose views about blackface differed at key points from those of the other Black participants. These were students who were not offended by blackface, and who in some cases were complicit in blackface incidents by "giving permission" to their white colleagues ("co-signing" blackface, according to some participants critical of the practice) and/or by participating in blackface incidents themselves.

There were three such students among the thirty Black student participants, and it so happens that these three were all international students. One student was from France, and attributed his lack of concern about blackface to the fact that he was not raised within the North American context. However, he claimed to "understand it in the context of the visceral reaction it can create within the Black community in the US considering the very close history of fighting for their civil rights" (U5BSOFGP3).[1] This student's perspective is

---

1 It is worth noting that the idea that blackface is not an issue in Europe is similar to the ways that Canada and Quebec disavow a historical connection to blackface, and thereby claim innocence. Much of Europe and certainly France (see, e.g., Smalls, 2003) were popular sites for minstrelsy in all its antiblackness. Thus, it is also interesting that this student seems to overlook Black reactions to blackface in Canada, only justifying Black objections to blackface in the United States.

not discussed further in this chapter since, in principle, he agrees with the majority of Black student participants that there is reason for Black people to be concerned about blackface in the context of slavery's afterlife, even if only in North America in his opinion, and even if he is not personally offended. The other two students, around whom this chapter revolves, were international students from the Caribbean. I draw on the significance of this positioning in the analysis below based on conversations with them. The source of their particular perspectives seems to be a bid for understanding that they might live Blackness differently than their counterparts in Canada, and an understandably only emergent understanding of the ways that race works here, coming as they do from majority Black countries. As I argue below, their perspectives may also be a function of the colonial conditions that make Canada attractive to many people from the Caribbean, and a clear lack of awareness of the antiblack terms of camaraderie upon which they are invited to belong among their white colleagues at university.

However, to be clear, I make no suggestion that this analysis can or should be extended to all Black international students, or to all Black international students from the Caribbean. Indeed, many of the other Black participants were international students who did not share the perspectives of the students who are the subject of this chapter. Further, there is a long tradition of Black international students, including those from the Caribbean, who come to Canada to attend university and have carved out space to think through and operationalize the radical project of Black freedom within and across national boundaries (see, e.g., Austin, 2013; Hudson & Kamugisha, 2014; McCartney, 2016; Walcott & Abdillahi, 2019, p. 58). In writing this chapter, then, I am doing the important work of attending to minoritarian perspectives within the study. The purpose is not to present these as idiosyncrasies as though to pathologize individuals. Rather, I argue that these students' ideas too are deeply informed by Canadian colonial, postracialist antiblackness and the way it seeks to seduce them into post-race perspectives through the politics of migration and multiculturalism – in much the same way that it attempts to seduce Black students attending K–12 schooling in Canada.

In what follows, I offer a reading of these "outlier" Black perspectives through the lens of anti-essentialism. Subsequently, I indicate the reasons that this analysis fails to fully account for the relationships of these Black dispositions to blackface and antiblackness, and complicate the analysis by drawing on the work of Frantz Fanon (1967) and Sylvia Wynter (2001).

Indifference to Blackface as an Anti-essentialist Bid

Janine, a participant in a focus group at University 1, shared her feelings about blackface as follows:

> I'm just sharing my views for the first time, but I'm not really that offended because I feel like there's so many things we do as Black people. … there's so many things we do and say – like, "You're acting like a white person" and stuff like that and I feel like Black people have to remember that we do stuff as well, that I think we're very racial, and I don't think we should be offended by stuff like that. … I talk to my friends, like Black friends I have, and you just do some stuff [and they're] just like, "Oh, you just think white! Oh, you're thinking that you need to be white!" … I think it goes both ways. (U1BSOFGP6)

Janine does not appear to necessarily give blackface a permanent or unconditional pass. Rather, her willingness to be lenient with blackface is expressed in relation to what she considers to be more troubling things that some Black people do – particularly around accusing each other of being white. She feels it is hypocritical for her Black colleagues to be offended at white people in blackface if they can also accuse her of being whitewashed. Perhaps, for her, blackface represents an attempt to essentialize Blackness through the stereotypical tropes associated with it. Thus, for Janine, both blackface and accusations of "whitewashed" flow from the same desire to fix Blackness in essentialist terms. Janine's declaration that she is "not that offended" at blackface seems to be a form of pushing back against her Black colleagues who question her Blackness based on superficial behavioural markers.

Charles, a student at University 2, expresses a similar sentiment:

> Even the sports I've chosen to play through my lifetime like swimming, rowing. And back home [a Caribbean country] it's multicultural, so everybody plays that. … I came to University 2, … there were only two of us that rowed who were coloured. And then people look at the opportunities that you have had in life like my parents being able to send me to University 2 and not have to take loans and that kind of business. They are making that assumption that you grew up in this white community, you have money, you are whitewashed, you think you are better than everybody else. But that is the furthest thing from the truth in terms of having money and even in terms of being better than everyone else. It's just a very simple way of thinking about life and people. (U2S2)

Interestingly, though Charles is Black-presenting, he refers to himself as "Coloured." "Coloured" is a dated term historically used in the Caribbean to distinguished between Black persons who were enslaved (referred to as Blacks) and those who were free, sometimes the offspring of white men and enslaved women (Simonsen, 2003, p. 256). Later the term would be one among many to distinguish the Black working class and the Black dispossessed from those more affluent Black persons, often lighter-skinned in a Caribbean pigmentocracy, who comprised the ruling classes after independence (Hall, 2018, p. 74). It is a terminology shot through with class distinctions, but which has largely fallen out of common usage.

Charles has encountered a group of Black students on campus who perform Blackness in what, to him, are stereotypical ways. In contrast to these, Charles sees himself as living Blackness differently. Having recently arrived in Canada, he feels his lifestyle differs in some ways from those of Black people who have lived in Canada for longer. He is frustrated by efforts to circumscribe what it means to be Black and to police the boundaries of Black identity. He surmises that his colleagues' responses to him are provoked by his Caribbeanness as well as his affluence, class position, and participation in certain associated activities, and he is frustrated that this is read as whiteness.

The relations to which Charles and Janine refer have been identified in Canada and beyond among Black people who come from affluent backgrounds, or have come into them through education, and who have come to identify with a particular mainstream class status. Those who identify this way ostensibly feel that their class status rearranges racial boundaries such that they now have much in common with middle-class white people, have less in common with other Black people, and struggle to belong within rigidly defined categories that conflate race and class (Gosine, 2008, p. 321; Rollock et al., 2012, p. 267). Other scholarship, notably that of Stuart Hall, also identifies the ways in which a strategic first moment in which Black people claim a unified political Blackness must necessarily give way to, and become complicated by, an overlapping second moment of Blackness without guarantees – of "new ethnicities" that recognize the "extraordinary diversity of subjective positions, social experiences and cultural identities which compose the category 'black'" (Hall, 1996, p. 444). This scholarship has identified the complexity of Black diasporic subjectivities, particularly Caribbean subjectivities, rightfully wanting to "make a differentiation between people who are black from one kind of society and people who are black from another" while not rejecting Blackness as a category within which they can all claim belonging (Hall, 2018, p. 80). Janine and Charles, at the intersection of affluence and Caribbeanness, seem to be experiencing some of this complexity of identification.

Consistent with Charles's and Janine's assessments, Michael, responding to Janine, opines on how he sees this complex politics of identity playing out, reflecting, in the Canadian context, the contingent Blackness advanced by Hall:

> I think Blacks in Canada feel a certain need to attempt to preserve their culture. And I think it's weird because there's so many cultures involved in Black that it very much will change depending on where you are in Canada. So in Toronto oftentimes a culture is this mesh of Afrocentricism – I don't know what the word is for that – of, like, the early 80s and 90s, mixed with like a current Jamaican culture, and then, like, other African cultures, and they sort of just blend into this thing they call Black. In Montreal it's very, very different, again because that culture is influenced more by Haitian people. But there is this sort of innate tendency for us to try to preserve our culture, preserve our way of talking and speaking, because we want to feel like we are still Black. Because increasingly, especially in Canada, we are amalgamating into a single culture, this single hybrid where Black is just really gonna turn into a skin colour if it continues to exist in the way it does. I think that's the way people sort of see things, so we try to create these lines where we sort of separate ourselves. (U1BSOFGP1)

While Michael's post-racism assessment that Black people are blending into "a single culture" where Blackness would be nothing more than a complexion seems highly implausible, he does seem to recognize the need to resist the postracialist climate that would deny the continued significance of antiblackness. At a superficial glance, it is possible to see the group of students Michael, Charles, and Janine refer to, who ostensibly live within stereotypical constructions of Blackness, as defensive essentialists (Gosine, 2002) who are choosing to reaffirm their identities as Black by embracing a limited set of cultural markers. Gosine asserts:

> Various social statuses interlock at particular moments and particular social locations to shape the production of essentialist, defensively situated collective identities on the part of racialized people ... [and these] defensively situated identities represent collective efforts to challenge or counteract dominant, negatively represented constructions of a given social group. (p. 95)

Despite the bricolage inherent in constructing such identities, where these essentialisms are reified, they risk erasing intra-group diversity, and at the limit become oppressive in their failure to recognize the complexities and intersectionalities of identity. It is perhaps against these tendencies that persons like Janine and Charles, whom we might refer to provisionally as the non-essentialists, push. They insist on the freedom not only to live their Blackness in its non–North American iterations, but also to engage/borrow/share across racial, class, and cultural boundaries with their non-Black colleagues at university.

Nevertheless, it is crucial to recall here that these non-essentialists are, at least initially, those who do not object to the blackface that occurs on campus, while those in the "defensive essentialist" category do oppose blackface. This gives reason for pause in light of my insistence that contemporary blackface in Canada is a powerful instantiation of the nation's extant antiblackness. Indeed, David Theo Goldberg (2009) cautions that anti-racism movements routinely run the risk of devolving into anti-racialist ones – a shift from contesting racist conditions to contesting racial categories (p. 10). Goldberg asserts that "as an end in itself, antiracialism, it turns out for the most part, is whiteness by another name, by other means, with recruitment of people of colour to act as public spokespersons for the cause" (p. 22). Moreover, while the "highly educated, upwardly mobile [read: affluent or middle-class] Black Canadians" in Gosine's study (2008, p. 309) resist stereotypical notions of Blackness – particularly where those do not conform to their classed self-perceptions – we also see that this sometimes plays out in a politics of Black exceptionality preoccupied with the idea that "being a Black person is about proving that you're not what they say you are, ... constantly having to, to fight ... to always challenge someone's assumptions about who you are" (p. 17), and "setting [one]self apart from the perceived Black culture that [one] depict[s] as incongruent with intellectual achievement" (p. 319). Indeed, in Gosine's study, the most outspoken resisters of stereotypical notions of Blackness were also those most committed to individualistic endeavours on the meritocratic terms of neoliberal capitalism with no sense of accountability to Black communities and collective Black politics (p. 328). They engaged the university primarily as a credentializing space and as one through which they forged new social identities – an engagement that has its foundations in antiblackness, as we saw in Chapter 5.

Taken together, then, we might ask to what extent Janine's and Charles's anti-racialism (or anti-essentialism) might be aiding and abetting whiteness, if not being whiteness's disguise? In what ways might it be antiblack in its aims? This question calls for us to complicate our initial anti-essentialism analysis. For this, Fanon's (1967) anti-colonial analysis and Sylvia Wynter's (2001) elaborations on Fanon's text seem particularly relevant given their focus in these writings upon Caribbean colonial subjects who migrate to colonial metropoles.

Coming to Canada

In Chapter 1 of *Black Skin White Masks* (1967), Fanon, focusing on language, examines the ways that colonial aspirations of the colonized seek to devalue the cultural practices of the colonized – in this case their creolized languages – relegating them to the realm of the primitive. This colonial dynamic imposes inferiority upon the colonized. Fanon (1967) writes:

> Every colonized people – in other words, every people in whose soul an inferiority complex has been created by the death and burial of its local cultural originality – finds itself face to face with the language of the civilizing nation; that is, with the culture of the mother country. The colonized is elevated above his [*sic*] jungle status in proportion to his adoption of the mother country's cultural standards. He becomes whiter as he renounces his blackness, his jungle. (p. 18; Wynter, 2001, p. 35; all gendered language in the original)

Wynter, building on Fanon, highlights that what is at stake is one's sense of one's humanity. Thus, Wynter writes, "in the European physiognomy and culture complex, it is to the extent that the Caribbean Negro 'renounces his blackness, his jungle' that he experiences himself as *more human* ... the logic of these new cultural standards has 'totemized' being fully human" (Wynter, 2001, p. 35, emphasis in original). Wynter elaborates:

> What Fanon enables us to see by analysis is not only the way in which the culturally imposed symbolic belief system of the French bourgeois *sense of self* also structures the *sense of self* of the colonized French Caribbean middle class Negro, but also that it is a *sense of self* for which the notion of "acting like a nigger," and thereby lapsing into non-being, ... serves as the internalized sanction system which motivates his/her behaviors. (p. 34, emphasis in original)

"Acting like a nigger" signifies not only falling short of whiteness and colonizer status, but falling short of being fully human (as per Western/colonial conceptions). However, at least in the colony, this feeling of non-white inferiority, of failing at being human, can be mitigated as long as the colonized chooses not to "act like a nigger" (p. 33) – that is, as long as they mimic the colonizer's language/culture and reject participating in the local language/culture.

Wynter (2001) further identifies what Fanon implies: that this insistent seduction by the colonial order to transcend Blackness, since the colonizer is set up as the full expression of humanity, is particularly experienced by the middle class (p. 33). And both Fanon and Wynter signal that it is also profoundly connected to (colonial) education (Fanon, 1967, p. 25; Wynter, 2001, p. 35). These middle classes have access to the schooling and the resources that open doors for them to participate in the colonizer's cultural behaviours and in so doing set themselves apart from the other (Black) people who apparently are happy to persist in their own (ostensibly subhuman) ways of life.

There is another hurdle to be cleared, however. Fanon (1967) notes that, despite whatever attempts at transcendence they succeed at in the colony, the colonized aspiring to colonizer status experience a sense of "amputation of [their full] being" (p. 23; Wynter, 2001, p. 38) as long as they remain in the colony. On the other hand, the promise of moving to the metropole, often to pursue further education, carries with it the promise of full Humanity. There, ostensibly, the metamorphosis from subhuman to full Human will be complete.

It is now several decades after Fanon's writing, when most Caribbean countries have achieved independence and therefore are at least nominally no longer colonies. Also, no country in the Caribbean has been a direct colony of Canada. Nevertheless, vestiges of colonial sensibilities remain within these ostensibly independent nations (as they do everywhere, since global colonialisms are ongoing, if manifested differently). More importantly, the globalization of whiteness and Euro-American hegemony, and Canadian implication in the slave economies and subsequent implication in markets in the Caribbean (Hudson, 2010; Walcott & Abdillahi, 2019, p. 54) perpetuate this colonial dynamic that Fanon identified in the 1960s, and make it applicable to migration to Canada today. For example, Cecil Foster (1996) writes about this dynamic when discussing his own migration to Canada more than a decade after independence in his native Barbados:

> As was the case of so many young people in the colonial Caribbean, the dream of self-fulfilment was built squarely on immigration. Even as the winds of independence blew out of Africa and raced across the islands in the late 1960s, they were not really intended for us. Independence was for those not so blessed with a chance to leave the region; the proclamation of sovereignty was to be an incentive for those left behind to make the

most of what few crumbs they would get from life's table, but not for anyone with personal ambition. Even as we mouthed the words to the new
national anthem, we never thought political independence was intended
for the better educated among us ... I can still recall how we felt whenever
one of our friends announced he or she was leaving for another country.
This gave them airs; it allowed them to ... take on the more worldly pose
of those plucked from among the wretched for good things. ... Immigration was a status symbol. (p. 35)

Foster too marks the ways in which schooling operated as both site
from which the desire to migrate was fostered and reason for which
to migrate (p. 37). He attends to the circumstances by which Canada
became a destination of choice for migrants from the Caribbean – a
combination of changing labour market needs and global geopolitics,
Canadian marketing of itself overseas, and the fictions that exist outside of Canada about its egalitarianism. Migrants to Canada often do
not expect to experience antiblackness here (p. 52). Important to the
analysis in this chapter, Foster further identifies the ways in which these
migration fictions and the fiction of Canadian egalitarianism set up a
pressure to "integrate fully" so as not to allow anyone to "think that any
of us had squandered a chance to make good in an adopted country"
(p. 37). Canadian postracialism created rifts between new migrants and
Black people who had been in Canada longer, and whom the migrants
indicted for not succeeding because they "were lazy" and then blaming lack of success on racism (p. 37). Migration flows to Canada, and
the dreams associated with them, are exacerbated and complicated by
the increasingly neoliberal global conditions that erode possibilities for
eking out a reasonable existence in Black nations and former European
colonies.

Those with ongoing relationships with/in the Caribbean can easily attest that little has changed over time in terms of the appetite for
migration, and some of the attitudes among prospective middle-class
migrants, who would be known as "economic," primarily "business
class" migrants in the terminology of current Canadian immigration
policy.

Revisiting the Anti-essentialism Argument: What Else Is Happening?

With these analytical tools, I now further consider what Charles had to
say. Charles was very vocal about his experiences, offering a lot more
of his opinion about blackface than did Janine. This may largely be
because he had participated in a blackface incident and felt he had more

to justify. I asked what it was that he felt made his Black peers see him as "whitewashed." Charles responds:

> Back then I was *culturally similar* to those [white] people that I hung out with, as opposed to the other coloured people in our dorm. I don't know how else to explain it, but I have to think about this ... I think sports is primarily it, the places I chose to go out to. Music, definitely not, because everybody used to complain about my music! (U2S2, emphasis added)

Recalling that Charles had been on a rowing team in the Caribbean, and now was on the rowing team at his university, we see that he refers to his sports involvement in terms that indicate proximity to whiteness and distance from Blackness. For Charles, participating in certain cultural practices, in this case rowing, opened up access to honorary whiteness, as does language in Fanon's analysis. I am not interested in making Charles entirely a dupe of colonialism, and his choice of music suggests complexity to the ways he identifies (or not) with white people and with whiteness. Nevertheless, his affluence and class position in the Caribbean had certainly made rowing more accessible to him there than to most of his compatriots. In Canada, it provided a point of commonality for him with his white, middle-class peers, and also was what he read as the source of the distance between him and his Black peers. Further, while it is impossible to know all the factors that might motivate an individual's choice of company, one cannot ignore the pervasive racial/colonial background against which these ostensible choices are made. Charles elaborates on the tension between him and his Black colleagues:

> But – [*pause*]. And just like – [*pause*]. Just like how certain – [*pause*]. Alright, so, I wasn't – [*long pause*]. Just like how someone would act [*long pause*], I don't know how else to say, but it was – [*long pause*]. Gotta choose these words, carefu—. You know – [*long pause*]. How do you – [*long pause*]? It's like those rappers. Again, I am not trying to speak badly about them. I understand where they're coming from, but it's like they wear the baggy pants, the twisted hats and have this, like, style about them, and have this, like, lethargic way about them. *And that is not something I want to be associated with.* And that was it! I just – yeah. They are very boisterous in their ways, and it's always like yelling and shouting – I don't know – just aggressive, basically. (U2S2, emphasis added)

In Charles's disdainful reference to "those rappers" who are "lethargic," boisterous," and "aggressive" it becomes clearer that he does not, in fact, simply advocate for a non-essentialist, mutual acceptance of different ways of performing Blackness. Instead, in its poignantly antiblack overtones there is a clear, colonially informed rejection of the Blackness that Charles's colleagues perform, whom Charles positions as "acting like niggers" (in Wynterian terms) – in many ways, as being less human. Charles wants nothing to do with them. Thus, while Charles might be resisting essentialist notions of Blackness, he is not doing so on terms that foster mutual respect; he is doing so in a manner consistent with an antiblack colonial logic that he reinforces.

Awakening

Charles's struggle to articulate exactly his discomfort with his Black colleagues is very evident in the previous excerpt. I suggest that his struggle is produced by the fact that he is talking about these experiences in the context of his participation in blackface – a participation that he now deeply regrets. In this context, the colonial ideas that have formed his identity and engagement with peers at university are becoming clear and being thrown into conflict with his growing awareness of the antiblack conditions within which all these experiences have taken place. He is in the process of a realization that, in the "metropole" (Canada in this instance), Fanon and Wynter make clear is always a rude awakening (Fanon, 1967, p. 112; Wynter, 2001, p. 38). Fanon writes of the violence of this rude awakening in the moment when, in the metropole, the Black person from the colonies meets the eyes of the white man (p. 112). In this moment, Wynter explains, one is met with the realization that for all one's attempts not to "act like one, s/he is, in white eyes, always already inescapably, a 'nigger'" (p. 38).

Yet, I argue that this realization is less abrupt and more temporally protracted in the contemporary postracialist moment in Canada, where the social is powerfully structured by antiblackness even as critical discourse about antiblackness is suppressed. In an effort to become fully Human on colonial terms, a status that is as yet, for students like Charles, not easily separated from whiteness and that they experience as just trying to be oneself, these students may be seduced into exploiting ostensible cultural similarities, and seeking out lighthearted post-race friendships with white people. These friendships, however, do not take place outside of the antiblack colonial frame, and so the ongoing effort to be accepted as fully Human by proving that one is part of the (normatively white) gang involves distancing oneself from Blackness. Only over time might these Black students find that an ingrained part of these post-race friendships is not only distance from Blackness, and the silencing of Black critique (as we saw in the previous chapter), but also a derision of Blackness that turns on them. Students like Charles must overlook this derision to maintain the illusion of inclusion and their honorary white/Human status. These are the circumstances under which we find Charles participating in blackface with his white colleagues, thereby endorsing their participation. Black participation in blackface, then, is one particularly disturbing outcome of the colonial dynamic that produces the antiblack terms for Black acceptance at university, and requires participation in one's own dehumanization.

We find evidence of Charles gaining insight into this dynamic only in retrospect, where he says:

> In my first and second year I had a lot of [white] friends and I know the reason why was because I was very much a novelty to them. You see it in terms of how they approach, the kind of jokes that they make. There's so many little actions that they do that show you that they're not your friend; you're just amusement to them ... Like just playing football, they would try to imitate my accent to ask me to pass the ball to them. Or I would go out with them and they would be like, "Listen to this guy talk! Listen to this guy talk! Listen to his accent!" You know, just things like that. At that age it was very – , it made me feel good to a certain extent because I didn't know where it came from. But I mean hindsight is always 20/20. So now that I see it, I'm just like, "Oh! That's where it came from!" (U2S2)

Looking back on his friendships with his white colleagues, Charles is able to discern that the relationships were unequal long before the blackface incident, and that his "friends" had often made fun at his expense. Now critically naming the colonial dynamics that informed his participation in blackface, he speaks of the "blissful ignorance" (to use his own words) that he is overcoming. He had been oblivious, perhaps wilfully so, because he felt that this meant acceptance.

Though Charles feels these colleagues would not participate in blackface again in the future, he is not sure that it is because they have allowed themselves to learn from pushback they received, but rather to avoid facing the same kind of backlash. His friendships with these white colleagues have cooled considerably since their participation together in blackface. As Charles became more aware of the history of blackface, and what its contemporary form might mean after the event, he tells us that his efforts to share this new knowledge with his colleagues were not welcomed and caused stiffness in their friendships. This makes sense through the analytical lenses that we have been using.

As Charles began to develop a more insightful analysis, the ground for his post-race friendships began to dissolve.

Perhaps Not *Just* Defensive Essentialists

In this light, then, perhaps the students who so far have been framed as defensive essentialists are involved in a rejection of the antiblack terms for their existence/inclusion on campus. In my research, I do not hear directly from any Black students who call others whitewashed (or at least who admit to doing so). Since we are hearing from them only by way of Charles, it is hard to determine whether they overplayed this position of resistance, resulting in the accusations they ostensibly made, or whether this was only Charles's reading of their position. The double bind of this situation is that within prevailing antiblack colonial logics, there are no ways of rejecting mimicry and reclaiming particular forms of Blackness that will not always already be assessed within this frame as confirming stereotypes of Blackness. Nevertheless, these students also exhibited a form of Black freedom that refused to tread carefully to avoid being stereotyped. They perhaps realize, consistent with Wynter's (2001) analysis, that any such care would be futile where one is always already deemed a "nigger" (p. 38). Steve Biko (2002 [1978]) describes it as a refusal that affirms:

> the value of their own standards and outlook. That urges black people to judge themselves according to these standards and not to be fooled by white society who have white-washed themselves and made white standards the yardstick by which even black people judge each other. (p. 30)

These students' use of the term "whitewashed" and other similar terms, if they were used, can be understood as an effort to call out colonial mimicry where they see it in their colleagues.

Nevertheless, we cannot dismiss the concerns of those positioned like Charles and Janine whose apprehensions, however poorly they play out, direct us to be mindful of the diverse ways in which Blackness can be lived, and of how we might address the problem of the colonizer within (all of us), promoting healing rather than alienation. If name-calling occurred, it is clear that this is not the most promising strategy for helping each other move past the effects of the antiblack colonial logics that incessantly seek to seduce us into postracialism. We should also be careful to avoid Charles's and Janine's dichotomous thinking, and instead to understand that name-callers are not representative of all Black persons on campus who reject mimicry. As the next chapter will show, there are many Black students, staff, and faculty who use much more fruitful approaches that are consistent with their show of love for *all* Black people, including those who have fallen prey to postracialism but who are open to learning.

Conclusion

I close by restating that it is not my intention to romanticize or demonize any participants, or the subject positions that I have discussed. Moreover, I do not intend to create or reify dichotomous notions of Black identity. The multiple and complex textures of Blackness, representing a variety of relationships to place of birth, citizenship, immigration, class, gender, activism, education, are reflected in my data and at Canadian universities in general in ways that defy reductive categorizations. This chapter therefore should not be read as an indictment of international students writ large, but rather points to the pitfalls for some Black international students who engage with the university and/or migration transactionally – as a means to escape "n***rdom" and access a whiteness understood as synonymous with humanity.

Instead, it has been my project to complicate how we might understand Janine's and Charles's experiences on campus, and to make sense of them in relation to their engagement with contemporary blackface in Canada and on campus. This chapter supplements chapters before it in affording us yet another view of the different ways that Black students grapple with living within a postracialist, antiblack context at university. As such, the gaze needs to remain squarely upon these dehumanizing antiblack structures and on how they might be dismantled.

9 Fugitive Learning: Countering Postracialism and Making Black Life at University

Black students clearly come to schools and universities to be educated, but what exactly does this mean in a context that is constitutively antiblack and a purveyor of knowledge in/through antiblackness? As others have noted, and consistent with the position I take in this book, schooling is a site for creating Blackness as excess – perpetually positioning it as disposable and "without," even as Blackness provides the indispensable foil against which the existence of the university, whiteness, and dominant conceptions of the Human become possible (McKittrick, 2011; Mustaffa, 2017, p. 711; Patel, 2016, p. 397; Sojoyner, 2013). Indeed, schooling (universities in particular) and the commodity they offer – education – are fraught with notions of meritocracy and credentialism that are always already antiblack. Yet there is little viable choice for Black people within current arrangements as to whether they will engage with schooling (Harney & Moten, 2013; Mustaffa, 2017, p. 711; Patel, 2016, p. 398). More importantly, Black students know full well that schools are and have been one site at which they can cull an education (where education is not synonymous with schooling), though this has always been on fugitive terms. There are four operating tenets of higher education (Mustaffa, 2017, p. 720). These include the enforced respectability politics informing the kinds of experiences that students like those in the previous two chapters have, and the ongoing exclusion of Black people from the university resulting in the "surprising" encounters discussed in Chapter 5. Mustaffa gathers these various forms under the rubric of educational violence, – a particular institutional corollary to state violence in educational institutions – and names blackface incidents on campus as one significant instantiation of this violence (p. 723).

Anti-racist and Equity/Diversity/Inclusion (EDI) initiatives notwithstanding, Walcott and Abdillahi (2019) note that within such a context

> incorporation is fundamentally impossible for "the Black." Furthermore, the conditions under which incorporation is understood [e.g., through EDI efforts] are so deeply freighted with the detritus of racial capital and white supremacist logics that incorporation can and only does occur at the symbolic level leaving all other Black beings or Black life forms marked for poverty and death as a repetition of modern life. (p. 76)

It is in the face of the impossibility of incorporation, indeed in the refusal of incorporation, that Black people might make Black life at the university. There are perhaps several responses that Black students might take in this regard if they are not to abandon themselves to the meritocratic illusion of the university. Among them: (1) one might make of the university a place one enters and leaves with all haste – both daily and with respect to completing one's studies. So very many students (and faculty) choose this option, understandably jaded by the antiblackness of the university's normative functioning. Making life elsewhere becomes a way of making Black life while at the university. (2) One might take it upon oneself to engage with/in the university through activism around causes affecting Black people. This may be either with an understanding that the university is redeemable, and therefore with a view to pressuring the university to reach its ostensible potential; or with a more radical understanding that the university is ontologically antiblack – where activism becomes about demystifying the university's claim to be otherwise, and grasping moments of racial fortuity and interest convergence (Bell, 1980, 2004) to attain temporary relief and improvements for Black people, or what have been called non-reformist reforms (Gilmore, 2017, p. 41; Kelley, 2016b, n.p.). (3) One might engage, while at the university, in a self-directed or group-based liberatory project of learning that takes place adjacent to the process of schooling. As Kelley, (2016b) has insisted, Black people have traditionally engaged in Black study by "repurposing university resources to instruct themselves and one another – to self-radicalize, in effect" (n.p.).

These processes are not mutually exclusive. As Choudry (2014) and others have argued, successful social movements, organizing, and activism are inherently educational processes. Indeed, hampton (2020) describes how engagement in activism in and around the university was eminently pedagogical for her while pursuing a degree program, variously "supplementing, complementing, and often challenging" (p. 8) what she was being taught in the classroom. Here, strategies 2 and 3 above overlap, and do not necessarily exclude strategy 1. Yet, in sepa-rating strategies 2 and 3, I signal that campus activism as it is most often understood is not the only crucible within which liberatory learning can be forged, nor is it to be considered a precondition for liberatory learn-ing, nor is everything that names itself campus activism necessarily a learning project. It is with these caveats in mind that Kelley (2016b) can urge that student activists "not cleave their activism from their intel-lectual lives" (n.p.), which indicates that they are not the same, but also indicates the ways in which they can, if engaged in an understanding of the history of Black struggle at university, lead to each other.

In this light, two points are particularly salient. First, schooling can-not be considered the same as learning or education, and to conflate them is to mystify the larger projects of injustice and coloniality upon which the university and its educational work are based (Patel, 2016). Learning as I mean it in this chapter must be conceived as a liberatory project envisioning freedom – "unruly rupture from the seductive mol-lification of school-based achievement" (Patel, 2016, p. 397).

The second point is that all three strategies mentioned above count as "Black life-making" – the multiple fugitive ways in which Black peo-ple preserve themselves, enact freedom, and carve out spaces for it in broader contexts of Black unfreedom (Mustaffa, 2017, p. 712). Walcott and Abdillahi (2019) draw our attention to

> the ways in which Black people break "rules," authorizing for themselves new ways of being in the world. These ways are often violently inter-dicted. Freedom is the gap or space between breaking the law and the re-imposition of the law or its variant – that is violence. The law is violence in this conception we are offering. The law, then, always curtails freedom for Black personhood in the West. It is the BLM call, that "we will win" in the face of contemporary state institutional (especially universities') vio-lences of all kinds that keeps open the possibility of a freedom yet to come. (pp. 69–70)

While Walcott and Abdillahi certainly speak quite literally of the law, I take their articulation of "the law" to also include the many other poli-cies, mandates, guidelines, and demands made upon Black people that perpetually seek to snuff out Black life and its expression. In specifically citing universities, the authors highlight the processes of educational violence instantiated through the normative operation of the university that punish Black freedom. Amid this, Walcott and Abdillahi identify the jurisgenerative practices (Harney & Moten, 2015) in which Black people engage as a practice of freedom.

In this chapter, I am interested in fugitive learning, or learning as marronage (Patel, 2016; N. Roberts, 2015) as a form of Black life-making and a jurisgenerative practice of freedom (Harney & Moten, 2015, p. 85) that takes place at the university. Given the context of this book, I attend along the way to those initiatives that students participate in related to challenging blackface and the broader postracialist iterations of educational violence.

Fugitive learning is constituted of the dialectical, not uncontradictory, processes of which Harney and Moten (2013) speak whereby the university is enclosure but might become refuge. Fugitive learning speaks to the sense in which Black people "sneak into the university and steal what [they] can" (Harney & Moten, 2013, p. 25). This "sneaking" and "stealing" signify that Black life-making in this way breaks "the law"that takes shape in the usual transactional terms of engagement at the university. Fugitive learning moves towards refusing the university (Grande, 2018). In this fugitive space, the end of learning is not the pursuit of a place in the world as it is, but rather the pursuit of freedom. This pursuit is less destination than way of being in the world where one can dream of and work towards a future where antiblackness and all forms of injustice are undone, while living freedom in the moment (Grande, 2018; Harney & Moten, 2013, 2015; Kelley, 2016b; N. Roberts, 2015).

In addition to data from my blackface study, in this chapter I draw on interviews, focus groups, and written responses to a multisite event I organized around the blackface issue. The event, held in October 2017, was called "The Arts Against Postracialism" (AAPR).[1] The purpose of AAPR was to share knowledge generated from my earlier research on blackface incidents with those most impacted by blackface – that is, the Black members of university communities. The project sought to build capacity for, and nuance within, the critical dialogue about blackface and antiblackness; to offer spaces of healing for Black people impacted by blackface, and to create intra- and inter-campus networks between campus organizations interested in challenging blackface, and antiblackness more broadly.

Curator and performance artist Camille Turner co-led this project with me. We invited a team of four artists, Anique Jordan, Esmaa Mohamoud, Nadine Valcin, and Quentin Vercetty, each of whom created an art installation inspired by the research. Participants in the event interacted

1 SSHRC Individual Connection Grant #611-2016-0429: The Arts Against Postracialism: Strengthening Resistance Against Contemporary Canadian Blackface.

with the installations and attended workshops, a panel discussion, and a lecture.

Fugitive Learning before University

Schooling is a key site at which Black children are inducted into the hegemonic national project, which, as we have seen, is postracialist and a threat to Blackness. Though this chapter builds from conversations with students at university, it acknowledges that fugitive learning for Black people does not necessarily begin at university. Understanding this helps us to grasp fugitivity as a/the way of life for Black people at all times within the afterlife of slavery. Understanding this also contests the university as place of enlightenment (Harney & Moten, 2013, p. 25), a position that we have seen it tries to claim, attempting to make that education which happens at university qualitatively different from the hegemonic project of schooling that leads up to university, and from what one is susceptible to learning from one's ostensibly unenlightened family or community.

Illustrating fugitive learning before university, Sonji recalls:

> I read a lot when I was younger too. I was very interested in history and things like that, and Black history and everything. And I remember in Grade 9 reading this book about the history of the KKK, and that book changed my life. It was so – ! (*makes gesture of enamouredness*) And it's just being aware. So I think the education is very important but unfortunately there isn't a lot of education that happens until you go out and seek it for yourself. (U2FGBSOP3)

The book that Sonji read in Grade 9 was not a book assigned by the teacher, and in this excerpt "Grade 9" acts only as a chronological marker in Sonji's life in the way that students often mark their stories. Sonji speaks to the learning that occurred for her through engagement with this book that she selected for herself, and signals the ways that students have to direct this learning themselves in the face of the stark omissions and silences of schooling. Sonji finds in this learning exercise what she would never have learned otherwise in school. It is *this* self-directed learning, and not what she gets in school, that Sonji experiences as transformative.

In a similar example of fugitive learning before university, Patrick tells us:

> Anything particularly anti-racist from K to 12 would have been non-existent, or would have been projects that *I* came up with. Like, I remember I was

cleaning stuff out of my room and I came across a Grade 10 English project assignment that was talking about slavery … those are the type of things that I would have to do myself or look at myself but there wasn't any anti-racist education that I can think of, or anything like that. (U7S1)

Here again, Patrick's Grade 10 project topic was not assigned to him by the school as part of the curriculum, but was a topic he chose as a way of fulfilling the requirements of a Grade 10 English Language Arts assignment. Of course, assignments that offer students choice are always good pedagogical strategy. However, they cannot stand in as a way to teach important knowledge that schools otherwise neglect. By juxtaposing his self-chosen topic with the complete absence of anything in the formal curriculum relevant to his Blackness and broader issues of race, Patrick communicates that this is exactly what happened in his case. Nevertheless, he actively repurposes this assignment for himself and his own learning.

These self-directed acts of learning are fugitive acts. They are practices of freedom to the extent that they are sites of learning and refuge created to make Black life apposite to the antiblackness of schooling that would not only ignore Black life, but snuff it out. They are also fugitive in another sense: in the way that they largely remain unnamed. Students are eking out an education in Blackness and Black histories hidden under the cover of the regular school curriculum into which they must insert it. The existence of these fugitive strategies as necessary for students to sustain their engagement with schooling – that is, to sustain Black life at school – remains largely unacknowledged, allowing schools to persist in a pretence of appropriately serving all their students, and even sometimes applauding themselves as the site where such learning about Blackness occurred. The students' extra educational labour over and above what their white colleagues have to do, and the ways that it supplements the labour for which teachers are paid, also disappear quietly, as fugitive.

Students' insertion of this fugitive learning, as a practice of freedom, is inherently disruptive if only because it highlights the knowledge that is actively negated in the official curriculum. Over and above the educational violence it is already responding to, it can activate other familiar forms of violence that desire to keep Blackness in check. Donovan recounts his experience of trying to create a site of fugitive Black learning when he was in high school:

We tried to have a Black History Month type of thing, and we were told that we couldn't do that; they said we couldn't have the auditorium. And we tried to practise in the hallways, and they said we were loitering. And I said, "Call the police!" You know, the mere fact that that's the type of environment in which people are learning, where someone would even be considering calling the police for trying to have, as I framed it when they called the police, I said, "There's a bunch of Black kids who are on the honour roll in the hallway trying to practise for a play after school, and they are calling you here!" Like, "Arrest me," you know what I mean? (U2FG2P1)

Donovan and his friends' work here is jurisgenerative. They *will* have a rehearsal for a Black History Month performance that may never take place given the school's refusal to give it space. They take to the halls when they are denied the auditorium. In response, the structure of schooling and its ingrained resistance to Black learning marked these students' activities as "out of place" and framed them as criminal. The school authorities – themselves "the law" to which Walcott and Abdillahi (2019, pp. 69–70) refer – were quite literally willing to bring "the law" in the form of police to discipline this act of fugitive learning and expression of Black freedom. Unsurprisingly, within the logic of schooling this seemed a more appropriate course of action than simply providing space and supervision for students seeking to make a place for Black knowledge and expression at school.

In addition to students' own acts, what communities and families do to counter the antiblackness of their children's schooling also constitutes the broader project of fugitive learning. This is evident in the numerous summer schools, after-school programs, and summer camps that exist, which I call Black Community Supplementary Education initiatives. The broader project includes the tradition of Black parental and maternal activism in Canada (Howard, 2013; Lawson, 2019) – which, in turn, involves the kind of parent-child coaching that we saw Sonji's mother engaging in in Chapter 7. It includes the work of Black teachers within schools who create conditions of survivability for their students (Aladejebi, 2012, 2015a; Howard, 2014b; Howard & James, 2019). It includes the activist work of Black scholars and teachers, which operates aside, apart from, and against existing forms of schooling to make Black life, work that results, for example, in such initiatives as the Africentric Alternative School in Toronto, the Black Lives Matter Freedom School, also in Toronto, and several other alternative Black learning sites (H. Codjoe, 2006; Dei & Kempf, 2013; Howard, 2013; James et al., 2017; Solomon & Palmer, 2004). Fugitive learning is a project that is in full effect long before a student arrives at the university.

At University: The Uncertain Status of Critical Coursework

Some critical education and Black learning does happen through the usual educational channels of the university – that is, coursework. Some students we interviewed spoke of learning about minstrelsy, blackface, and why they might be racist and, more broadly, of learning about structural racism and antiblackness in courses they took. We cannot, however, misconstrue this to simply suggest that the university in its normative institutional iteration is a site of critical Black learning. Students made a point of contrasting these courses with the majority of other courses in their programs and at the university, and therefore with those that characterize the normative education the university had to offer. For example, a student at University 3, speaking about a recent incident of blackface at their university, says:

> I also think that the institution needs to be more accountable to – Like, the whole silence that University 3 has over issues is just bullshit. I think that they need people who actually know why these incidents are so offensive and use them as teaching moments. I have only had one professor who found out about something that was happening on campus and was, like, "OK. We are talking about this in class because this needs to be addressed." Most professors just don't care, and most administrators will just silence things. (U3FGP1)

This white student points out that their professor, who is racialized, is an exception among other professors for being willing to teach about race and address racist events happening at the university. The "don't care" approach that this respondent identifies in other professors reminds us of the attitudes of Sonji's teachers at elementary school, as well as those professors at university who stood by as Sonji was lambasted by her colleagues (Chapter 7). Another student confesses:

> I am studying diaspora studies, and in our tutorial for my history class in that program we always joke about that if you go into [the History Department's] history major, you can literally circumvent learning anything about the Caribbean, anything about Aboriginal history, and graduate from [University 2] with a history major. So basically you are just learning Eurocentric white history, and then you can say, like, "I'm an expert. I graduated with a history major." So, like, I guess there obviously is stimulating debate in our course, but it's something that is constantly joked about in class all the time. (U2FG1P6)

Here again, the respondent marks the exceptionality of the kind of critical knowledge they are receiving in a few courses, and the ways that the normative practices of the university lead in a very different direction. Many more students in the study identified, instead, how they have been subjected to antiblackness through both official curriculum and (not so) hidden curriculum at university. Therefore, the critical education that takes place in some classrooms is not because of the university, but rather despite the university.

In most cases, the critical courses students spoke of were offered by Black, Indigenous, and other racialized instructors. Of these courses, those specifically concerning Blackness represent forms of fugitivity and Black life-making. In a kind of tautology, they are seldom offered under the rubric of Black Studies or within Black Studies departments, and there are few Black Studies departments across the country within which such courses could be offered. The courses the students describe therefore exist on fugitive terms and undercover (despite themselves) as niche offerings or special topics within other disciplinary formations, and/or under non-specific, wholly inadequate headings such as anti-racism, critical race, multiculturalism, area studies, and diaspora studies (Hudson & Kamugisha, 2014, p. 7; Walcott, 2014a, p. 276). They are also spaces that (usually, but not exclusively) Black instructors offer to carve out sites of fugitive study for themselves and for students who would not otherwise find spaces to study Black life. Yet fugitive spaces are, definitionally, sites both of freedom/refuge *and* of risk, and this is especially so in these courses. Black professors and instructors who participated in my research study and Black, Indigenous, and racialized scholars in the educational literature (see, e.g., Bannerji, 1991; Daniel, 2019; Dei, 2017; Monture, 2009; Ohito, 2016, 2020) refer repeatedly to the personal costs of doing this critical work in the university, and to the difficulty of adequately meeting their Black, Indigenous, and racialized students' learning needs in their courses. As Ohito (2020) writes:

> Classrooms like mine that are anchored to "vision driven justice" … are atypical; therefore, there are few places available for Black students to aerate their unfiltered perspectives and feelings about whiteness and anti-Blackness, which may rightfully include rage and anger (hooks, 1995; Thomson, 2017). The crux of the tension described here is the impossibility of Black and white cohabitation in an interracial classroom designed to propel flight from whiteness and anti-Blackness, and the (ethical?) dilemmas of constructing curricular and pedagogical spaces that promise all students sanctuary and well-being when only some (i.e., Black students) are most adversely affected by inhaling the noxious airs of whiteness and anti-Blackness. (pp. 214–15)

Ultimately, then, courses in the university, even when they focus on Black study, offer an uncertain refuge and are inherently dangerous –

both for Black students and for Black professors who teach them. Fortunately they are not the only spaces of fugitive learning at the university.

Fugitive Learning in/through Black Sociality at University

Fugitive Learning Sites and/as Self-recovery

Many Black students enter the predominantly white, largely non-Black institutions – which all Canadian universities are – understandably hoping to make friends and find community at a significant juncture in their lives. They may expect to find this community across racial lines given the ways that the university represents itself as a site of open-mindedness, family, and diversity (Kelley, 2016b, n.p.). Instead, some Black students face outright rejection. Njeri tells us:

> We're just so few, especially if you're first year and you don't know any other Black students around. You just feel like "Oh my God! Where am I?" You go to class and you're the only Black kid, and no one wants to talk to you, and you're just, like, "What's happening?," you know. You thought you're gonna make friends, but they are not ready to make friends with you. Like, they just look at you and no one wants to say anything to you. … and on the floor the don is trying to … force people to make friends with me. (U1BSOFGP4)

As an international student from the African continent accustomed to Black majority settings, Njeri grapples with her new reality that the number of Black students at her university is very small, and with the implications for finding community, particularly as a new student. When she looks to her non-Black colleagues, Njeri's experience is that they are not interested in forming friendships with her, and she finds the interventions by the residence don to contrive such friendships counterproductive and insulting. Fortunately, by the time we spoke to Njeri, she had located one of the Black student organizations on her campus and found community there.

Other Black students may not face outright rejection, but experience "incorporation" on very particular terms. Valerie speaks about her struggle with belonging:

> Even through my whole first year, I never really felt like I was a part of that family at Cambridge Residence. *They* were all pretty much family, but they were all white, they were all Italian, they were all – , you know, they

all had this in common and I had nothing in common with them. And I didn't like that. I didn't really like myself. And I was always being judged, whether it was indirectly or even directly, I was always being judged on something. Like my hair – always my hair – or my body. Yeah, that's probably the most two things, but yeah, I was never really accepted, I feel. (U2BSOFGP2)

Unlike Njeri, Valerie claims to have had friends, but the postracialism of schooling and the university made the terms upon which these friendships were formed deeply antiblack. Valerie's "friendships" were all with white peers, who constantly evaluated her being and who fixated on Black hair and the Black body much as blackface perpetrators do. This constant positioning as spectacle foreclosed on any sense of acceptance and community that might normally be associated with friendship. In the end, it amounts to rejection, which Valerie internalized.

Yet, as with Njeri, the rest of Valerie's story is one of the power and importance of Black sociality in these circumstances. We met Valerie in a focus group session with members of a Black student organization (BSO) at University 2. Naturally, we were interested in how she had transitioned from seeking community but experiencing rejection in an all-white friendship group to now being a member of a BSO. She tells us:

What made me join was just everyone that was on the BSO at the time was just so loving and welcoming. They reminded me of my family, like my own family and home. I was like, "Wow, I have to join this group," … I think they were having this event … and they were all just dancing on the campus. I was like, "This is really cool!" And then the president just came up to me and she's like, "Come dance! Come get food!" It was just so welcoming, and it was just a natural connection that happened. So then I joined. … I was like, "I do not feel like this at Cambridge Residence. At Cambridge Residence I am always trying to fit in; I'm pushing to fit in. I am never just comfortable. It's like I can't breathe. But just this one interaction, it was so comfortable, so natural. So I joined. (U2BSOFGP2)

For Valerie, meeting Black people at the BSO event where members welcomed and encouraged her to get involved was a starkly different experience than what she had been used to. She was drawn to "jurisgenerative black social life walking … dancing" (Harney & Moten, 2015, p. 81) on a campus that she had otherwise experienced as suffocating. She was invited into this context where she did not have to force herself to fit in ways that violated her very being as a Black woman. Valerie found respite from the pervasive antiblackness of the university, and it afforded her a site of self-recovery. She relates:

> It's going to sound really corny but joining the BSO really changed me. Like, it made me embrace myself and love myself. Because I was always around people who were different than me and judging me that I don't look like them, like "Oh, you're too curvy," "Your hair is a different texture," this and that. And now I am around people who just like me and embrace me for me, and it made me love myself and like, yeah, embrace my Blackness, you know? (U2BSOFGP2)

Here, Valerie connects the transformation of her consciousness – an essential learning for her – with the non-judgmental manner in which the BSO reached out to her, and the nurturing space that it continued to provide. These qualities of the BSO might be contrasted with the accusations of being whitewashed that Charles and Janine mention experiencing in Chapter 8, and which seemed at least partially responsible for their non-engagement with Black people at the university. As Janine mentioned, the accusation of being whitewashed has the potential to feel similar to the ways that black-face tries to fix Blackness in essentializing terms. Valerie openly admits to having been "ignorant" (to use her words) prior to her involvement with the BSO, engaging in behaviours that could have left her open to accusations of being "whitewashed." However, her experience with the BSO on her campus did not put her Blackness on trial. It neither rejected her for her Blackness like her white peers did, nor rejected her for the post-race ways of being that she had been socialized into. Consequently, the BSO felt like family, a welcoming, and she attached herself to it.

This BSO's thoughtful approach is an important one that is able to see past the individual and resist pathologizing individual Black people. Instead, it understands the pathological social structures within which we live and are educated and the ways they impact us all to varying degrees. This approach not only serves as a means of attracting Black students into community, but is also one condition of possibility for fugitive learning and for self-recovery from the imposed post-racism. This particular BSO at University 2 at the time understood its crucial pedagogical role in providing community as a fugitive site for Black learning and healing.

Fugitive Learning and Epistemic Community

Lance, who like Valerie tended to dismiss his embodied responses to blackface and other forms of antiblackness to maintain friendships with white people, has experienced a similar self-recovery and now also finds community within the University 2 BSO. Lance no longer allows his friendships with white people to cause him to overlook antiblackness. He tells us:

> I guess now I am not as passive with white people as I was before … now I find that instead of just laughing about it or kind of ignoring it, I educate about it and I wouldn't be ashamed to, and I wouldn't feel weird about doing that. … Now I don't even care. If they say something, I am going to call them out on it and let them know why you can't say stuff like that, why that's not fine with me! At least like, "Don't say that because of this, this, this." (U2BSOFGP1)

Lance does not attribute his new resolve directly to the BSO, but does attribute it to increased engagement with Black people. Responding to the question about how he had come to his current way of being, he says:

> Honestly, for me I think two things: (1) growing up, and (2) getting closer with my Black friends. I had Black friends, but they weren't my close friends. They were kind of like I talked to them here and there. But I really got close to them and I could just talk about things that I couldn't talk about with my other friends, and I was like, "Okay, yeah." And I wouldn't have to be like, "Do you kind of get what I'm saying?" They know what I'm saying! I don't have to ask, "Do you get it?" They just got it! It sounds weird but it empowered me in some way. (U2BSOFGP1)

As Lance continued to have experiences with antiblackness at the university, and as he matured – ostensibly to where he was less concerned about being rejected by his white peers – he moved into more meaningful relationships with his Black friends. He no longer viewed them through a post-race lens as friends who just happened to be Black, but instead viewed their Blackness as essential to the quality of relationship he could have with them. With these friends with whom he shared particular experiences of Blackness, he did not have to negotiate the barrier of a dominant mandatory post-racism to find empathy (see Tatum, 2003, p. 60). Having these kinds of relationships to understand and anchor him became epistemic community – a place to share ways of knowing and being. Epistemic community was fugitive learning that transformed Lance and allowed him to take a more unapologetic stance when responding to antiblackness.

Black sociality not only constitutes fugitive learning, but creates a desire to further such learning. Valerie's experience with the BSO led her to seek out more knowledge that would help her understand her experiences as a Black woman. She sought out course offerings of the type described earlier in this chapter:

> And my mind is just so open now like regarding that. So, yeah, I think that is what changed. And also some classes I have been taking have really opened my mind as well, like to Blackness and to, like, what's right and what's wrong. Like, I feel like I was really sheltered and closed growing up pertaining to these issues, especially in high school, which is kind of why I think I was like that in my first year. (U2BSOFGP2)

Here Valerie signals that her earlier orientation was not some kind of "natural" or "blank slate" state, but something that had been actively cultivated in her through her educational experience. Black sociality at university offers a corrective. It does not impose a way of being or seeing upon students like Lance and Valerie. Rather, recalling that they both had been suppressing their embodied negative reactions to black-face and other forms of antiblackness, we can see that Black sociality offered them a way of understanding their lives that no longer required them to negate their experiences as Black people. This learning acquired in fugitive spaces at the university worked to undo the effects of their earlier education and the ways it undermines what Black families and Black communities endeavour to teach these students. Ultimately, Black sociality provides epistemic community within the wider context of educational violence.

Other students we interviewed also indicate the value of the epistemic community provided by Black friends and BSOs at their universities. Aminata at University 5 tells us:

> I think I joined the graduate BSO because I realize that it is good, especially being new to City 5 into grad school, it's good to have a community of people that you can ask questions, to share concerns with, if need be. (U5BSOFGP2)

Similarly, Franklin at University 2 tells us:

> I felt like I benefited so much from spaces like the BSO, or just like radical spaces where people listen and thread a thought. ... So a lot of students on campus here, we came together through the BSO ... I felt like I was able to talk to them, and like bounce ideas off them as well. Also last year, there was a don at Tower Residence. She was also very, like, anti-racism oriented and I liked that a lot, and so I was able to bounce my ideas off of

her ... within the other very forward-thinking Black dons that I've met, probably the most powerful thing, the powerful tool they have, was just like affirmation, being like, "You're not crazy! it's true! It's messed up!" I felt that was really strong and really good. ... There aren't many other Black dons and so it's been interesting because, like, that definitely pushed me to hold events on anti-racism last year. (U2S1)

For Franklin, the epistemic community he had with members of the BSO and other Black dons sustained his mental health, built his knowledge, and supported him in making decisions to act on antiblackness at the university. Armed with this confidence, in his role as residence don, Franklin planned and held events for the largely non-Black residents, which he hoped might pre-empt blackface incidents and raise residents' critical understanding of race.

Epistemic community forged in these fugitive spaces where Black people are able to share and think together about their lives is an important site of fugitive learning in the broader university context that is hostile to Black thought. Both for Black students accustomed to having to direct their own fugitive learning alone and against the grain of their schooling, and for students who are newly recovering from schooling that has not been in their interest, these spaces afford some safety to discuss concerns and questions, and even to try out new ideas, while feeling more confident that what they learn in these spaces will be in their interest. They are spaces of Black life-making within, but not of, the university.

Fugitive Learning and/as Collective Action

The learning that comes of epistemic community is intertwined with willingness to contest conditions of antiblackness, as Lance's and Franklin's experiences suggest. With specific reference to blackface, Lance's and Valerie's claims above about how they might respond in the future are largely speculative. However, as members of their BSO's executive team they have actively demonstrated their willingness to act from their new perspectives through leading BSO events. In these roles, they organized various events that allow for the kind of learning we have been talking about and that act on their antiblack surroundings, whether these approaches flow from more liberal or more radical visions, and though the two types of visions are not necessarily mutually exclusive (Kelley, 2016a, 2016b). They spoke of organizing discussions where Black students could share their experiences of the university, debates to discuss broader social and political issues salient to

Black people, and outreach events for high school students with a view towards increasing levels of Black student enrolment at their university. These initiatives are opportunities to learn – both for the organizers and for those who attend. As such, BSOs, as one expression of Black sociality, offer a platform for this kind of learning through organizing and acting on one's environment.

The identity formation/development and the organizing that take place in these spaces are co-constitutive (Choudry, 2014; hampton, 2020, p. 8). Yonas at University 5 speaks about how a BSO at his university worked in this manner for him:

> Back then, you wouldn't think I would be joining an organization such as this BSO that I have joined now. The turning point is when I accepted to come to this program, and the first day we came in and over 182 students were sitting down in a big auditorium. And there's a certain silence before the dean speaks, and you glance over and you see a predominantly white group except for a few sparkles here and there. And instantly, you may not even recognize it for a second, you just count. There are only seven [Black] kids ... You just subconsciously say, "Wait a second! 1-2-3-4-5-6-7." And then you are like, "Is this something that needs to be addressed?" ... Then came this BSO. This is one of those organizations that is at the forefront of this issue. (U5BSAFGP4)

An international student from an African country, Yonas says understandably that he did not claim a Black identity (not the same as an African identity) before coming to University 5, and that it would have been unlikely for him to have joined a group organized around such an identity. The under-representation of Black students that became evident to him on his very first day immediately provoked a resolve to challenge it, which led him to the BSO that had been working on this issue. Through this affiliation, Yonas simultaneously discovered the alignment of his concerns with those of other Black people at the university, and the ways in which the presentation of his body interpellated him as Black within Canada despite his personal sense of self up until that point (Fanon, 1967, p. 110; Wynter, 2001). The processes are inseparable. In and through this organizing work, Yonas began to identify more deliberately as Black, and this identification informed his organizing work.

Like Black under-representation, blackface incidents often also stand out to Black students as instantiations of the antiblackness of university. Black students and other Black members of university communities therefore frequently organize around this issue, and these events also become sites of fugitive learning.

At the University of Toronto after a blackface incident in 2009, a BSO there – the Black Students Association (BSA) – organized a town hall, which drew an attendance of between three hundred and five hundred (Kyei et al., 2009; Powell, 2009). The BSA garnered support for the event from the University of Toronto Students' Union (UTSU), but notably received no support for the event from the University of Toronto administration (Kyei et al., 2009). The town hall consisted of lectures and discussions led largely by Black faculty about the blackface issue (Powell, 2009). It also called for apologies from the students involved in the blackface incident, apologies (to be printed in campus newspapers) from the student unions that had failed to stop or condemn the incident and had, in one case, rewarded the blackface costumes (Mahoney, 2009; Powell, 2009); and a statement from the university (Kyei et al., 2009; Powell, 2009). The offending students and student unions issued apologies (of varying depth) at the event (Powell, 2009). The university administration eventually issued a statement (Office of the Vice-Provost – Students, 2009), only because of the persistence of the BSA and UTSU, that fell short of condemning the incident and was issued a week after the town hall and almost a full month after the incident (Kyei et al., 2009). The statement was sent privately only to the team of six (two students and four faculty) who had met with the administration to call for action, then was finally posted on the university's Equity website upon further calls from the team for the letter to be made public (Kyei et al., 2009).

Thus, while the town hall was open to the broader university community and served as an educational opportunity for all, it was in many respects a fugitive space carved out by Black people in the "undercommons" (Harney & Moten, 2013) of the university – taking up space within and against the university and its antiblack values and commitments. It offered a place where Black students could be "heard" (Powell, 2009), where they could develop a framework for understanding their (antiblack) experiences of the university, and from which they could act against antiblackness at the university. The town hall as a vehicle for Black collective action to protest blackface was both result of and site for Black fugitive learning and Black life-making at this university.

Fugitive Learning through the AAPR Event

In this section, I turn more specifically to interviews and focus groups from the "Arts Against Postracialism" event organized to contemplate blackface and its effects. Here again, I am interested in what fugitive learning looked like in these spaces, and how it operated as Black life-making. Many of the themes discussed earlier repeat in this setting. Participants interviewed and surveyed found this event to be a space of fugitive learning in that they felt they were learning things that they simply do not learn through the universities' normal channels, and because they felt it contested the pervasive antiblackness of the university.

First, for the participants, the AAPR event served to convene Black students and break the isolation that results from their small numbers on campus. Shana told us:

> It has to do with that low – very, very low – number [of Black people on campus], and what that does to you as a young adolescent and an individual who is finding your way in your early twenties or late teens on a campus where you're walking a tightrope of hypervisibility and invisibility at the same time. So what this exhibit represented, I think, was something bigger than blackface. It was just kind of looking at the different ways in which antiblackness literally infuses itself into our everyday life and at the institutions, the universities ... So I think a lot of why you got people unified or coming together around this exhibit ... was because at University C, we don't often get to speak and talk about antiblackness, about racism, as an independent, isolating force that really affects so many of the students here on campus, and people of colour in general on the University C campus. (UCFGP1)

Here, Shana highlights the relationships among the university's antiblackness, the low numbers of Black people on campus, the resulting isolation yet positioning as spectacle (surprise), and the lack of opportunity to process this entire dynamic. The isolation and limited opportunity for Black people to come together in numbers is itself a way that the Canadian university atmosphere forecloses on Black learning. For Shana, the AAPR event represented more than just an opportunity to talk about blackface, but rather was an opening – a rift in the university's normative fabric, and a defiance of the terms of isolation it imposes – allowing Black people at University C to occupy themselves with themselves and their own interests.

In the same vein, Fatima at University A told us:

> It created a safe space because you were allowed to have awkward conversations. You were allowed to kind of confide in each other, which you don't usually get to do, you know what I mean? Like most times there isn't really a space for Black students to sort of talk to each other, you know? And we just see each other in passing. And it's kind of weird if you try

and be friends with other Black students, if that makes sense, like, because you don't want to bother people, you know what I mean, or whatever? ... Like I remember one girl in particular was telling me [during the event] how there is a lot of offensive stuff going on at her university, but there's no space to really talk about it, you know what I mean? And the conversation that me and her were having, she needed that, you know, as much as I did, too. (UAFGP1)

While it makes total sense that Black students would be interested in having these kinds of conversations, Fatima's designation of them as "awkward" and as requiring permission, along with her repeating bids for affirmation as she spoke to us ("you know what I mean?" "If that makes sense"), indicate the ways in which these conversations are not fostered in the postracialist, antiblack university. There is limited opportunity for Black people at the university to have these conversations and process their experiences together. Fatima and her new acquaintance grasped the opportunity provided by this event to reflect on their similar experiences across different institutions. They found a place of healing and solidarity in a broader context that militates against this kind of connection.

Diane at University D experiences this healing through personal reflection she undertook after interacting with one of the installations. She writes:

I think there is a pressure that racialized individuals endure in silence and isolation. I think the pressure is invisible because the discourses we hear are often in conflict with our experience as Black. ... I think living in an environment and a time where we hear so many discourses about equality, equity, justice, freedom and so many beautiful values conflicting with racism confuses the way I generally feel about contemporary Canadian blackface. I sometimes feel like my experience is not real, ... I think this [event] ... communicated some aspect of reality I was not able to put into words. It was similar to what I felt like watching *Get Out*, *Insecure*, or *Black-ish*, and reading *Beloved*. Now I know how real it is for me. I can no longer invalidate my experience based on the discourses I hear. (UDWR1)

Diane signals the insistent post-racism that is evident in hegemonic, postracialist university discourse around equity and social justice, which conflicts with the way she experiences the university. She refers to the impossible work of articulating Black life in relation to dominant, post-racism versions of these concepts. For Diane, the negative mental health implications of this demand for post-racism, only magnified by experiences of isolation, were countered in a fugitive space of Black sociality. The space of Black fugitive learning valorized Black knowledge, and gave her confidence to trust her embodied experience of the world.

As it did for participants mentioned earlier, fugitive learning bolsters students' confidence to challenge antiblackness. DeWayne at University C experienced this new sense of being able to act against the antiblack terms of his life at the university:

> I think it gives students a different approach and a different mentality to an issue such as blackface where it pretty much informs students such as myself that, ahm, you don't have to internalize it. ... I've been on University C campus for a while and I've seen a lot ... and I've internalized a lot. ... There were certain instances where it would affect someone I was close with, you know, a good friend and ... we would discuss this experience ... And a lot of times those thoughts, those emotions are just pretty much internalized. There's nothing that follows up, whether it's me not speaking up, whether it's me not going to some of the resources that are on campus, you know. Those have been pretty much all locked in a box ... Now I feel like I have other people around me that are just as invested, and are also expressing themselves publicly. And that allows myself to say, "Okay. It is okay to publicly tackle these issues!" So it's more of a confidence booster for me to be able to deal with an issue, this kind of racism in that community. (UCFGP2)

The isolation that DeWayne usually experiences on campus causes him to feel that he cannot do much more than internalize his experiences – that is, absorb the negative effects of incessant antiblackness without outlet to respond. He experiences the fugitive learning space of AAPR and the community it offers as energizing, a realization that there are others who share his concerns, and that they do not have to just go along to get along. Fatima at University A feels similarly:

> I feel better equipped [to deal with blackface incidents] going through other people. It kind of feels like you need a support system, like a system of people, instead of just like a small group. [Alone] you just look mad, you know what I mean? But when you have other people to support the reason why something isn't okay it's a little bit easier, you know? Because a lot of the time we're like alone, you know.

Fugitive Learning and/as Refreshing and Taking Up Space

DeWayne described the effects of the AAPR event for other members of the BSO on his campus who had shared their reactions with him. He told us, "So students at University C find this refreshing opportunity to come in and shut out everything around them and, you know, partake in this safe space to be able to express things they have been experiencing for years" (UCFGP2). Building on this theme, Shana says, "I thought for the fellow Black students who attended it definitely gave them life. Like, people walked out energized and renewed and just more so confident ... So for the students, the response was definitely one of renewal" (UCFGP1). Shana indicates that daily life at University C means being worn down by the space, but that the AAPR event offered an opportunity for renewal. DeWayne relates the "refreshing" that "gave them life" to the opportunity to "shut out everything." Of course, antiblackness, as a structure and not simply a series of events, continues to prevail around the students, and there is no way, in these terms, to really shut it out. As such, it is the fugitive act of taking time and space to turn attention to issues relevant to Black people when everything at the university militates against it that constitutes the refreshing, and the life they speak of. Such fugitive spaces are "life-giving" in the context of the afterlife of slavery at the university that always already tends towards Black erasure and the negation of Black thought. Taking space to think the "position of the unthought" (Hartman & Wilderson, 2003; Sexton, 2016) at the university constitutes the learning that is Black life-making at the university.

The idea of fugitive learning as taking the space for Black thought is intertwined with the idea of fugitive learning as simply taking up space. DeWayne says:

The event was able to transform space which was funded by this white donor centuries ago, right? So to transform that space which represents more so that white face of the university and that dominance, you guys were able to transform that space literally, physically, as well as through the conversations that took space. So for our BSO too that shows us how we can transform the space physically, verbally, and with, like, different types of dialogues and narratives that we can set forth here on [University C] campus. (UCFGP2)

DeWayne speaks here about a building in which an AAPR event took place. It stands out to him as an icon of the university's whiteness. He understands it as white space because of its history and the way it is usually appointed. It is a building that many of the Black students at this university say they had never visited. For DeWayne, the building was transformed as it became a site for exhibiting the Black art installations of the project, *and* for critical conversations about Blackness and antiblackness. DeWayne understands the physical make-over and the conversations that happened during the event as mutually reinforcing and intertwined. Indeed, he speaks of the conversations as "taking *space*"! He has begun to think forward about the ways his BSO might similarly transform spaces at the university by repurposing them for Black learning, even if only for the duration of an event. Fugitive learning happens where Blackness takes up space.

Letitia, at University D, feels similarly:

> I think just by convening, like meeting this many Black folks that are artists, just having this much Black thought and attention, not in February, for me, was powerful because it's not something that – and I've been around campus a long time – it's not something that gets viewed ... I feel like that was really powerful. We don't often get that opportunity ... And so to anticipate something and to witness something – And I went, "Wow. What's that feeling? Oh right, that's the desire to be with, to sit in a space and to listen to this many Black folks think about something, and just to sit in a lecture hall and have that many Black folks at the front of a stage." It's really powerful! And it's really, just, even the presence was just, the idea of convening and taking up space for me was really extremely, ahm, exciting! (UDFGP4)

That Black people were gathered together to contemplate Black issues and to think together made this a fugitive learning experience. However, for Letitia, simply having Black people in numbers in one location contrary to the usual geography of Blackness at the university, and the expectancy associated with it as the date approached, were themselves instructive. This was a phenomenon contrary to the normative order of the university. Here, Blackness and Black knowledge were taking up space – jurisgeneratively spilling over the restrictive boundaries of the time (February as Black History Month) and space into which they are normally squeezed. Occupying space, too, is fugitive learning and Black life-making. As one participant wrote in their feedback, "[AAPR] was a good reminder to proudly occupy spaces with my black body" (UDWR3).

Final Insights

This chapter has looked at various ways that fugitive learning takes place within but against the university and the pervasive antiblackness of its educational projects. Fugitive Black learning does not, and cannot, take place through the official channels of the university. Indeed, it is by definition refuge from the university. Even where some courses might be considered to offer this kind of learning, they are exceptional and often perilous by definition for the Black people found in these spaces. Spaces of Black sociality at the university are much more conducive to fugitive learning.

There are a few insights that have emerged through this exploration. Students do not necessarily arrive at university with Black political identities fully formed. This is hardly surprising given the antiblackness that defines the Canadian nation state and its educational systems – and particularly because, having been accepted to university, they are those who have best succeeded on the educational pathways to university that educate away from a healthy Blackness. The first insight, then, is that there can therefore be no sharp ontological distinctions between the "activist" student and the (currently) non-activist student; between those who come already ready to engage in what typically gets named activism and those who are not yet sure. The audience that is imagined for fugitive learning projects must be broader than those who already know they need to be engaged. The non-activist student might often be a potential activist student grappling with the antiblackness into which they have been seduced. This chapter has reinforced that fugitive spaces of Black sociality and the fugitive learning that takes place there provide an important site at which students can recover from hegemonic commitments to postracialism that hinder them from being involved in projects towards their own freedom. Being involved in Black community is an important pathway to activism and action, both by fostering understandings of what it means to be Black and by giving students confidence to act.

Second, and related, Black student organizations are crucial to Black life-making at the university. In addition to creating other fugitive endeavours (such as Black social events), BSOs have a crucial role to play in fugitive Black learning – the learning that must take place because it is not given space in the university. They have the important role of holding space for all Black students[2] – for loving Blackness even when its expression has been distorted by the educational and social violence to which it is constantly subject. Understanding and undertaking this role holds open a pathway for Black self-recovery for Black people.

---

2 This is, of course, also true of Black professors and Black staff. However, that analysis is beyond the scope of the present study.

Third, in thinking about fugitive Black learning, we must think less in terms of whatever tidbits of *information* might be gathered in these fugitive spaces. It is not a heady or unembodied pursuit. Fugitive learning is not even limited to the critical pedagogy notion of literacy as "reading the word and the world" (Freire & Macedo, 1987). We must think of fugitive learning more in terms of the way that fugitive spaces and what occurs in them themselves *constitute* learning. What is experienced in fugitive spaces through conversation and sharing is inseparable from the politics of Black existence at the university and in the world. Fugitive Black learning produces and is synonymous with self-recovery, epistemic community, collective action, resistance, and refreshing. It both takes up space and *is* the taking up of space. It is jurisgenerative.

Mustaffa (2017) is quite right that "Black life-making cannot just highlight education violence to show moments of resistance; it must also start to define a future beyond the logics that make the past and present circumstances possible" (p. 724), and in thinking about this in relation to fugitive learning we must dwell with this jurisgenerative moment. This is the law of being that defies educational violence. Black fugitive learning takes place in opposition to the normative functioning of the university, and defies the rules that refuse space for Black thought and Black being. In contrast to the conceptions of academic freedom that define and measure themselves in terms of antiblackness,[3] this is Black freedom that says freedom can't wait, won't wait until the university gets it right. It is the moment of self-love, the moment of falling in love with oneself, the moment of loving Black people. Fugitive Black learning is "learning as marronage" (Patel, 2016), however fleeting its moment necessarily is (Harney & Moten, 2015; Walcott & Abdillahi, 2019, p. 69). It makes it possible for Black people, individually and collectively, to sustain their presence at the university. It is finding, making, taking freedom in a context where we are not yet free. It is Black life-making that flagrantly refuses the constraints of an antiblack world.

---

3 A clear case in point is the October 2020 letter signed by more than 500 white professors claiming their "right" to use the "n-word" un-euphemized in their classes, identifying this as a matter of their academic freedom. This took place despite the loud objections of Black students and faculty, and even as worldwide protests against gratuitous antiblack violence and death continued to rage after the assassination of George Floyd.

References

ABC News. (1995). *Good Ol Boys Roundup, ABC News, with clips from the actual video*. Internet Archive. https://archive.org/details/GOBRoundup_201809

Adjei, P.B. (2018). The (em)bodiment of blackness in a visceral anti-black racism and ableism context. *Race Ethnicity and Education, 21*(3), 275–87. https://doi.org/10.1080/13613324.2016.1248821

Agbaire, E. (2019). *Microaggressions: Black students' experiences of racism on campus* [Unpublished master's thesis]. University of Ottawa. https://ruor.uottawa.ca/bitstream/10393/39694/5/Agbaire_Ejiro_2019_thesis.pdf

Ahmed, S. (2006). The nonperformativity of antiracism. *Meridians, 7*(1), 104–26. https://doi.org/10.2979/mer.2006.7.1.104

Ahmed, S. (2012). *On being included: Racism and diversity in institutional life*. Duke University Press.

Aiello, G. (2006). Theoretical advances in critical visual analysis: Perception, ideology, mythologies, and social semiotics. *Journal of Visual Literacy, 26*(2), 89–102. https://doi.org/10.1080/23796529.2006.11674635

Aladejebi, F. (2012). "I didn't want to be anything special. I just wanted to teach school": A case study of Black female educators in Colchester, Ontario, 1960. *Southern Journal of Canadian Studies, 5*(1–2), 146–59. https://doi.org/10.22215/sjcs.v5i1.292

Aladejebi, F. (2015a). RESISTANCE: Send little outbursts across the school: Black women teachers and micro-resistive strategies in Ontario schools, 1960s–1980s. *Education Matters, 4*(1), 16–22.

Aladejebi, F. (2015b). 'We got our quota': Black female educators and resistive pedagogies, 1960s–1980s. *Ontario History, 107*(1), 111–29. https://doi.org/10.7202/1050681ar

Allen, K. (2010, 3 November). KKK costume wins first prize at Legion Halloween party. *Toronto Star*. https://www.thestar.com/news/gta/2010/11/03/kkk_costume_wins_first_prize_at_legion_halloween_party.html

Alvarez, N., & Johnson, S. (2011). Minstrels in the classroom: Teaching, race, and blackface. *Canadian Theatre Review, 147*, 31–7. https://doi.org/10.3138/ctr.147.31

Arat-Koc, S. (2005). The disciplinary boundaries of Canadian identity after September 11: Civilizational identity, multiculturalism, and the challenge of anti-imperialist feminism. *Social Justice, 32*(4), 32–49.

Arceneaux, M. (2012, 11 December). Serena Williams's body is no joke. *Ebony Magazine*. https://www.ebony.com/entertainment/caroline-wozniacki-mocks-serena-williams-999/

Archemdis. (2013, 22 July). Black face is not funny! Black face is insulting and demeaning. *Archemdis's Blog*. https://archemdis.wordpress.com/2013/07/22/black-face-is-not-funny-black-face-is-insulting-and-demeaning/

Armstrong, J. (2013, 4 November). *Peel school board investigating VP's blackface costume*. Global News. https://globalnews.ca/news/945587/peel-school-board-investigating-vps-blackface-costume/

Austin, D. (2007). All roads led to Montreal: Black power, the Caribbean, and the Black radical tradition in Canada. *The Journal of African American History, 92*(4), 516–39. https://doi.org/10.1086/jaahv92n4p516

Austin, D. (2013). *Fear of a Black nation: Race, sex, and security in sixties Montreal*. Between the Lines.

Axelrod, P., & Reid, J.G. (1989). *Youth, university, and Canadian society: Essays in the social history of higher education*. McGill-Queen's University Press.

Bakan, A. (2008). Reconsidering the Underground Railroad: Slavery and racialization in the making of the Canadian state. *Socialist Studies/Études socialistes, 4*(1), 3–29. https://doi.org/10.18740/s4c59d

Bakhtin, M. (1984). *Rabelais and his world*. Indiana University Press.

Baldwin, J. (1966). Unnameable objects, unspeakable crimes. In *The Editors of Ebony Magazine* (Ed.), *The white problem in America* (pp. 173–81). Johnson Publishing.

Baldwin, J. (1984). On being "white" ... and other lies. *Essence, 14*(12), 90–92.

Bannerji, H. (1991). Re: Turning the gaze: Racism, sexism, knowledge and the academy. *Resources for Feminist Research, 20*(3/4), 5–11.

Bannerji, H., Carty, L., Dehli, K., Heald, S., & McKenna, K. (Eds.). (1991). *Unsettling relations: The university as a site of feminist struggles*. Women's Press.

Barnes, A. (2009). Displacing danger: Managing crime through deportation. *Journal of International Migration and Integration/Revue de l'integration et de la migration internationale, 10*(4), 431–45. https://doi.org/10.1007/s12134-009-0107-y

Bashi, V. (2004). Globalised anti-Blackness. *Ethnic and Racial Studies, 27*(4), 584–606. https://doi.org/10.1080/0141987042000216726

Béland, R. (2012, 12 April). *Réal Béland Le Gala des Oliviers* [Video]. YouTube. https://youtu.be/KsMb4G5Kh80

Bell, D.A., Jr. (1980). Brown v. Board of Education and the interest convergence dilemma. *Harvard Law Review, 93*(3), 518–33. https://doi.org/10.2307/1340546

Bell, D.A., Jr. (2004). *Silent covenants: Brown v. Board of Education and the unfulfilled hopes of racial reform.* Oxford University Press.

Benedictson, M. (2013, 29 October). *Winnipeg nightclub blasted for blackface photo.* CBC News. https://www.cbc.ca/news/canada/manitoba/winnipeg -nightclub-blasted-for-blackface-photo-1.2255492

Benjamin, A. (2003). *The Black/Jamaican criminal: The making of an ideology.* University of Toronto.

Bernard, C., Thomas Bernard, W., Ekpo, C., Enang, J., Joseph, B., & Wane, N. (2000). "She who learns teaches": Othermothering in the Academy: A dialogue among African Canadian and African Caribbean students and faculty. *Journal of the Motherhood Initiative for Research and Community Involvement, 2*(2), 66–84.

Berry, B. (2014, 26 March). Criticisms surrounding frat party are valid. *The Cord.* https://thecord.ca/criticisms-surrounding-frat-party-are-valid

Best, K. (2008). Making cool things hot again: Blackface and Newfoundland mummering. *Ethnologies, 30*(2), 215–48. https://doi.org/10.7202/019953ar

Biko, S. (2002). *I write what I like: Selected writings* (A. Stubbs, Ed.). University of Chicago Press. (Original work published 1978 by The Bowerdean Press.)

Billig, M. (2001). Humour and hatred: The racist jokes of the Ku Klux Klan. *Discourse and Society, 12*(3), 267–89. https://doi.org/10.1177 /0957926501012003001

Black Learners Advisory Committee (BLAC). (1994). *BLAC report on education: Redressing inequity, empowering Black learners.* Halifax.

Blatchford, C. (2019, 23 September). Christie Blatchford: Urgent questions for Justin Trudeau after last week's blackface revelations. *National Post.* https:// nationalpost.com/opinion/christie-blatchford-urgent-questions-for-justin -trudeau-after-last-weeks-blackface-revelations

Bowe, R. (2019, 1 October). Local Green Party candidate apologizes for Mr. T costume. *Orillia Matters.* https://www.orilliamatters.com/local-news/local -green-party-candidate-apologizes-for-mr-t-costume-1724532

Bramble, M. (2000). Black Education in Canada: Past, Present and Future. In T. Goldstein & D. Selby (Eds.), *Weaving connections: Educating for peace, social, and environmental justice* (pp. 99–119). Sumach Press.

Breaux, R. (2012). Nooses, sheets, and blackface: White racial anxiety and Black student presence at six Midwestern flagship universities, 1882–1937. In M. Gasman & R.L. Geiger (Eds.), *Higher education for African Americans before the civil rights era, 1900–1964* (pp. 43–73). Transaction.

Breeze, M. (2018). Imposter syndrome as a public feeling. In Y. Taylor & K. Lahad (Eds.), *Feeling academic in the neoliberal university: Feminist flights, fights and failures* (pp. 191–219). https://doi.org/10.1007/978-3-319-64224-6_9

Bullen, P.E. (2007). *Facing intolerance: Toronto Black university students speak on race, racism, and in(e)(i)quity*. University of Toronto.

Butcher, L. (1971). The Anderson affair. In D. Forsythe (Ed.), *Let the niggers burn: The Sir George Williams University affair and its Caribbean aftermath* (pp. 76–109). Black Rose Books.

Calliste, A. (1994). Race, gender and Canadian immigration policy: Blacks from the Caribbean, 1900–1932. *Journal of Canadian Studies, 28*(4), 131–48. https://doi.org/10.3138/jcs.28.4.131

Canadian Federation of Students-Ontario. (2010). *The final report of the Task Force on Campus Racism*. https://www.uwindsor.ca/antiblackracism/sites/uwindsor.ca.antiblackracism/files/cfs_final_report_task_force_on_campus_racism_2009.pdf

Canadian Press. (2012, 31 October). Leafs' Bozak criticized for blackface Michael Jackson costume. *CBC News*. https://www.cbc.ca/sports/hockey/nhl/leafs-bozak-criticizedfor-%0Dblackface-michael-jackson-costume-1.1213129

Cannon, M. (2007). Revisiting histories of legal assimilation, racialized injustice, and the future of Indian status in Canada. In J.P. White, E. Anderson, & W. Cornet (Eds.), *Aboriginal policy research: Moving forward, making a difference* (Vol. 5, pp. 35–48). Thompson Educational Publishing.

Carty, L. (1991). Black women in academia: A statement from the periphery. In H. Bannerji, L. Carty, K. Dehli, S. Heald, & K. McKenna (Eds.), *Unsettling relations: The university as a site of feminist struggles* (pp. 13–44). Women's Press.

CBC News. (2013a, 4 September). *Black statue allegedly lynched in effigy at Leon's store*. https://www.cbc.ca/news/canada/nova-scotia/black-statue-allegedly-lynched-in-effigy-at-leon-s-store-1.1323962

CBC News. (2013b, 5 September). *Leon's black statue lynching case probed by police*. https://www.cbc.ca/news/canada/nova-scotia/leon-s-black-statue-lynching-case-probed-by-police-1.1323960

CBC News. (2013c, 29 October). *Trayvon Martin, blackface Halloween costumes spur debate*. https://www.cbc.ca/news/canada/montreal/trayvon-martin-blackface-halloween-costumes-spur-debate-1.2286606

CBC News. (2014a, 10 April). *Leon's Furniture ordered to pay ex-worker for racial discrimination*. https://www.cbc.ca/news/canada/nova-scotia/leon-s-furniture-ordered-to-pay-ex-worker-for-racial-discrimination-1.2605486

CBC News. (2014b, 4 November). *Brock University students in blackface win Halloween contest*. https://www.cbc.ca/news/canada/hamilton/headlines/brock-university-students-in-blackface-win-halloween-contest-1.2822958

CBC News. (2014c, 10 November). *Nightclub responds to complaints after blackface controversy.* https://www.cbc.ca/news/canada/manitoba/nightclub -responds-to-complaints-after-blackface-controversy-1.2829525

CBC News. (2014d, 21 December). *P.K. Subban blackface in Théâtre du Rideau Vert play deemed offensive by some.* https://www.cbc.ca/news/canada /montreal/p-k-subban-blackface-in-théâtre-du-rideau-vert-play-deemed -offensive-by-some-1.2880720

CBC News. (2015, 14 January). *P.K. Subban blackface portrayal denounced by Montreal artists.* https://www.cbc.ca/news/canada/montreal/p-k-subban -blackface-portrayal-denounced-by-montreal-artists-1.2900288

CBC News. (2016a, 23 November). *Queen's University investigates "shockingly racist" student costume party.* https://www.cbc.ca/news/canada/ottawa /costume-party-photos-queen-s-university-1.3863522

CBC News. (2016b, 7 December). *Backlash over blackface in Chatham, Ont.* https://www.cbc.ca/news/canada/windsor/blackface-tradition-chatham -grocery-store-1.3884973

CBC News. (2017, 18 October). *Quebec's controversial consultations into systemic racism get new mandate, name.* https://www.cbc.ca/news/canada/montreal /quebec-consultations-systemic-racism-overhaul-1.4360661

CBC News. (2018, 4 January). *London police officer apologizes for blackface incident.* https://www.cbc.ca/news/canada/london/london-police-blackface-1.4473127

CBC News. (2019, 20 September). *What we know about Justin Trudeau's blackface photos – and what happens next.* https://www.cbc.ca/news/politics/canada -votes-2019-trudeau-blackface-brownface-cbc-explains-1.5290664%0D%0A

CBC News. (2020, 15 June). *Racist video posted on social media prompts Montreal police investigation.* https://www.cbc.ca/news/canada/montreal/montreal -police-racist-video-social-media-high-school-1.5613201

Cho, S. (2008). Post-racialism. *Iowa Law Review, 94,* 1589–1649.

Choudry, A. (2014). Activist research for education and social movement mobilization. *Postcolonial Directions in Education, 3*(1), 88–121.

Cockrell, D. (1997). *Demons of disorder: Early blackface minstrels and their world.* Cambridge University Press.

Codjoe, H. (2006). The role of an affirmed Black cultural identity and heritage in the academic achievement of African-Canadian students. *Intercultural Education, 17*(1), 33–54. https://doi.org/10.1080/14675980500502271

Codjoe, H.M. (2001). Fighting a 'public enemy' of Black academic achievement: The persistence of racism and the schooling experiences of Black students in Canada. *Race Ethnicity and Education, 4*(4), 343–75. https:// doi.org/10.1080/13613320120096652

Cole, C.M. (2012). American ghetto parties and Ghanaian concert parties. In S. Johnson (Ed.), *Burnt cork: Traditions and legacies of blackface minstrelsy* (pp. 223–57). University of Massachusetts Press.

Cole, D. (2020, 29 May). Remembering Black, Indigenous, and other people of colour killed by Canadian police. *Pyriscence.* https://www.pyriscence.ca /home/2020/5/29/cdnpolice

Collins, P.H. (2000). *Black feminist thought: Knowledge, consciousness, and the politics of empowerment.* Routledge.

Cooper, A. (2002). Black women and work in nineteenth-century Canada: Black woman teacher Mary Bibb. In N.N. Wane, K. Deliovsky, & E.S. Lawson (Eds.), *Back to the drawing board: African-Canadian feminisms* (pp. 117–25). Sumach Press.

Cooper, A. (2006). *The hanging of Angelique: The untold story of Canadian slavery and the burning of Old Montreal.* HarperCollins.

Cooper, A., Baylis, F., Cameron, C., Francis, A., Lovejoy, P., States, D., Tillotson, S., Whitfield, H.A., & Williams, N. (2019). *Report on Lord Dalhousie's History on Slavery and Race.* Dalhousie University.

Crawford, B. (2017, 29 November). Bowing to protests, Dutch grocer, school end Christmas tradition of "Black Pete." *Ottawa Citizen.* https:// ottawacitizen.com/news/local-news/bowing-to-protests-dutch-grocer -school-end-christmas-tradition-of-black-pete

CTV Atlantic. (2019, 17 May). *Picture of Citadel student in blackface shared to social media.* CTV News. https://atlantic.ctvnews.ca/picture-of-citadel -student-in-blackface-shared-to-social-media-1.4428035

CTV News. (2010, 4 November). *We're not racist, KKK costumes a mistake: Former cop.* https://www.ctvnews.ca/we-re-not-racist-kkk-costumes-a -mistake-former-cop-1.570760

Daniel, B.-J. (2019). Teaching while Black: Racial dynamics, evaluations, and the role of white females in the Canadian academy in carrying the racism torch. *Race Ethnicity and Education, 22*(1), 21–37. https://doi.org/10.1080 /13613324.2018.1468745

Day, I. (2015). Being or nothingness: Indigeneity, antiblackness, and settler colonial critique. *Critical Ethnic Studies, 1*(2), 102–21. https://doi.org/10.5749 /jcritethnstud.1.1.0086

Dei, G.J.S. (1995). Examining the case for "African-centred" schools in Ontario. *McGill Journal of Education, 30*(2), 179–98.

Dei, G.J.S. (1996). *Anti-racism education: Theory and practice.* Fernwood Publishing.

Dei, G.J.S. (2003). Challenges for anti-racist educators in Ontario today. *Orbit, 33*(3), 2–5. http://anyflip.com/vzpm/zpkp/basic

Dei, G.J.S. (2017). *Reframing Blackness and Black solidarities through anti-colonial and decolonial prisms.* Springer.

Dei, G.J.S., & Kempf, A. (2013). *New perspectives on African-centred education in Canada.* Canadian Scholars' Press.

Dei, G.J.S., Mazzuca, J., McIsaac, E., & Zine, J. (1997). *Reconstructing "dropout": A critical ethnography of the dynamics of Black students' disengagement from school.* University of Toronto Press.

Dempsey, A., & Allen, K. (2010, 4 November). Campbellford reels after Halloween costume furore. *Toronto Star*. https://www.thestar.com/news /ontario/2010/11/04/campbellford_reels_after_halloween_costume _furore.html

DiManno, R. (2014, 2 May). Racist attacks on Habs' P.K. Subban stain storied Bruins-Habs rivalry. *Toronto Star*. https://www.thestar.com/sports/hockey /2014/05/02/racist_attacks_on_habs_pk_subban_stain_storied_bruinshabs _rivalry_dimanno.html

D'Sa, P. (2020, 6 July). *Man shows up to Toronto anti-Black racism protest in blackface*. Huffington Post Canada Online. https://www.huffpost.com/archive/ca /entry/toronto-blackface-protest-police_ca_5edd04f5c5b6b22606b4ae15

Du Bois, W.E.B. (1920). The souls of white folk. In *Darkwater: Voices from within the veil* (pp. 29–52). Harcourt, Brace & Howe.

Du Bois, W.E.B. (1940). *Dusk of dawn: An essay toward an autobiography of a race concept*. Harcourt, Brace & Co.

Dumas, M.J. (2018). Beginning and ending with Black suffering: A meditation on and against racial justice in education. In E. Tuck & K.W. Yang (Eds.), *Toward what justice? Describing diverse dreams of justice in education* (pp. 29–45). Routledge.

Dunlevy, T. (2016, 6 February). Morissette, Radio-Canada can't swat away blackface controversy. *Montreal Gazette*. https://montrealgazette.com /entertainment/morissette-radio-canada-cant-swat-away-blackface -controversy

Durocher, S. (2016, 10 February). Normand Brathwaite a fait du blackface! *Journal de Montréal*. https://www.journaldemontreal.com/2016/02/10 /normand-brathwaite-a-fait-du-iblackface-i

Eggerston, L. (1995, 22 July). RCMP attended racist picnic, U.S. senator reveals at inquiry; Canadian officials probe allegation. *Ottawa Citizen*, A4.

Ellison, R. (1958). Change the joke and slip the yoke. *Partisan Review*, 25(2), 212–22.

Fanon, F. (1961). *The wretched of the earth*. Grove Press.

Fanon, F. (1967). *Black skin, white masks*. Grove Press.

Farley, A.P. (1997). The Black body as fetish object. *Oregon Law Review*, 76, 457–536. https://heinonline.org/HOL/LandingPage?handle=hein.journals /orglr76&div=22&id=&page=

Fellows, M.L., & Razack, S. (1997). The race to innocence: Confronting hierarchical relations among women. *Journal of Gender, Race and Justice*, 1, 335–52.

Forsythe, D. (1971). By way of introduction: "The Sir George Williams affair." In D. Forsythe (Ed.), *Let the niggers burn: The Sir George Williams University affair and its Caribbean aftermath* (limited ed., pp. 7–21). Black Rose Books.

Foster, C. (1996). *A place called heaven: The meaning of being Black in Canada.* HarperCollins.

Foster, C. (2015, 9 November). Canada's blacks: Still waiting for their moment of "real change." *Globe and Mail.* https://www.theglobeandmail.com /opinion/canadas-blacks-still-waiting-for-their-moment-of-real-change /article27175310/

Frankenberg, R. (1993). *White women, race matters: The social construction of whiteness.* University of Minnesota Press.

Freire, P., & Macedo, D. (1987). *Literacy: Reading the word and the world.* Bergin & Garvey.

Freud, S. (1960). *Jokes and their relation to the unconscious.* Penguin Books.

Gill, R. (2009). Breaking the silence: The hidden injuries of the neoliberal university. In R. Gill & R. Ryan-Flood (Eds.), *Secrecy and silence in the research process: Feminist reflections* (pp. 228–44). Taylor & Francis.

Gilmore, R.W. (2017). In the shadow of the shadow state. In INCITE! Women of Color Against Violence (Ed.), *The revolution will not be funded* (pp. 41–52). https://doi.org/10.1515/9780822373001

Giroux, H. (1997). Rewriting the discourse of racial identity: Towards a pedagogy and politics of whiteness. *Harvard Educational Review, 67*(2), 285–321. https://doi.org/10.4135/9781446261705

Goldberg, D.T. (1993). *Racist culture: Philosophy and the politics of meaning.* Blackwell.

Goldberg, D.T. (2002). *The racial state.* Blackwell.

Goldberg, D.T. (2009). *The threat of race: Reflections on racial neoliberalism.* Wiley-Blackwell.

Goldberg, D.T. (2012). When race disappears. *Comparative American Studies, 10*(2–3), 116–27. https://doi.org/10.1179/1477570012Z.0000000008

Goldberg, D.T. (2015). *Are we all postracial yet?* Polity Press.

Gosine, K. (2002). Essentialism versus complexity: Conceptions of racial identity construction in educational scholarship. *Canadian Journal of Education, 27*(1), 81–99. https://doi.org/10.2307/1602189

Gosine, K. (2008). Living between stigma and status: A qualitative study of the social identities of highly educated black Canadian adults. *Identity: An International Journal of Theory and Research, 8*(4), 307–33. https://doi.org /10.1080/15283480802365304

Government of Canada. (1985). *Canadian Multiculturalism Act*, RSC, 1985, c 24 (4th Supp).

Grande, S. (2018). Refusing the university. In E. Tuck & K.W. Yang (Eds.), *Toward what justice? Describing diverse dreams of justice in education* (pp. 47–65). Routledge.

Greenhill, P. (1993). Ben Johnson jokes: Flaws in the Canadian mosaic. *Fabula, 34*(1–2), 78–89. https://doi.org/10.1515/fabl.1993.34.1-2.78

Griffin, J.H. (1961). *Black like me*. Penguin Books.

Hall, S. (1996). New ethnicities. In D. Morley & K.-H. Chen (Eds.), *Stuart Hall: Critical dialogues in cultural studies* (pp. 442–51). Routledge.

Hall, S. (2018). Old and new identities; Old and new ethnicities [1991]. In D. Morley (Ed.), *Essential essays* (Vol. 2, pp. 63–82). https://doi.org/10.1515/9781478002710

hampton, r. (2010). Black learners in Canada. *Race and Class, 52*(1), 103–10. https://doi.org/10.1177/0306396810371770

hampton, r. (2020). *Black racialization and resistance at an elite university*. University of Toronto Press.

hampton, r., & Rochat, D. (2019). To commit and to lead: Black women organizing across communities in Montreal. In T. Kitossa, E.S. Lawson, & P.S.S. Howard (Eds.), *African Canadian leadership: Continuity, transition and transformation* (pp. 149–69). University of Toronto Press.

Hannaford, E. (2011, 22 September). HEC Montreal froshies wear blackface. *McGill Daily*. https://www.mcgilldaily.com/2011/09/hec-montreal-froshies-wear-blackface/

Haque, E. (2012). *Multiculturalism in a bilingual framework: Language, race and belonging in Canada*. University of Toronto Press.

Harney, S., & Moten, F. (2013). *The undercommons: Fugitive planning & Black study*. Minor Compositions.

Harney, S., & Moten, F. (2015). Michael Brown. *Boundary 2: An International Journal of Literature and Culture, 42*(4), 81–7. https://doi.org/10.1215/01903659-3156141

Harris, T. (1984). *Exorcising Blackness: Historical and literary lynching and burning rituals*. Indiana University Press.

Hartman, S.V. (1997). *Scenes of subjection: Terror, slavery, and self-making in nineteenth-century America*. Oxford University Press.

Hartman, S.V. (2007). *Lose your mother: A journey along the Atlantic slave route*. Farrar, Straus and Giroux.

Hartman, S.V., & Wilderson, F.B., III. (2003). The position of the unthought. *Qui Parle, 13*(2), 183–201.

HEC Montréal. (2020). *Facts and figures*. https://www.hec.ca/en/about/facts-and-figures/index.html

Heidelmann. (2012, 28 November). *Re: McGill University: Black students – We don't want to ruin your good time* [Online forum post]. Stormfront. https://www.stormfront.org/forum/t928424/

Henry, A. (1992). African Canadian women teachers' activism: Recreating communities of caring and resistance. *The Journal of Negro Education, 61*(3), 392–404. https://doi.org/10.2307/2295256

Henry, A. (1993). Missing: Black self-representations in Canadian educational research. *Canadian Journal of Education, 18*(3), 206–22. https://doi.org/10.2307/1495383

Henry, F., & Tator, C. (Eds.). (2009). *Racism in the Canadian university: Demanding social justice, inclusion, and equity*. University of Toronto Press.

Hernandez-Ramdwar, C. (2009). Caribbean students in the Canadian academy: We've come a long way? In F. Henry & C. Tator (Eds.), *Racism in the Canadian university: Demanding social justice, inclusion, and equity* (pp. 106–27). University of Toronto Press.

Holthouse, D. (2007, 31 May). Shirley Q. Liquor: The most dangerous comedian in America. *Rolling Stone*. https://www.rollingstone.com /culture/culture-features/shirley-q-liquor-the-most-dangerous-comedian -in-america-188700/

hooks, bell. (1992a). *Black looks: Race and representation*. South End Press.

hooks, bell. (1992b). Representing whiteness in the Black imagination. In L. Grossberg, C. Nelson, & P. Trichler (Eds.), *Cultural Studies* (pp. 338–46). Routledge.

hooks, bell. (1994). *Teaching to transgress: Education as the practice of freedom*. Routledge.

Howard, P.S.S. (2004). White privilege: For or against? A discussion of ostensibly antiracist discourses in Critical Whiteness Studies. *Race, Gender & Class, 11*(4), 63–79.

Howard, P.S.S. (2006). On silence and dominant accountability. In *Anti-colonialism and education: The politics of resistance* (pp. 43–63). Sense Publishers.

Howard, P.S.S. (2010). Turning out the center: Racial politics and African agency in the Obama era. *Journal of Black Studies, 40*(3), 380–94. https://doi.org /10.1177/0021934709352990

Howard, P.S.S. (2013). The smack of self-determination: A Fanonian analysis of the Africentric schooling debate in Toronto. In G.J.S. Dei & M. Lordan (Eds.), *Contemporary issues in the sociology of race and ethnicity* (pp. 43–68). Peter Lang.

Howard, P.S.S. (2014a). Drawing dissent: Postracialist pedagogy, racist literacy, and racial plagiarism in anti-Obama political cartoons. *Review of Education, Pedagogy, and Cultural Studies, 36*(5), 386–402. https://doi.org/10.1080/1071 4413.2014.958379

Howard, P.S.S. (2014b). Taking the bull by the horns: The critical perspectives and pedagogy of two Black teachers in anglophone Montreal schools. *Race Ethnicity and Education, 17*(4), 494–517. https://doi.org/10.1080/13613 324.2012.759921

Howard, P.S.S. (2018). A laugh for the national project: Contemporary Canadian blackface humour and its constitution through Canadian anti-blackness. *Ethnicities, 18*(6), 843–68. https://doi.org/10.1177 /1468796818785936

Howard, P.S.S. (2020). Getting under the skin: Antiblackness, proximity, and resistance in the SLĀV affair. *Theatre Research in Canada, 41*(1), 126–48. https://doi.org/10.3138/tric.41.1.126

Howard, P.S.S., & James, C.E. (2019). When dreams take flight: How teachers imagine and implement an environment that nurtures Blackness at an Africentric school in Toronto, Ontario. *Curriculum Inquiry, 49*(3), 313–37. https://doi.org/10.1080/03626784.2019.1614879

Hudson, P.J. (2010). Imperial designs: The Royal Bank of Canada in the Caribbean. *Race & Class, 52*(1), 33–48. https://doi.org/10.1177/0306396810371762

Hudson, P.J., & Kamugisha, A. (2014). On Black Canadian thought. *The CLR James Journal, 20*(1), 3–20. https://doi.org/10.5840/clrjames201492216

HueyFreeman222. (2007, 6 February). Racist winter carnival blackface @Wilfrid Laurier University [video].

Huffington Post Canada. (2013, 2 December). *Joachim Stroink, Nova Scotia MLA, criticized for blackface photo.* https://www.huffpost.com/archive/ca/entry/joachim-stroink-blackface-photo_n_4372073

Human Rights Watch. (2005). *Ethiopia: Events of 2004.* Retrieved 17 December 2019 from https://www.hrw.org/world-report/2005/country-chapters/ethiopia

Ibrahim, A. (2014). *The rhizome of Blackness: A critical ethnography of hip-hop culture, language, identity, and the politics of becoming.* Peter Lang.

Ibrahim, A. (2019). *Black immigrants in North America: Essays on race, immigration, identity, language, hip-hop, pedagogy, and the politics of becoming Black.* Myers Education Press.

Jackson, S.J. (2004). Exorcizing the ghost: Donovan Bailey, Ben Johnson and the politics of Canadian identity. *Media, Culture and Society, 26*(1), 121–41. https://doi.org/10.1177/0163443704039496

James, C.E. (1995). Multicultural and anti-racism education in Canada. *Race, Gender & Class, 2*(3), 31–48.

James, C.E. (2005). *Race in play: Understanding the socio-cultural worlds of student athletes.* Canadian Scholars' Press.

James, C.E. (2012). *Life at the intersection: Community, class and schooling.* Fernwood Publishing.

James, C.E., Turner, T., George, R., & Tecle, S. (2017). *Towards race equity in education: The schooling of Black students in the greater Toronto area.* York University. https://edu.yorku.ca/files/2017/04/Towards-Race-Equity-in-Education-April-2017.pdf

Johnson, S. (2012). Introduction: The persistence of blackface and the minstrel tradition. In S. Johnson (Ed.), *Burnt cork: Traditions and legacies of blackface minstrelsy* (pp. 1–17). University of Massachusetts Press.

Johnson, S. (2017). "Shield us from this base ridicule": The petitions to censor blackface circus clowns, Toronto, 1840–43. In H. Davis-Fisch (Ed.), *Canadian Performance Histories and Historiographies: New essays on Canadian theatre* (pp. 254–79). Playwrights Canada Press.

Jones, D.A. (2013). Black politics but not Black people: Rethinking the social and "racial" history of early minstrelsy. *TDR/The Drama Review, 57*(2), 21–37. https://doi.org/10.1162/DRAM_a_00259

Joshee, R. (2004). Citizenship and multicultural education in Canada: From assimilation to social cohesion. In J.A. Banks (Ed.), *Diversity and citizenship education: Global perspectives* (pp. 127–56). Jossey-Bass/Wiley.

Kambhampaty, A.P., Carlisle, M., & Chan, M. (2019, 18 September). Justin Trudeau wore brownface at 2001 "Arabian Nights" party while he taught at a private school. *Time Magazine.* https://time.com/5680759/justin-trudeau-brownface-photo/

Karstens-Smith, G., & Rushowy, K. (2013, 12 November). "Blackface" controversy at Mayfield Secondary School. *Toronto Star.* https://www.thestar.com/news/gta/2013/11/12/blackface_controversy_at_mayfield_secondary_school_in_caledon_not_the_first.html

Kelland, A. (2017, 31 October). *Halloween costumes weren't intended to offend, law enforcement group says.* CBC News Online. https://www.cbc.ca/news/canada/newfoundland-labrador/law-enforcement-torce-run-offensive-halloween-1.4380748

Kelley, R.D.G. (2016a, 1 March). Forum final response: Black study, Black struggle. *Boston Review.* http://bostonreview.net/forum/black-study-black-struggle/robin-d-g-kelley-robin-d-g-kelleys-final-response

Kelley, R.D.G. (2016b, 7 March). Black study, Black struggle. *Boston Review.* http://bostonreview.net/forum/robin-d-g-kelley-black-study-black-struggle

Kenrick, J. (2010). *Musical theatre: A history.* Bloomsbury Publishing.

Kincheloe, J.L., & Steinberg, S.R. (1998). Addressing the crisis of whiteness: Reconfiguring white identity in a pedagogy of whiteness. In J.L. Kincheloe, S.R. Steinberg, N.M. Rodriguez, & R.E. Chennault (Eds.), *White reign: Deploying whiteness in America* (pp. 3–29). St: Martin's Press.

Kirby, K. (1998). Re-mapping subjectivity: Cartographic vision and the limits of politics. In *Body space: Destabilizing geographies of gender and sexuality* (pp. 45–55). Routledge.

Kyei, D., Samuel, D., Hawkins, S., Newton, M., Trotz, A., & Walcott, R. (2009, 26 November). *Public statement from University of Toronto faculty and students condemning the University of Toronto administration's inappropriate response to the "blackface" incident.* University of Toronto Students' Union. https://www.newswire.ca/news-releases/public-statement-from-university-of-toronto-faculty-and-students-condemningthe-university-of-toronto-administrations-inappropriate-response-to-theblackface-incident-539024691.html

Lafortune, G., & Balde, A. (2012). Cheminement scolaire des élèves québécois originaires des Antilles : Un double aperçu à partir de données quantitatives et qualitatives / Educational pathways among Quebec students originating from the Caribbean: A survey of both quantitative and qualitative data. *Diversité urbaine, 121,* 49–68. https://doi.org/10.7202/1019211ar

Larsen, K. (2019, 20 September). *Langley Conservative candidate mum on connection to blackface performers.* CBC News Online. https://www.cbc.ca /news/canada/british-columbia/langley-conservative-candidate-mum -on-connection-to-blackface-performers-1.5291357

Law Enforcement Torch Run Newfoundland and Labrador. (n.d.). *About* [Facebook page]. Facebook. Retrieved 17 December 2019 from https:// www.facebook.com/NLLETR/

Lawson, E.S. (2013). The gendered working lives of seven Jamaican women in Canada: A story about "here" and "there" in a transnational economy. *Feminist Formations, 25*(1), 138–56. https://doi.org/10.1353/ff.2013.0002

Lawson, E.S. (2019). Mercy for their children: A feminist reading of Black women's maternal activism and leadership practice. In T. Kitossa, E.S. Lawson, & P.S.S. Howard (Eds.), *African Canadian leadership: Continuity, transition and transformation* (pp. 190–210). University of Toronto Press.

Le Camp, L. (2005). *Racial considerations of minstrel shows and related images in Canada.* University of Toronto.

Lee, E., Menkart, D., & Okazawa-Rey, M. (Eds.). (1998). *Beyond heroes and holidays: A practical guide to K-12 anti-racist, multicultural education and staff development.* Network of Educators on the Americas.

Lensmire, T.J., & Snaza, N. (2010). What teacher education can learn from blackface minstrelsy. *Educational Researcher, 39*(5), 413–22. https://doi.org /10.3102/0013189X10374980

Leonardo, Z., & Porter, R.K. (2010). Pedagogy of fear: Toward a Fanonian theory of "safety" in race dialogue. *Race Ethnicity and Education, 13*(2), 139–57. https://doi.org/10.1080/13613324.2010.482898

Lexier, R. (2007). "The backdrop against which everything happened": English-Canadian student movements and off-campus movements for change. *History of Intellectual Culture, 7*(1), 1–18. http://www.ucalgary.ca/hic

Lhamon, W.T., Jr. (1998). *Raising Cain: Blackface performance from Jim Crow to hip hop.* Harvard University Press.

Lhamon, W.T., Jr. (2003). *Jump Jim Crow: Lost plays, lyrics, and street prose of the First Atlantic popular culture.* Harvard University Press.

Lhamon, W.T., Jr. (2012). Turning around Jim Crow. In S. Johnson (Ed.), *Burnt cork: Traditions and legacies of blackface minstrelsy* (pp. 18–50). University of Massachusetts Press.

Lightstone, J.N. (2014, 4 November). Blackface Halloween costumes, and a lesson in historical consciousness. *Brock News.* https://brocku.ca/brock -news/2014/11/blackface-halloween-costumes-and-a-lesson-in-historial -consciousness/

Lomax, L.E. (1966). The white liberal. In The Editors of Ebony Magazine (Ed.), *The white problem in America* (pp. 39–46). Johnson Publishing Company.

London Free Press. (2017, 29 December). London police probe online photos of officer painted brown, in apparent traditional African clothing. *London Free Press*. https://www.stthomastimesjournal.com/2017/12/29/london-police-probe-online-photos-of-officer-painted-brown-in-apparent-traditional-african-clothing

Lorde, A. (1993). *Zami; Sister outsider; Undersong*. Quality Paperback Book Club.

Lott, E. (1993). *Love & theft*. Oxford University Press.

MacKinnon, P. (2018). *University commons divided: Exploring debate and dissent on campus*. University of Toronto Press.

MacMillan, J. (2005, 1 December). Race, racism & blackface. *Queen's Journal*. https://www.queensjournal.ca/story/2005-12-01/news/race-racism-and-blackface/

Magnan, M.O., Collins, T., Darchinian, F., Kamanzi, P.C., & Valade, V. (2021). Student voices on social relations of race in Québec universities. *Race Ethnicity and Education*, 1–17. https://doi.org/10.1080/13613324.2021.1890564

Mahoney, J. (2009, 11 November). Apology sought after U of T students cause uproar with blackface for Halloween. *Globe and Mail*. https://www.theglobeandmail.com/news/toronto/apology-sought-after-u-of-t-students-cause-uproar-with-blackface-for-halloween/article4292207/

Martis, E. (2020). *They said this would be fun: Race, campus life, and growing up*. McClelland & Stewart.

Marwick, A., & Lewis, R. (2017). *Media manipulation and disinformation online*. http://www.chinhnghia.com/DataAndSociety_MediaManipulationAndDisinformationOnline.pdf

McAndrew, M., Ledent, J., & Ait-Said, R. (2006). L'école québécoise assure-t-elle l'égalité des chances ? Le cheminement scolaire des jeunes noirs au secondaire. *Cahiers québécois de démographie*, *35*(1), 123–48. https://doi.org/10.7202/017751ar

McCartney, D.M. (2016). Inventing international students: Exploring discourses in international student policy talk, 1945–75. *Historical Studies in Education/Revue d'histoire de l'éducation*, *28*(2), 1–27. https://doi.org/10.32316/hse/rhe.v28i2.4457

McGill Daily. (2012, 1 November). Editorial: Safe space not blackface. *McGill Daily*. https://www.mcgilldaily.com/2012/11/safe-space-not-blackface/

McKittrick, K. (2002). "Their blood is there, and they can't throw it out": Honouring Black Canadian geographies. *Topia: Canadian Journal of Cultural Studies*, *7*, 27–37. https://doi.org/10.3138/topia.7.27

McKittrick, K. (2006). *Demonic grounds: Black women and the cartographies of struggle*. University of Minnesota Press.

McKittrick, K. (2011). On plantations, prisons, and a black sense of place. *Social and Cultural Geography, 12*(8), 947–63. https://doi.org/10.1080 /14649365.2011.624280

McLaren, K. (2004). "We had no desire to be set apart": Forced segregation of Black students in Canada West public schools and myths of British egalitarianism. *Social History/Histoire sociale, 37*(73), 27–50.

McPherson, K. (2020). Black girls are not magic; they are human: Intersectionality and inequity in the Greater Toronto Area (GTA) schools. *Curriculum Inquiry, 50*(2), 149–67. https://doi.org/10.1080/03626784.2020 .1729660

Mills, S. (2016). *A place in the sun: Haiti, Haitians, and the remaking of Quebec.* McGill-Queen's University Press.

Miss World 2003. (2019, 16 December). In *Wikipedia.* https://en.wikipedia. org/w/index.php?title=Miss_World_2003&oldid=931015243

Mogadime, D. (2000). Black girls/Black women-centered texts and Black teachers as othermothers. *Journal of the Association for Research on Mothering, 2*(2), 222–33.

Mogadime, D. (2002). Black women in graduate studies: Transforming the socialization experience. In *Back to the Drawing Board: African-Canadian Feminisms* (pp. 129–57). Sumach Press.

Montpetit, J. (2011, 15 September). *Blackface stunt backfires at Montreal university frosh-week event.* Global News. https://globalnews.ca/news/155216 /blackface-stunt-backfires-at-montreal-university-frosh-week-event/

Monture, P. (2009). "Doing academia differently": Confronting "whiteness" in the university. In F. Henry & C. Tator (Eds.), *Racism in the Canadian university: Demanding social justice, inclusion, and equity* (pp. 76–105). University of Toronto Press.

Moon, D.K. (1999). White enculturation and bourgeois ideology: The discursive production of "good (white) girls." In T.K. Nakayama & J.N. Martin (Eds.), *Whiteness: The social communication of identity* (pp. 177–97). Sage.

Morgan, A. (2012, 27 March). *La grève et les minorités.* Huffington Post Canada Online. https://www.huffpost.com/archive/qc/entry/greve-etudiante -minorites_b_1383521

Morreal, D. (2005). Humour and the conduct of politics. In S. Lockyear & M. Pickering (Eds.), *Beyond a joke: The limits of humour* (pp. 63–78). Palgrave Macmillan.

Morrison, T. (1992). *Playing in the dark: Whiteness and the literary imagination.* Vintage.

Moten, F. (1999). Review of the books *Scenes of subjection: Terror, slavery, and self-making in nineteenth-century America* by S.V. Hartman, and *Soul: Black power, politics, and pleasure,* edited by M. Guillory and R.C. Gree. *TDR/The Drama Review, 43*(4), 169–74. https://doi.org/10.1162/dram.1999.43.4.169

Moten, F. (2013). Blackness and nothingness (Mysticism in the flesh). *South Atlantic Quarterly, 112*(4), 737–80. https://doi.org/10.1215/00382876-2345261

Mueller, J.C., Dirks, D., & Picca, L.H. (2007). Unmasking racism: Halloween costuming and engagement of the racial other. *Qualitative Sociology, 30*(3), 315–35. https://doi.org/10.1007/s11133-007-9061-1

Mustaffa, J.B. (2017). Mapping violence, naming life: A history of anti-Black oppression in the higher education system. *International Journal of Qualitative Studies in Education, 30*(8), 711–27. https://doi.org/10.1080/09518398.2017.1350299

Myles, S. (2014, 19 February). *Some joker takes the P.K. Subban blackface thing and brings it to Sochi.* Yahoo! Sports. https://ca.sports.yahoo.com/blogs/eh-game/joker-takes-p-k-subban-blackface-thing-brings-205115456.html

Nangwaya, A. (2013, 25 July). *Fact sheet on police violence against the African community in Canada.* Toronto Media Co-Op. http://toronto.mediacoop.ca/blog/ajamu-nangwaya/18378

NBC 15. (n.d.). *The original Crichton leprechaun news story from LOCAL 15 News, WPMI* [Video]. YouTube. https://youtu.be/K1ljOcl39PQ

Nelson, C. (2016). *Slavery, geography and empire in nineteenth-century marine landscapes of Montreal and Jamaica.* Routledge.

Nelson, C. (2017, 21 July). The Canadian narrative about slavery is wrong. *The Walrus.* https://thewalrus.ca/the-canadian-narrative-about-slavery-is-wrong/

Nichols, R. (2014). Contract and usurpation: Enfranchisement and racial governance in settler-colonial contexts. In A. Simpson & A. Smith (Eds.), *Theorizing native studies* (pp. 99–121). Duke University Press.

Nicks, J., & Sloniowski, J. (2010). Entertaining Niagara Falls, Ontario: Minstrel shows, theatres, and popular pleasures. In J. Nicks & B.K. Grant (Eds.), *Covering Niagara: Studies in local popular culture* (pp. 285–310). Wilfrid Laurier University Press.

Nova Scotia Department of Education. (2009). *African Canadian Studies 11: Implementation draft.* African Canadian Services Division.

Office of the Vice-Provost – Students. (2009, 20 November). Letter to Black Students Association regarding "blackface" costumes. https://www.viceprovoststudents.utoronto.ca/announcements/letter-to-black-students-association-regarding-blackface-costumes-november-20-2009/

Ohito, E. (2016). Refusing curriculum as a space of death for Black female subjects: A Black feminist reparative reading of Jamaica Kincaid's "Girl." *Curriculum Inquiry, 46*(5), 436–54. https://doi.org/10.1080/03626784.2016.1236658

Ohito, E. (2020). "The creative aspect woke me up": Awakening to multimodal essay composition as a fugitive literacy practice. *English Education, 52*(3), 186–222.

Oprah Winfrey Network. (2019, 15 October). *Why comedian Dave Chappelle walked away from $50 million* [Video]. YouTube. https://youtu.be/tlScX2stRuo

Patel, L. (2016). Pedagogies of resistance and survivance: Learning as marronage. *Equity and Excellence in Education, 49*(4), 397–401. https://doi.org/10.1080 /10665684.2016.1227585

Pérez, R. (2013). Learning to make racism funny in the "color-blind" era: Stand-up comedy students, performance strategies, and the (re)production of racist jokes in public. *Discourse and Society, 24*(4), 478–503. https://doi .org/10.1177/0957926513482066

Pérez, R. (2016). Brownface minstrelsy: "José Jiménez," the Civil Rights Movement, and the legacy of racist comedy. *Ethnicities, 16*(1), 40–67. https://doi.org/10.1177/1468796814548233

Pérez, R. (2017). Race, gender, and comedy awards: From civil rights to color-blindness. *Comedy Studies, 8*(1), 68–80. https://doi.org/10.1080/2040610X .2017.1294413

Petchesky, B. (2010, 12 March). *Yup, that's some blackface at a hockey game.* Deadspin. https://deadspin.com/yup-thats-some-blackface-at-a-hockey -game-5492171

Phillips, R.S. (1997). Mapping men. In *Mapping men and empire: A geography of adventure* (pp. 45–67). Routledge.

Pieterse, J.N. (1992). *White on Black: Images of Africa and Blacks in Western popular culture.* Yale University Press.

Pitcher, B. (2014). *Consuming race.* Routledge.

Poole, C. (2012). "Not of the nation": Canadian history textbooks and the impossibility of an African-Canadian identity. *Southern Journal of Canadian Studies, 5*(1–2), 81–102. https://doi.org/10.22215/sjcs.v5i1.290

Powell, K. (2009, 12 November). *A lesson on blackface.* Torontoist. https:// torontoist.com/2009/11/a_lesson_on_blackface/

Prestwich, E. (2013, 2 July). *Daytona Bitch, Toronto drag queen, fired from Pride over "blackface."* Huffington Post Canada Online. https://www.huffpost .com/archive/ca/entry/daytona-bitch-blackface_n_3519836

Prestwich, E. (2016, 6 December). *Zwarte Piet, or Black Pete, part of Edmonton Sinterklaas celebrations.* Huffington Post Alberta Online. https://www .huffpost.com/archive/ca/entry/zwarte-piet-black-pete_n_13460622

QMI Agency. (2014, 20 February). Fan in blackface wearing P.K. Subban jersey spotted in Sochi. *Sarnia Observer.* https://www.theobserver.ca/2014/02/19 /fan-in-blackface-wearing-pk-subban-jersey-spotted-in-sochi

Queen's Encyclopedia. (n.d.) *Sutherland, Robert (c. 1830-1878).* Retrieved 18 September 2020 from https://www.queensu.ca/encyclopedia/s /sutherland-robert-c

Ram gopal. (2013, 22 July). *Novak Djokovic imitates Serena Williams … the best one ever!!!* [Video]. YouTube. https://youtu.be/gMUeS-kORpo

Razack, S. (2002). When place becomes race. In S. Razack (Ed.), *Race, space, and the law: Unmapping a white settler society* (pp. 1–20). Between the Lines.

Reay, D. (2001). Finding or losing yourself?: Working-class relationships to education. *Journal of Education Policy, 16*(4), 333–46. https://doi.org/10.1080/02680930110054335

Reay, D., Crozier, G., & Clayton, J. (2009). "Strangers in paradise"?: Working-class students in elite universities. *Sociology, 43*(6), 1103–21. https://doi.org/10.1177/0038038509345700

Reynolds, C. (2016, 22 February). U of T to track race-based data of its students. *Toronto Star.* https://www.thestar.com/news/gta/2016/02/22/u-of-t-to-track-race-based-data-of-its-students.html

Richmond, R. (2018, 3 January). *Ont. cop under fire after blackface pics surface on Instagram.* Canoe.com. https://canoe.com/news/national/ont-cop-under-fire-after-blackface-pics-surface-on-instagram

Roberts, J. (2011, 20 September). Racial tension builds: HEC students caught in blackface on campus. *The Link* (Concordia University). https://thelinknewspaper.ca/article/racial-tension-builds

Roberts, N. (2015). *Freedom as marronage.* University of Chicago Press.

Robinson, C.J. (2012). Blackface minstrelsy and Black resistance. In *Forgeries of memory and meaning: Blacks and the regimes of race in American theater and film before World War II* (pp. 127–79). University of North Carolina Press.

Roediger, D.R. (1999). White skins, Black masks: Minstrelsy and white working class formation before the Civil War. In *The wages of whiteness: Race and the making of the American working class* (115–131). Verso.

Rogers, R.A. (2006). From cultural exchange to transculturation: A review and reconceptualization of cultural appropriation. *Communication Theory, 16*(4), 474–503. https://doi.org/10.1111/j.1468-2885.2006.00277.x

Rollock, N., Vincent, C., Gillborn, D., & Ball, S. (2012). "Middle class by profession": Class status and identification amongst the Black middle classes. *Ethnicities, 13*(3), 253–75. https://doi.org/10.1177/1468796812467743

Saltwire Network. (2014, 10 April). *Human Rights Commission sides with former Dartmouth Leon's employee in racism complaint.* https://www.saltwire.com/atlantic-canada/federal-election/human-rights-commission-sides-with-former-dartmouth-leons-employee-in-racism-complaint-84057/

Sammond, N. (2015). *Birth of an industry: Blackface minstrelsy and the rise of American animation.* Duke University Press.

Schick, C. (2002). Keeping the ivory tower white: Discourses of racial domination. In S.H. Razack (Ed.), *Race, space, and the law: Unmapping a white settler society* (pp. 99–119). Between the Lines.

Schlueter, J. (2013). "How you durrin?" Chuck Knipp, Shirley Q. Liquor, and Contemporary Blackface. *TDR/The Drama Review, 57*(2), 163–81. https://doi.org/10.1162/DRAM_a_00266

Seiler, R.M. (2002). Selling patriotism/selling beer: The case of the "I AM CANADIAN!" commercial. *American Review of Canadian Studies, 32*(1), 45–66. https://doi.org/10.1080/02722010209481657

Severin, K. [erroneously attributed to A.D. online]. (2014, 26 March). "Jamaican Me Crazy" event shut down. *The Cord*. https://thecord.ca/jamaican-me -crazy-event-shut-down/

Sexton, J. (2008). *Amalgamation schemes: Antiblackness and the critique of multiracialism*. University of Massachusetts Press.

Sexton, J. (2010). People-of-color-blindness: Notes on the Afterlife of Slavery. *Social Text, 28*(2), 31–56. https://doi.org/10.1215/01642472-2009-066

Sexton, J. (2016). The Vel of slavery: Tracking the figure of the unsovereign. *Critical Sociology, 42*(4–5), 583–97. https://doi.org/10.1177/0896920514552535

Shah, M. (2019, 21 September). *Green Party leader speaks out about one of her own candidates wearing blackface in the past*. Global News. https://globalnews.ca /news/5934682/green-party-candidate-blackface/

Shingler, B. (2018, 9 January). *Quebec opposition parties against marking mosque shooting with day against Islamophobia*. CBC News. https://www.cbc.ca /news/canada/montreal/quebec-mosque-shooting-islamophobia-1.4478861

Simonsen, G. (2003). Skin colour as a tool of regulation and power in the Danish West Indies in the eighteenth century. *The Journal of Caribbean History, 37*(2), 256–276.

Simpson, J.S., James, C.E., & Mack, J. (2011). Multiculturalism, colonialism, and racialization: Conceptual starting points. *Review of Education, Pedagogy, and Cultural Studies, 33*(4), 285–305. https://doi.org/10.1080/10714413.2011.597637

Simpson, N. (2020, 2 June). Canada has race-based police violence too. We don't know how much. *The Tyee*. https://thetyee.ca/Analysis/2020/06 /02/Canada-Race-Based-Violence/

Smalls, J. (2003). "Race" as spectacle in late-nineteenth-century French art and popular culture. *French Historical Studies, 26*(2), 351–81. https://doi .org/10.1215/00161071-26-2-351

Sojoyner, D.M. (2013). Black radicals make for bad citizens: Undoing the myth of the school to prison pipeline. *Berkeley Review of Education, 4*(2), 241–63. https://doi.org/10.5070/b84110021

Solomon, P., & Palmer, H. (2004). Schooling in Babylon, Babylon in school: When racial profiling and zero tolerance converge. *Canadian Journal of Educational Administration and Policy, 33*. https://journalhosting.ucalgary .ca/index.php/cjeap/article/view/42713

Spillers, H.J. (1987). Mama's baby, papa's maybe: An American grammar book. *Diacritics, 17*(2), 65–81. https://doi.org/10.2307/464747

SSMU University Affairs. (n.d.) *McGill History: 1848: William Wright becomes the first Black medical doctor in British North America*. Retrieved 18 September 2020 from https://ua.ssmu.ca/history/

Staff, S. (2012, 31 October). *Bozak defends MJ costume, says it's not racist.* Sportsnet. https://www.sportsnet.ca/hockey/nhl/maple-leafs-tyler-bozak-blackface-michael-jackson/

Tate, G. (2003). *Everything but the burden: What white people are taking from Black culture.* Broadway Books.

Tatum, B.D. (2003). *Why Are all the Black kids sitting together in the cafeteria? And other conversations about race* (revised ed.). Basic Books.

TheBctechGroup. (2012, 16 July). *Les survivants du cabinet Real Beland – Sandra Paul* [Video]. YouTube. https://youtu.be/miA9RnoeYlE

The Post Millennial [@TPostMillennial]. (2018, 28 September). *A new high quality video of @JustinTrudeau dancing in blackface* [Video attached] [Tweet]. Twitter. https://twitter.com/TPostMillennial/status/1178027994285260800

Thobani, S. (2007). *Exalted subjects: Studies in the making of race and nation in Canada.* University of Toronto Press.

Thomas, B. (1987). Anti-racist education: A response to Manicom. In J. Young (Ed.), *Breaking the mosaic: Ethnic identities in Canadian schooling* (pp. 104–7). Garamond Press.

Thompson, B.C. (2015). *Anthems and minstrel shows: The life and times of Calixa Lavallée, 1842–1891.* McGill-Queen's University Press.

Toronto Mike. (2010, 12 March). Subbanator Habs fans find new way to offend. https://www.torontomike.com/2010/03/subbanator_habs_fans_find_new/

TVA Nouvelles. (2017, 1 November). *Le costume d'un directeur d'école soulève l'indignation.* https://www.tvanouvelles.ca/2017/11/01/le-costume-dun-directeur-decole-souleve-lindignation

Urback, R. (2009, 11 November). Innocent Halloween costume or blackface? *Macleans.* https://www.macleans.ca/education/uniandcollege/editorial-innocent-halloween-costume-or-blackface/

US Senate Judiciary Committee. (1996). *Good Ol' Boy Roundup report executive summary.* US Department of Justice. https://oig.justice.gov/sites/default/files/archive/special/9603/exec.htm

Van Dijk, T.A. (1991). *Racism and the press.* Routledge.

Van Dijk, T.A. (1993). *Elite discourse and racism.* Sage.

Van Dijk, T.A. (2000). New(s) racism: A discourse analytical approach. In S. Cottle (Ed.), *Ethnic minorities and the media* (pp. 33–49). Open University Press.

Vargas, J.H.C. (2018). *The denial of antiblackness: Multiracial redemption and Black suffering.* University of Minnesota Press.

Vidal, J. (2003, 18 April). Ethiopia's worst famine in 20 years. *The Guardian.* https://www.theguardian.com/world/2003/apr/18/famine.ethiopia

Walcott, R. (2000). "Who is she and what is she to you?" Mary Ann Shadd Cary and the (im)possibility of Black/Canadian studies. *Atlantis: Critical Studies in Gender, Culture & Social Justice, 24*(2), 137–46.

Walcott, R. (2001). Caribbean pop culture in Canada: Or, the impossibility of belonging to the nation. *Small Axe, 5*(1), 123–39. https://doi.org/10.1353/smx.2001.0011

Walcott, R. (2003a). A tough geography: Towards a poetics of Black space(s) in Canada. In *Black like who: Writing Black Canada* (pp. 43–55). Insomniac Press.

Walcott, R. (2003b). *Black like who? Writing Black Canada.* Insomniac Press.

Walcott, R. (2014a). Shame: A polemic. *The CLR James Journal, 20*(1), 275–9. https://doi.org/10.5840/clrjames201492318

Walcott, R. (2014b). The Book of Others (Book IV): Canadian multiculturalism, the state, and its political legacies. *Canadian Ethnic Studies, 46*(2), 127–32. https://doi.org/10.1353/ces.2014.0018

Walcott, R. (2014c). The problem of the human: Black ontologies and "the coloniality of our being." In S. Broeck & C. Junker (Eds.), *Postcoloniality – Decoloniality – Black critique: Joints and fissures* (pp. 93–105). Campus.

Walcott, R. (2018). Against social justice and the limits of diversity: Or Black people and freedom. In E. Tuck & K.W. Yang (Eds.), *Toward what justice? Describing diverse dreams of justice in education* (pp. 85–99). Routledge.

Walcott, R. (2019). The end of diversity. *Public Culture, 31*(2), 393–408. https://doi.org/10.1215/08992363-7286885

Walcott, R., & Abdillahi, I. (2019). *BlackLife: Post-BLM and the struggle for freedom.* ARP Books.

Wane, N.N. (2009). Black Canadian feminist thought: Perspectives on equity and diversity in the academy. *Race Ethnicity and Education, 12*(1), 65–77. https://doi.org/10.1080/13613320802650964

Watts, E.K. (1997). An exploration of spectacular consumption: Gangsta rap as cultural commodity. *Communication Studies, 48*(1), 42–58. https://doi.org/10.1080/10510979709368490

Wavywebsurf. (2018, 21 November). *The REAL story behind the Alabama leprechaun* [Video]. YouTube. https://youtu.be/PJcz37ERPKQ

Weaver, S. (2010a). Developing a rhetorical analysis of racist humour: Examining anti-Black jokes on the internet. *Social Semiotics, 20*(5), 537–55. https://doi.org/10.1080/10350330.2010.513188

Weaver, S. (2010b). Liquid racism and the Danish prophet Muhammad cartoons. *Current Sociology, 58*(5), 675–92. https://doi.org/10.1177/0011392110372728

Weaver, S. (2011). Jokes, rhetoric and embodied racism: A rhetorical discourse analysis of the logics of racist jokes on the internet. *Ethnicities, 11*(4), 413–35. https://doi.org/10.1177/1468796811407755

Weaver, S. (2013). *The rhetoric of racist humour: US, UK and global race joking.* Ashgate Publishing.

Weheliye, A.G. (2008). Pornotropes. *Journal of Visual Culture, 7*(1), 65–81. https://doi.org/10.1177/1470412907078570

Weheliye, A.G. (2014a). Depravation: Pornotropes. In *Habeas viscus: Racializing assemblages, biopolitics, and Black feminist theories of the human* (pp. 89–112). Duke University Press.

Weheliye, A.G. (2014b). *Habeas viscus: Racializing assemblages, biopolitics, and Black feminist theories of the human*. Duke University Press.

Wetherell, M., and Potter, J. (1988). Discourse analysis and the identification of interpretive repertoires. In C. Antaki (Ed.), *Analysing everyday explanation* (pp. 163–83). Sage.

Wilder, C.S. (2014). *Ebony and ivy: Race, slavery, and the troubled history of America's universities*. Bloomsbury Publishing.

Wilderson, F.B., III. (2003). Gramsci's black Marx: Whither the slave in civil society? *Social Identities, 9*(2), 225–40. https://doi.org/10.1080/1350463032000101579

Wilderson, F.B., III. (2010). *Red, white & black: Cinema and the structure of US antagonisms*. Duke University Press.

Williams, D. (1997). *The road to now: History of Blacks in Montreal*. Véhicule Press.

Williams, D. (2020, 30 June). *When it comes to systemic racism, history belies your words, Mr. Legault*. CBC News. https://www.cbc.ca/news/canada/montreal/systemic-racism-quebec-historian-1.5608397

Willis, S. (1991). I want the Black one. In *A Primer for Daily Life* (1st ed.) (pp. 89–109). Routledge.

Wingfield, A.H. (2010). Are some emotions marked "whites only"? Racialized feeling rules in professional workplaces. *Social Problems, 57*(2), 251–68. https://doi.org/10.4324/9781315631011-31

Winks, R.W. (1997). *The Blacks in Canada: A history* (2nd ed.). McGill-Queen's University Press.

Wolfe, P. (2006). Settler colonialism and the elimination of the native. *Journal of Genocide Research, 8*(4), 387–409. https://doi.org/10.1080/14623520601056240

Wynter, S. (1979). Sambos and minstrels. *Social Text, 1*, 149–56. https://doi.org/10.2307/466410

Wynter, S. (1994a). A Black Studies manifesto. *Forum N.H.I.: Knowledge for the 21st Century, 1*(1), 3–11.

Wynter, S. (1994b). "'No humans involved": An open letter to my colleagues. *Forum N.H.I.: Knowledge for the 21st Century, 1*(1), 42–73.

Wynter, S. (1995). 1492: A new world view. In V.L. Hyatt & R.M. Nettleford (Eds.), *Race, discourse, and the origin of the Americas: A new world view* (pp. 5–57). Smithsonian Institution Press.

Wynter, S. (1996). Is "development" a purely empirical concept, or also teleological?: A perspective from "we the underdeveloped." In A.Y. Yansané (Ed.), *Prospects for recovery and sustainable development in Africa* (pp. 299–316). Praeger.

Wynter, S. (2001). Towards the sociogenic principle: Fanon, identity, the puzzle of conscious experience, and what it is like to be "Black." In A. Gomez-Moriana & M. Duran-Cogan (Eds.), *National Identities and Socio-Political Changes in Latin America* (1st ed., pp. 30–66). Routledge.

Wynter, S. (2003). Unsettling the coloniality of being/power/truth/freedom: Towards the human, after man, its overrepresentation – An argument. *New Centennial Review, 3*(3), 257–337. https://doi.org/10.1353/ncr.2004.0015

Wynter, S. (2006). On how we mistook the map for the territory, and re-imprisoned ourselves in our unbearable wrongness of being, of *desêtre*: Black Studies toward the human project. In L.R. Gordon & J.A. Gordon (Eds.), *A Companion to African-American Studies* (pp. 107–18). https://doi.org/10.1002/9780470996645.ch9

Yousman, B. (2003). Blackophilia and Blackophobia: White youth, the consumption of rap music, and white supremacy. *Communication Theory, 13*(4), 366–91. https://doi.org/10.1111/j.1468-2885.2003.tb00297.x

Zembylas, M. (2007). Mobilizing anger for social justice: The politicization of the emotions in education. *Teaching Education, 18*(1), 15–28. https://doi.org/10.1080/10476210601151516

Index